This book – the only history of friendship in classical antiquity that exists in English – examines the nature of friendship in ancient Greece and Rome from Homer (eighth century BC) to the Christian Roman Empire of the fourth century AD. Although friendship is throughout this period conceived of as a voluntary and loving relationship (contrary to the prevailing view among scholars), there are major shifts in emphasis from the bonding among warriors in epic poetry, to the egalitarian ties characteristic of the Athenian democracy, the status-conscious connections in Rome and the Hellenistic kingdoms, and the commitment to a universal love among Christian writers. Friendship is also examined in relation to erotic love and comradeship, as well as for its role in politics and economic life, in philosophical and religious communities, in connection with patronage and the private counsellors of kings, and in respect to women; its relation to modern friendship is fully discussed.

KEY THEMES IN ANCIENT HISTORY

Friendship in the classical world

KEY THEMES IN ANCIENT HISTORY

EDITORS

Dr P. A. Cartledge
Clare College, Cambridge
Dr P. D. A. Garnsey
Jesus College, Cambridge

Key Themes in Ancient History aims to provide readable, informed and original studies of various basic topics, designed in the first instance for students and teachers of Classics and Ancient History, but also for those engaged in related disciplines. Each volume is devoted to a general theme in Greek, Roman, or where appropriate, Graeco-Roman history, or to some salient aspect or aspects of it. Besides indicating the state of current research in the relevant area, authors seek to show how the theme is significant for our own as well as ancient culture and society. By providing books for courses that are oriented around themes it is hoped to encourage and stimulate promising new developments in teaching and research in ancient history.

Other books in the series

Death-ritual and social structure in classical antiquity, by Ian Morris
Literacy and orality in ancient Greece, by Rosalind Thomas
Slavery and society at Rome, by Keith Bradley
Law, violence, and community in classical Athens, by David Cohen
Public order in ancient Rome, by Wilfried Nippel

FRIENDSHIP IN THE CLASSICAL WORLD

DAVID KONSTAN

Professor of Classics and Comparative Literature, Brown University

CAMBRIDGE
UNIVERSITY PRESS

CAMBRIDGE UNIVERSITY PRESS
Cambridge, New York, Melbourne, Madrid, Cape Town, Singapore, São Paulo

Cambridge University Press
The Edinburgh Building, Cambridge CB2 2RU, UK

Published in the United States of America by Cambridge University Press, New York

www.cambridge.org
Information on this title: www.cambridge.org/9780521454025

First published 1997

A catalogue record for this publication is available from the British Library

Library of Congress Cataloguing in Publication data
Konstan, David.
Friendship in the classical world / David Konstan.
p. cm. – (Key themes in ancient history)
Includes bibliographical references and index.
ISBN 0 521 45402 6 (hardback). – ISBN 0 521 45998 2 (paperback)
1. Friendship – History. I. Title. II. Series.
BF575.F66K66 1996
302.3´4´0938 – dc20   96–22245   CIP

ISBN-13 978-0-521-45402-5 hardback
ISBN-10 0-521-45402-6 hardback

ISBN-13 978-0-521-45998-3 paperback
ISBN-10 0-521-45998-2 paperback

Transferred to digital printing 2005

For Pura

Contents

Acknowledgements

I began devoting my research entirely to the history of classical friendship in the summer of 1991. I have been most fortunate in the support I have received for this project, and am eager to express my gratitude. A sabbatical semester, generously granted by Brown University in the autumn term of 1991, permitted uninterrupted study. I spent part of this period as a fellow at King's College, Cambridge, which gave me access not only to the splendid University Library, but also to conversation with stimulating colleagues who endured some of my early reflections on the present theme. A month at the Rockefeller Foundation's Center in Bellagio, Italy, late in 1991 enabled me to write up materials in an idyllic ambience, and I offer sincere thanks to the Foundation. I spent another month as a visitor at the American Academy in Rome, and wish to thank the entire staff of the Academy for their hospitality.

In August of 1993, I was visiting professor in the Classics Department at the University of Natal in Durban, where I gave a series of seminars on friendship. I thank my colleagues there for their unfailing warmth and spirited dialogue. In the academic year 1994–5, I was free to work exclusively on the book at the National Humanities Center in North Carolina, thanks to a grant from the Center and from the Guggenheim Memorial Foundation. I am deeply grateful to both institutions, and to the staff and fellows at the Center for their constant encouragement.

I have also enjoyed support both personally and intellectually from colleagues, friends and family. I have been lucky in the devotion of my friends, whose example has made the subject of this book especially congenial to me. It is not possible to list all those who have contributed to this project by their love; I trust they will be content with an anonymous expression of my appreciation. I must mention, however, five friends who provided specific commentary and thoughtful conversation at critical stages of the work: Mary Barnard, Jonathan Haynes, Phillip Mitsis, Elisa Romano, and, as always, Khachig Tölölyan. I wish also to acknowledge the special encouragement of Paul Cartledge, who first introduced me to the series in which this book appears and gave advice with his customary care and magnanimity. I am likewise grateful to Peter Garnsey as co-editor of the series, and to Pauline Hire of Cambridge University Press.

I am privileged to have been invited to speak on ancient friendship at several universities and professional congresses, and I take this opportunity to thank collectively the many colleagues who offered suggestions and criticisms on these occasions. To my colleagues at Brown University, special thanks.

My daughter, Eve (called Tupi) Mothner, her husband John, and my son, Geoff, have been, as ever, a source of gladness and comfort. I thank my brothers, Larry and Michael, for their love and all that they have meant to me. During two summers and part of a winter I worked on this book in the bright air of Salamanca, in the home of my mother-in-law, Catalina Hernández Hernández, who provided the perfect conditions in which to think and study; to her, I express my deepest gratitude.

Finally, I dedicate this book to my wife, María de la Purificación Nieto Hernández, in thanks for her love, for the wisdom and learning with which she commented on every aspect of this book, and for the joy of her companionship.

Abbreviations

AJAH	*American Journal of Ancient History*
AJP	*American Journal of Philology*
ANRW	*Aufstieg und Niedergang der Römischen Welt*, ed. W. Haase and H. Temporini. Berlin (1972–)
AP	*Ancient Philosophy*
CAG	*Commentaria in Aristotelem Graeca*, ed. H. Diels. Berlin
CB	*Classical Bulletin*
CJ	*Classical Journal*
CP	*Classical Philology*
CQ	*Classical Quarterly*
Cron. Erc.	*Cronache Ercolanesi*
D-K	*Fragmente der Vorsokratiker*, ed. H. Diels and W. Kranz. 6th edn. Berlin (1951–2)
EE	*Eudemian Ethics*
EN	*Nicomachean Ethics*
Ep.	*Epistle*
GRBS	*Greek Roman and Byzantine Studies*
ICS	*Illinois Classical Studies*
JHS	*Journal of Hellenic Studies*
JRS	*Journal of Roman Studies*
K-A	*Poetae Comici Graeci*, ed. R. Kassel and C. Austin. Berlin (1983–)
LCM	*Liverpool Classical Monthly*
LSJ	*A Greek-English Lexicon*, ed. H. G. Liddell and R. Scott; 9th edn. revised by H. S. Jones. Oxford (1940)
MM	*Magna Moralia*
Or.	*Oration*
PG	Patrologiae cursus completus, series Graeca, ed. J.-P. Migne. Paris (1857–66)

PL	Patrologiae cursus completus, series Latina, ed. J.-P. Migne. Paris (1841–55)
QUCC	_Quaderni Urbinati di Cultura Classica_
RAC	_Reallexikon für Antike und Christentum_, ed. E. Dassmann _et al._ Stuttgart (1941–)
SO	_Symbolae Osloenses_
SVF	_Stoicorum veterum fragmenta_, ed. H. Von Arnim. Leipzig (1903–24)
TAPA	_Transactions of the American Philological Association_
TLS	_Times Literary Supplement_
ZPE	_Zeitschrift für Papyrologie und Epigraphik_

Introduction

The subject of this book is the history of the relationship we call friendship in the classical world, beginning with the Homeric epics and concluding in the Christian empire of the fourth and fifth centuries AD. While the idea of friendship is not uniform over various cultures or even within a single culture at any given moment, the core of the relationship with which we shall be concerned may be characterized as a mutually intimate, loyal, and loving bond between two or a few persons that is understood not to derive primarily from membership in a group normally marked by native solidarity, such as family, tribe, or other such ties. Friendship is thus what anthropologists call an achieved rather than an ascribed relationship, the latter being based on status whereas the former is in principle independent of a prior formal connection such as kinship or ethnicity.

An achieved relationship does not necessarily mean one that depends essentially on free or personal choice. One may meet friends by accident and be drawn to them for mysterious reasons having little to do with decision, as is often the case with erotic attraction, for example. Arranged marriages and those based on individual sentiment or infatuation may from a certain point of view seem like two kinds of constraint; the fifth-century BC rhetorician Gorgias thus held that *erōs* or erotic passion was involuntary (*Helen* 19), and in canon law infatuation may be grounds for annulment because marriage was not entered into freely. In addition, friendship is "socially patterned" by numerous factors such as class or age. The role of election in discussions of friendship, though commonly insisted upon in modern accounts, appears to be historically variable.[1]

---

[1] "Socially patterned": Allan 1989: 47; class: ibid., 130–42; election: e.g. Black 1980: 5; Little

The description of friendship offered above may seem to be so minimal as to be a human constant across all societies, like the capacity to love or to grieve. In fact, however, it is commonly supposed to be much more restricted, and some have argued that friendship in the modern sense emerged only with the Renaissance or indeed still more recently, as late perhaps as the eighteenth or even nineteenth century. Thus, one writer remarks: "one cannot help thinking that easy equal friendship is a late development in Western culture." And he adds: "Think of the depressing overtones of the word 'friend' in eighteenth-century politics and the posturing associated with most classic and much vaunted friendships, like Montaigne's with La Boétie" (Furbank 1995). Anthropologists, moreover, have popularized the idea that "there are kinship-oriented *v.* friendship-oriented societies" (Paine 1969: 508).[2] In particular, it has been denied that the terms that are translated as "friend" or "friendship" in ancient Greek or Latin involve the personal intimacy and affection that are associated with the modern conception. Thus, Malcolm Heath (1987: 73–4) writes that *philia* (friendship) in classical Greece "is not, at root, a subjective bond of affection and emotional warmth, but the entirely objective bond of reciprocal obligation; one's *philos* [friend] is the man one is obliged to help, and on whom one can (or ought to be able to) rely for help when oneself is in need." Simon Goldhill (1986: 82) remarks in a similar vein: "The appellation or categorization *philos* is used to mark not just affection but overridingly a series of complex obligations, duties and claims."

What is more, the predominant view concerning the classical Greek vocabulary of friendship is that it did not distinguish between friends in the modern sense and a wide range of relationships from family ties to those between fellow-citizens. For example, Paul Millett (1991: 113) writes: "It is true that from the viewpoint of comparative sociology, to say nothing of our own experience, the all-inclusive quality of Greek friendship is anomalous." Millett cites the article on "Friendship" by Odd Ramsøy in the *International Encyclopedia of the Social Sciences* (1968: 12) for the generalization that "most other important social relationships exclude friendship," which "tends to be incompatible with such relationships as those of mother and child, lovers, and employer and employee." Millett goes on to

1993: 39; but contrast Cucó Giner 1995: 26–8, 36–8 for the view that even institutionalized friendships are voluntary.
2   Cf. also Paine 1969: 513; Cohen 1961: 352.

observe that Greek usage, as illustrated for example by Aristotle, admits of the term *philos* or "friend" in respect to "parents, brothers, benefactors, fellow-tribesmen and fellow-citizens," as well as to "husbands and wives, fellow-voyagers, comrades-in-arms, guest-friends, and cousins," and he adds that "perhaps the clearest illustration comes from the *Memorabilia* of Xenophon, plotting the extension of *philia* both inside and outside the family circle." A somewhat different but comparable reduction of the emotive aspect of the Roman conception of *amicitia* is reflected in the narrowly political interpretation defended by Sir Ronald Syme (1939: 157):

> Roman political factions were welded together, less by unity of principle than by mutual interest and by mutual services (*officia*), either between social equals as an alliance, or from superior to inferior, in a traditional and almost feudal form of clientship: on a favourable estimate the bond was called *amicitia*, otherwise *factio*.

Peter Brunt cites the German scholar Wilhelm Kroll for the view that "*amicus* means in the everyday language of [Cicero's] time no more than a political follower."[3]

THE ANTHROPOLOGICAL TURN

The views represented above are not radical or eccentric; on the contrary, they represent the dominant and indeed almost universal conception of ancient friendship, especially Greek friendship, in current scholarly literature.[4] It is appropriate to trace the development of this interpretation before proceeding to indicate the kinds of evidence that tell against it and which will be examined in detail in the chapters of this book.

An important shift in the understanding of ancient society occurred with what might be called the recent anthropological turn in classical historiography, represented in the English-speaking world by Moses Finley and his disciples, and in French above all by the heirs of Louis Gernet.[5] Finley, in an essay entitled "Anthropology and the Classics" (1986 [orig. 1972]: 118), described anthropology as the "mentor" of the classics, which might provide, if not a theory, then "an approach, a habit of thought – I might say, a methodology." One of the fundamental insights adopted from anthropology was the emphasis on systems of exchange in pre-modern

---

[3] Brunt 1988: 352–3 summarizing Kroll 1933: 55ff; cf. Powell 1995.
[4] Further discussion in Konstan 1996.   [5] See Kurke 1991: 90–7.

societies. Building on the work of Bronislaw Malinowski (1922: 176), Marcel Mauss, a student of Emile Durkheim, wrote in his seminal monograph, *The Gift* (1967 [orig. 1923-4]: 140): "If friends make gifts, gifts make friends. A great proportion of primitive exchange, much more than our own traffic, has as its decisive function this latter, instrumental one: the material flow underwrites or initiates social relations." As Leslie Kurke explains: "In contrast to commodity exchange, gift exchange depends on a personalized relationship between transaction partners which endures over time."[6]

In his extraordinary book, *The World of Odysseus* (1977 [orig. 1954]), Finley applied the concepts developed by Malinowski, Mauss, Gernet, and Karl Polanyi (1944; 1969) to the societies represented in the Homeric epics.[7] Friendships, especially between foreigners, were now interpreted as elements in a network of social relations that constituted the fabric of pre-civic communities regulated by custom rather than law. Walter Donlan (1980: 14) remarks on the "complex system of guest-friendship (*xeniē*), which afforded individual protection in a hostile tribal world, fostered the expansion of 'foreign' contact and increased the prestige of individuals and their *oikoi* [households]." Although the precise characterization of Homeric society might vary, many scholars have agreed that in Homer obligatory reciprocity outweighs sentiment in interpersonal relations. In particular, "Homeric 'friendship' appears as a system of calculated cooperation, not necessarily accompanied by any feelings of affection."[8]

The reason, it is supposed, why friendship assumed so pragmatic a form in the archaic world is that it served as a matrix for relations that in modern societies are governed by autonomous economic and legal practices. In *The Ancient Economy* (1985 [orig. 1973]), Finley argued that the societies of classical Greece and Rome did not possess an economy in the modern sense of the term. Rather, the economy was inextricably embedded in a complex of social relations that included personal bonds. To impose modern categories by separating out economic exchange or other transactions as a distinct domain of social activity obliterates the difference between the ancient world and contemporary capitalism.

The roots of Finley's thesis may be found in the social theories

---

[6] Kurke 1991: 93, with reference to Mauss 1967: 34-5; Bourdieu 1977: 171.
[7] See Millett 1991: 15-23; Van Wees 1992: 26-8; on Polanyi, see Humphreys 1978: 31-75.
[8] Millett 1991: 121, with reference to Adkins 1963.

proposed by the eighteenth-century liberal Scots thinkers such as Adam Ferguson, David Hume, Francis Hutcheson, and Adam Smith. Allan Silver has explained how these Enlightenment figures understood the difference between ancient and modern friendship:

precommercial societies do not offer the possibility of disinterested relations, ungoverned by the clash and calculation of interests; only the development of the market does so, in those domains falling outside the market itself and therefore newly distinguishable from the interplay of interest. (Silver 1990: 1484–5)

This is why in pre-modern societies such as ancient Greece "the purpose of friendship ... was to help friends by defeating enemies" (Silver 1990: 1487); this sordid and calculating mode of interaction was unavoidable, Silver writes in his summary of Adam Ferguson's argument, because

in such settings vital resources are obtained largely through what modern culture and theory see as personal relations ... In contrast, the Scots conceive of personal relations in commercial society as benefiting those involved at no cost to others; friendship becomes simultaneously a private virtue and a public good. (Silver 1990: 1484–5, 1487, 1496)

The qualities of disinterestedness and intimacy are peculiar to modern friendship, then, because individual bonds now occupy the space freed up by the emergence of the economic sphere governed by market relations.

It is now apparent that one strand of the argument developed in this book, according to which friendship in the classical world is understood centrally as a personal relationship predicated on affection and generosity rather than on obligatory reciprocity, challenges prevailing assumptions about the nature of social relations in antiquity. Rather than conceiving of Greek and Roman friendship as seamlessly embedded in economic and other functions, I am claiming for it a relative autonomy comparable to the status it presumably enjoys in modern life. The implications of this view are considerable. There is obviously a world of difference between ancient and modern social systems, although it has been argued that the Athenian economy in fact achieved a certain autonomy in the fourth century BC and perhaps earlier.[9] But both societies – perhaps for entirely

---

[9] Fourth-century autonomy: Cohen 1992: 4–7; for the economic transformation of Athens following the Persian invasion and Athens' new role as imperial center, see Frost 1976 and Garnsey 1988: 89–164; Graham 1995: 8–10 remarks on the high level of organized trade testified to by Homer.

distinct reasons – did produce a space for sympathy and altruism under the name of friendship that stands as an alternative to structured forms of interaction based on kinship, civic identity, or commercial activity. This resemblance or continuity in the nature of friendship has consequences, as the following chapters will indicate, for how one writes the history of classical ethics, politics, and trade.

FRIENDSHIP AND OTHER RELATIONS

Social concepts do not exist in a vacuum. Friendship in any society is bounded by a set of alternative relationships that mark off its specific dimensions and properties. Semiotic theory posits the necessity of contrast in the construction of cultural ideas; as Umberto Eco (1976: 73) observes: "A cultural unit 'exists' and is recognized insofar as there exists another one which is opposed to it." Stephen Nimis (1987: 9–10) rightly adds that language "is much too complex to be thought of in terms of a series of binary correlations ... A cultural unit is a *nodal point* arising from a series of criss-crossings of numerous oppositional axes."

The controversy over whether friendship existed in contrast to kinship, citizenship, and other ascribed roles in classical antiquity has already been noted; part of the argument of this book consists in demonstrating that it did, more or less analogously to the way modern friendship does. But friendship also takes its contours from other achieved relations that abut upon it, such as romantic love, the bonds that exist between mates and comrades, voluntary partnerships, neighborliness, and, in classical Greece, the special connection between foreign friends called *xenia*. The structure of erotic attraction, for example, in ancient society is not identical to that in twentieth-century England or the United States; one point of difference is the constitutive role played in the construction of Greek *erōs* by pederastic relations between men and boys, which produced a rather sharp distinction between amatory and amicable ties. Again, whether friendship assumes the same form among women as it does among men, and whether it is acknowledged as the name of a relationship between women and men, are not constants. Moreover, the numerous public feasts and other collective activities that marked the social life of the classical polis, along with common service in political office and in military units by men residing in different and often non-contiguous villages throughout the territory of Attica, especially after the reforms of Cleisthenes shuffled and reorganized local demes into larger patch-work units, all contributed to the formation of friendships among people living at a distance from one another, and thus to a distinct differentiation between friends and neighbors.[10] The several inclusions and exclusions that operate among these categories vary not only between cultures but in the course of classical antiquity itself, and thereby articulate different moments in the history of ancient friendship.

Such variations are of course not specific to classical antiquity, and it is salutary to remind oneself of divergences in modern conceptions of friendship that occur over a brief period of time or reflect differences in local culture, class, or point of view. Thus, we took note earlier of Odd Ramsøy's (1968: 12) claim that relationships between parents and children, brothers, lovers, or workers and bosses tend to "exclude friendship." More recently, Janet Reohr (1991: ix), in a sociological study of modern friendship, affirms:

What seems intriguing about friendship is its inclusive nature, whereas other relations often maintain exclusionary boundaries. It is possible for two people to be friends and have no other relational connections yet it is also possible to be siblings and friends, spouses and friends, colleagues and friends.

A writer who comments that "Over the years probably the most universal restriction on friendships has been to limit them to persons of the same sex," dedicates his book on friendship to "my wife and friend."[11]

The criteria or differentiae that discriminate friendship from other affective bonds are of several sorts. To the extent that friendship excludes relationships marked by kinship or by differences of age, gender, and class (e.g. between masters and slaves), it invites a sociological analysis. Friendship may also be approached psychologically by way of the quality of the emotion specific to it. On this basis, Laurence Thomas (1993: 59) would efface the distinction between love and friendship: "I do not believe that there is a deep formal difference between friendship and romantic love." Alternatively, one may insist on the phenomenological differences between the experience of friendship and that of love, pointing, for example, to the

[10] On the specific character of women's friendships, see, e.g.: Rubin 1959; Wright 1982; Raymond 1986; Eichenbaum and Orbach 1988; Allan 1989: 63–84; on collective activities in the polis, Schmitt-Pantel 1990a; on common service, Osborne 1990: 283.

[11] Bell 1981: 95; cf. Black 1980: 112–13.

relative absence of jealousy and possessiveness in friendship as opposed to romantic love. Again, the presence or absence of particular practices, such as sex, may motivate a conceptual distinction between two kinds of relationship. The emphasis in this book will fall on social aspects of friendship, but account will be taken where possible of alterations in what may be called the structure of feeling characteristic of the relationship.[12]

SOURCES AND THE PROBLEM OF LANGUAGE

Knowledge of friendship in classical Greece and Rome is based almost exclusively on the interpretation of textual sources. Images on pottery give some idea of the companionship of the symposium. Archaeology may suggest something about the material conditions of ancient society, but it is mute on the nature of a relationship like friendship, except insofar as it may illuminate a social context that for independent reasons is presumed to have a bearing on it: a case in point are size and density of population, which are sometimes supposed to affect the possibility or quality of friendships. When Walter Donlan (1985a: 301) observes of archaic Greece that "within the villages and village-clusters that made up the early *demos* [people], the majority of households were probably linked by ties of blood and marriage," he is inferring from physical remains the small space available for personal and optional bonds between non-kin. A semi-urban region like classical Athens, then, with a population perhaps upward of 150,000 people (including women, children, and slaves), may be thought to have permitted the emergence of friendship as a primary social category, although modern evidence for the effect, good or bad, of urbanization on the formation of friendships is not unambiguous. Occasionally, the visual arts may supplement written sources, as in the case of archaic vase paintings illustrating Achilles' special friendship with Ajax.[13]

Determining the parameters of ancient friendship, then, is fundamentally a philological task, which must begin by identifying the vocabulary of friendship and specifying its connections both with terms denoting other bonds in Greek or Latin and with the modern

---

[12] Phenomenological differences: Alberoni 1990: 33; structure of feeling: Williams 1977: 128–35.

[13] Urbanization: Fischer 1982: 114–22; Cucó Giner 1995: 20–1; Achilles and Ajax: Moore 1987: 158–9.

lexicon. We have already noted that the noun *philos*, which is the Greek word normally translated as "friend," has been understood variously by scholars. For those who have supposed that its extension is so broad as to include blood relatives and fellow citizens, rendering it as "friend" will not be accurate. Thus, Mary Whitlock Blundell, in her book *Helping Friends and Harming Enemies* (1989: 40–4), classifies Greek conceptions of friendship under three main heads or circles: the family, fellow-citizens, and "the third main group of *philoi* [plural of *philos*]" that "approximates most closely to modern conceptions of a friend." I shall present evidence to show that in fact *philos* as a substantive is normally restricted to the last category, but plainly such a demonstration involves a close analysis of texts, especially where critics of the highest caliber have disagreed over so fundamental a matter.

A further question involves the relationship between the concrete noun *philos* and other forms derived from the same root, such as the verb *philein*, which means "to love," and the abstract noun *philia*, commonly rendered as "friendship." As it happens, the form *philia* does in fact cover relationships far wider than friendship, including the love between kin and the affection or solidarity between relatively distant associates such as members of the same fraternity or city. Thus, it is often misleading or simply wrong to translate it as "friendship," although the practice is quite general, as for example in English versions of the eighth and ninth books of Aristotle's *Nicomachean Ethics*. The different range of meanings of the terms *philos* and *philia* has contributed, I believe, to the prevalent confusion over the significance of the concrete noun, leading scholars to suppose that its use is as broad as that of *philia*. Hence the denial that Greek has a word corresponding to the English "friend," though it would indeed be true to say that there is no single Greek term quite equivalent to "friendship."

Similar problems arise with related vocabulary, such as the archaic term *xenos*, commonly translated as "guest-friend." At the other temporal extreme of classical antiquity, one observes that the classical vocabulary of friendship tends to be eschewed by some Christian writers, while the word "brother" is used of members of the faith generally, and hence may be applied to non-kin, including friends, as well as to kin (e.g. Basil, *Ep.* 64, in reference to Elpidius who is no relation). In each case, the only procedure for getting at the sense is a patient examination of usage and contexts, inevitably

motivated by certain expectations which may be consciously maintained on theoretical grounds or else vaguely supported by intuition
or common sense (the latter being nothing but the implicit endorsement of hypotheses formulated by others).

The issue of the extent to which Greek and Latin terminology for
friendship corresponds to modern nomenclature raises sticky problems pertaining to the history of culture and of ideas generally.
How is it possible to penetrate the hermeneutic barrier between
distinct languages and social systems, especially given the idiosyn-
cratic nature of the ancient city-state communities?[14] With what
assurance do we even begin the search for continuities in meaning
over so vast a time period as two millennia and more? If, as we have
suggested, every "cultural unit" is bounded by an array of concepts
specific to a given historical moment, what sense is there in seeking
equivalences between single elements of the two systems taken in
isolation? In general, the value and reliability of such comparisons
become manifest, if at all, in the results produced by investigation:
where ancient and modern meanings are congruent, and also where
they are not, should shed light both on the sense of specific passages
in classical texts and on larger ideological configurations.

Of the connection between ancient and modern signs, Jacques
Derrida (1982: 254) remarks:

While acknowledging the specific function of a term within its system, we
must not, however, take the signifier as perfectly conventional. Doubtless,
Hegel's Idea, for example, is not Plato's Idea; doubtless the effects of the
system are irreducible and must be read as such. But the word *Idea* is not an
arbitrary *X*, and it bears a traditional burden that continues Plato's system
in Hegel's system.

Hegel was aware that the expression "idea" was transliterated from
the Greek. In the case of friendship, where the signifiers *philos*,
amicus, and friend are distinct, Derrida (1993: 366–7) affirms more
cautiously: "we should not forget that we are speaking first of all
from within the tradition of a certain concept of friendship, within a
given culture ... Now, this tradition is not homogeneous, nor is the
determination of friendship within it." Derrida proposes to identify
"the major marks of a tension, perhaps ruptures, and in any case
scansions, at the interior of this history of friendship, of the
canonical figure of friendship." *Philos* does not exactly equal

<hr>

[14] Cf. Roussel 1976: 6, 311–12.

"friend." The instabilities in both the ancient and the modern senses of the term "friend," which are precisely what endow it with a history, demand an approach that reckons with the transformations within a concept that has been shown to be in some essential respect continuous.

OVERDETERMINATION OF FRIENDSHIP

We have said that cultural concepts are the precipitate of "criss-crossings" of multiple oppositions; their meaning is thus overdetermined, and different aspects or emphases may be elicited in specific contexts. It is not impossible that certain concretizations of a complex term like friendship should even appear contradictory. Aristotle observed that not all inquiries permit of equal rigor (*akribes*), and that social matters in particular admit of "great discrepancy and deviation, so that they seem to be exclusively a product of custom rather than of nature" (*EN* 1.2,1094b15–16). Ludwig Wittgenstein (1958: 24–6) took the thought further:

When we talk of language as a symbolism used in an exact calculus, that which is in our mind can be found in the sciences and in mathematics. Our ordinary use of language conforms to this standard of exactness only in rare cases. Why then do we in philosophizing constantly compare our use of words with one following exact rules? The answer is that the puzzles which we try to remove always spring from just this attitude towards language.

The effect of intersecting determinations of the idea of friendship may be observed in connection with the requirement of loyalty, which is usually expected between friends and was posited at the beginning of this introduction as one of the signs or conditions of friendship. Loyalty may take various forms; in Greek texts of the classical period (and also later), it is frequently interpreted as the obligation to come to a friend's assistance in time of crisis. Failure to provide such help in turn is the mark of a false friend. That is simple logic (argument from the contrapositive). But it is entirely natural to suppose further that a display of fidelity is proof of friendship. Insofar as close kin prove faithful in an emergency, they may accordingly be described as friends, and this usage indeed occurs in a few passages in Greek tragedy where there is a strong emphasis on the theme of mutual services and aid (e.g. in Euripides' *Orestes*). The paradox thus arises that one of the criteria of friendship, namely loyalty, generates instances of the use of the word "friend" that appear to violate the

premise that friendship is not an ascribed relationship, that is, that it
is not an aspect of kinship or other status connections.

A few such cases have buttressed the view that the term *philos* has
as wide an extension as the abstract noun *philia*, which denotes
affection in the broadest sense. One may, however, acknowledge a
certain margin of ambiguity in Greek as in English without obliter-
ating the distinction between friends and kin. The polarity of the two
categories is amply attested, for example, in disjunctive expressions
of the sort, "friends and relatives," as, for example, when the fifth-
century BC orator Antiphon remarks (1.29): "they summon and bring
as witnesses both friends and relatives [*kai philous kai anankaious*]."

A further complication in the use of *philos* derives from the Greek
tendency to pair the term with its opposite, *ekhthros* or "enemy." In
such contexts (which are relatively restricted), the disjunction is often
treated as exhaustive, as in the English expression "friend or foe,"
which is presumed to cover all the possibilities. Enemies seek each
other's harm, and in Greek, just as in English, one may label as an
enemy a relative who does one an injury or – what amounts to the
same thing – abandons kin in time of need (e.g. Euripides, *Medea*
765–7, 797, 809). If disloyalty between blood relations proves them
enemies, then the polarity between *philoi* and *ekhthroi* suggests that
benevolence renders them friends. In this way too, there understandably occur instances in which members of the same family are
called *philoi*, apparently blurring the boundary between friends and
kin. Similarly, one may say in English that relatives who have had a
falling out have made friends again. Neither usage warrants the
conclusion that the term "friend" is in principle all-inclusive. As
always, a sense of context is indispensable. My daughter and I
happen to be good friends, but when I introduce her to an
acquaintance I do not say, "This is my friend Tupi," any more than
a Greek or Roman would have done.

The expectation of mutual assistance between friends is the
ground of another tension in the concept of friendship that is rather
less amenable to resolution by way of linguistic protocols. Friendship
is commonly assumed, both today and in antiquity (as will be
illustrated in the following chapters), to be an expression of uncoerced love or altruism. The demand for reciprocity appears to
introduce into the heart of friendship a mercantile element that
would confirm the low opinion of ancient amicability entertained by
the Scots Enlightenment thinkers. In fact, Greek and Roman writers

were unabashed about celebrating the usefulness of friends, and popular maxims are in accord with the philosophers in recommending friendship as a source of security and succor.

That there are practical advantages to friendship does not necessarily reduce it to a set of transactions based on interest and obligation rather than selfless affection. Modern views too, moreover, acknowledge the material benefits that derive from friendship, as witnessed by the phrase "a fair-weather friend" (cf. the Latin expression *temporaria amicitia*, Seneca, *Epist. mor.* 9.9). With a characteristically contemporary twist, one authority notes that "it is beginning to be realised that, for some reason, people with fewer friends are more prone to tonsillitis and cancer"; in addition, "people who are poor at making friends have been shown to have worse teeth and to get more serious illnesses."[15]

Nevertheless, there is a certain discomfort or ambivalence about emphasizing the utilitarian aspect of friendship. In a sociological study of friendship in contemporary Britain, Graham Allan (1989: 20) notes that it is correct to say that

friendships *are* used instrumentally; that friends regularly provide a variety of services for one another; and that these services play a larger part in the routine organisation of daily life than is normally assumed. Nonetheless it is true that friendships must not be defined in these terms. In other words, while friends can be used to achieve a variety of objectives, their instrumentality should not be the basis or rationale for the relationship.[16]

Although the arguments differ, ancient treatments of friendship also regularly subordinate its instrumental value to more disinterested motives.

Modern philosophical analyses, which often presuppose a notion of the individual as an isolated subject, have raised the question of the possibility of altruism or action for the sake of another.[17] It must be said that the classical philosophers, including Epicurus, normally take for granted the existence of other-regarding motives; Aristotle indeed includes disinterestedness ("one must wish good things for a friend for his sake," *EN* 8.2,1155b31) as one of the defining characteristics of friendship. In this respect, the ancient thinkers (who do not operate with the modern concept of the individual) recognize a domain of human sympathy uncontaminated by the desire for

---

[15] Duck 1983: 7–8, citing Lynch 1977.
[16] Cf. Wolf 1966: 13; Pitt-Rivers 1971: 138–9; Saller 1982: 12; Dixon 1993: 452–5.
[17] Cf. Nagel 1970; Blum 1980: 117–39; Gill (forthcoming).

personal advantage or gain and accordingly disembedded from the patterns of exchange and reciprocity that characterize social relations such as marriage and commerce.

Aristotle's views will be examined later in greater detail. If, however, there remains in his exposition an implicit contradiction between altruism and self-interest, it may be a sign of an ideological overdetermination of the concept of friendship that persists even today and reflects the double characterization of friendship as a spontaneous and unconstrained sentiment and as a social institution with its particular code of behavior. Robert Paine (1969: 514) reflects rather than resolves the difficulty when he remarks:

Inasmuch as friendship is recognised as a social relationship, it is an institution in the limited and rather loose sense of bestowal of recognition; and this is commonly the extent of its institutionalisation in our culture, where it amounts to a kind of institutionalised non-institution.

Jacqueline Wiseman (1986: 203–5) refers to the "unwritten contract" that obtains between friends. Robert Bell (1981: 13) notes crisply that "in most societies love between friends is not allowed to depend on the vague bonds of moral sentiment alone."

The antinomy in the nature of friendship may be irreducible. But it is also possible that Greek and Roman views are not subject to the same cultural pressures as are certain modern ideals of friendship. In this respect, they may serve to cast new light on contemporary conundrums, and at the same time exhibit more clearly features specific to the ideology of classical societies. At all events, the theoretical problems associated with the notion of altruism may serve as a caution against the casual assumption that ancient friendship was more compromised than modern in respect to its objective or quasi-contractual status.[18]

ANCIENT VS. MODERN FRIENDSHIP

Despite the ostensible continuities between classical and modern conceptions of friendship as a mutual, voluntary, loving, and unselfish relationship, there are deep differences between them that reflect diverse values and psychological assumptions. For example, one aspect of friendship universally emphasized in modern discussions is

[18] Irreducible antinomy: Annis 1987; Derrida 1993: 382; contractual status of ancient friendship: Springborg 1986: 198–9.

the need for self-disclosure as the basis for intimacy and trust between friends. Thus, Steve Duck (1983: 67) affirms: "The main feature that stabilises, establishes and develops relationships of all types is proper and dexterous control of *self-disclosure*; that is, the revelation of personal layers of one's self, personal thoughts, or even one's body." Acquaintanceship falls short of friendship precisely because it "is not a relationship of intimacy or exchange of confidences," even though "a great amount of information may be passed between those who are acquaintances" (Bell 1981: 22).[19]

In antiquity, frankness or candor among friends is a value (e.g. Aristotle, *EN* 9.9), although it becomes prominent in discussions of friendship only in the Hellenistic and Roman periods, for reasons that will be examined in the chapters that follow. Honesty is prized because it discriminates the true friend from the toady. In addition, it is recognized that people require criticism, provided it is constructive, in order to recognize their faults; the Hellenistic philosophical schools devoted particular attention to frank speech in the context of friendly instruction. In tense political times, moreover, openness was understood to be possible only among friends, as Cicero intimates in his treatise on friendship (cf. *audeas*, "be so bold," 6.22); he begins a letter to his lifelong friend Atticus (1.18 = 18, dated 20 January 60): "Know that what I miss most now is a man with whom I can communicate all the things that cause me any anxiety, a man who loves me, who is wise, with whom I can speak without pretending, without dissimulating, without concealing anything." Plainspokenness and the liberty to express dangerous views, however, are not the same as the injunction to self-disclosure. Never in antiquity, so far as I am aware, is the revelation of personal intimacies described as necessary to the formation of friendships. Contrast Laurence Thomas (1987: 223): "The bond of trust between deep friends is cemented by the equal self-disclosure of intimate information."[20]

Modern discussions often suppose that the basis of attraction between friends resides in their individual or personal qualities: "The person who is a friend must be appreciated as a unique self rather than simply a particular instance of a general class" (Suttles 1970: 100). In a survey of modern views on friendship, Jacqueline Wiseman (1986: 198) writes that, however they may "describe

---

[19] On self-disclosure, cf. also Jourard 1971; Chelune 1979.
[20] Further bibliography in Thomas 1987: 235n.9.

characteristics they believe are integral to their friends' make-up, respondents often imply a uniqueness in their combination." Ancient writers, on the contrary, tend to emphasize traits that are good (on some definition of good) rather than singular; while excellence may be rare, it is always of a kind.

Uniqueness and self-disclosure are related: one reveals what is peculiar to oneself. Because each person is distinctive, a special value attaches to the possibility of communicating. In a study of friendship in the United States, Myron Brenton (1974: 45) writes: "All of us, regardless of our capacity for intimacy, want to be understood." Friendship is thus imagined as opening a special window onto an interior self that is ordinarily opaque or hidden. Acquaintances, by contrast, know "of the other only what he is toward the outside."[21]

The unique individual seeks in communication with friends an antidote to loneliness, which is the condition of lack characteristic of the isolated self. Ronald Sharp (1986: 4–5) attributes "the recent plight of friendship" to "those elements of modernity that have been variously associated with existential *angst*, narcissism, rootlessness, nihilism, alienation, the breakdown of community, and general estrangement," and he concludes that "in the face of that painful loneliness, friendship seems to have reemerged as something both highly valued and intensely desired."

The Greeks and Romans were sociable peoples, and to be deprived of human company was normally perceived as the extreme of suffering, at least until monastic ideals took root late in the Christian era; Euripides was thought to be strange on account of his penchant for solitude (Alexander Aetolus fr. 7). In Sophocles' *Philoctetes*, the hero, who has been abandoned on a desolate island, laments his condition as "wretched, alone, deserted and friendless" (227–8). Aristotle (*EN*, 8.1.1155a19–22) remarks that the traveler always delights to encounter fellow human beings – "at least," the second-century AD commentator Aspasius soberly adds, "if they are not perverted by acquisitiveness" (160.3 Heylbut). Virgil's Achaemenides prefers to die by human hands than to survive among the Cyclopes (*Aeneid* 3.606). But isolation is not loneliness. The Greeks and Romans did not see in friends a cure for the "bone loneliness that eats its way into the psyche" (Sarton 1977: 59).

The themes of individuality, separateness, confession and commu-

---

[21] Simmel 1950: 320; cit. Bell 1981: 23.

nion are dimensions of a sense of self that is characteristic of a contemporary sensibility. William Sadler (1970: 201) writes that

when we sense that a friend really understands us and truly communicates with us, then we know that cynicism and despair are unnecessary because loneliness is not revelatory of the ultimate character of human life...When interpreted from within the perspective of love, the experience of loneliness is transformed into an awareness of our singular identity. This identity is accepted and affirmed by a true friend.

In a world in which a subject conceives of itself as different in essence from other humans, a monad constituted by unique attributes, intimacy has a special significance. Only by a mysterious contact across the boundaries of self can one escape existential loneliness; to be understood, not just heard, is the important thing. Communication with other beings is presumed to be a difficult matter. Hence the need for relationships – a term often employed in place of friendship in modern discussions.[22]

It is beyond the scope of this book to inquire whether this sensibility is grounded in a distinctly modern conception of the self. In a perceptive article, Christopher Gill expands upon Lionel Trilling's (1972) intuition that the Renaissance inaugurated a notion of authenticity or sincerity that has no analogue in classical antiquity. Gill (1994: 4600) explains modern sincerity as follows:

behind the social self, the bearer of roles and participant in communal action, there is another, deeper and more private self. Although it is the social self which is conventionally treated as the author of morally significant action and the recipient of moral judgement, the need to be true to one's "real" self is taken to constitute a more profound claim and one that is potentially in conflict with conventional moral requirements.

Kantian ethics, on this view, is an attempt "to ground morality from the perspective of this asocial self" (Gill 1994: 4601). Gill (4638) argues that ancient thinkers, on the contrary, do not posit the self as the "bearer of a unique personal identity."[23]

It may be that the new sensibility is already evident in Montaigne's exclamation concerning his friend La Boétie: "If you press me to tell why I loved him, I feel that this cannot be expressed except by

---

[22] Cf. Sharabany 1994: 157–61.
[23] On authenticity, see also Taylor 1989; "asocial self": cf. MacIntyre 1984: 60; contrast Friedman 1993: 67–8: "the self is inherently *social*"; on personal identity in ancient thought, Stern-Gillet 1995: 8, 14 and also 172–3 and Laín Entralgo 1985: 41 on the implications of Aristotle's description of a friend as another self; cf. Batstone 1993: 143–50 on the rhetorical presentation of self in classical lyric poetry.

answering: Because it was he, because it was I" ("Of Friendship," in Pakaluk 1991: 192). Lorna Hutson (1994: 61), however, has challenged the common view that sixteenth-century literature on friendship reflects the "transition from the instrumental and socially unequal ties of friendship fostered by feudal society, to a new 'modern' concept of friendship as pure affection, preceding and exceeding all instrumentality." There may in fact be no precise moment at which to date such a transformation: at any time, including today, sundry conceptions of friendship co-exist, and not all conform to the dominant fashion.[24] Many writers have perceived a decline in the quality of friendship in modern society as a consequence of alienation and the commodification of personal relations; Stuart Miller (1983: 20–6) lists the market economy, Protestantism, philosophical monadism, individualism, technology, rationalism, professionalism, and mobility as "all tending to destroy intimacy" (26). In contrast to the psychologizing tendency of recent literature on friendship, other voices continue to stress virtue or utility or the mere passing of time together:

Ours had been an intermittent and night-time friendship, based more on similar tastes in alcohol...than on some kind of shameful confession, which we never or almost never fell into. As respectable drinkers, we both mistrusted the excesses of feeling and friendship that drink and night bring with them. (Muñoz Molina 1987: 24)

The idea of friendship not only is overdetermined as the site of multiple oppositions, but is also dispersed, assuming different configurations depending on social environment and even on transient concerns. Some forms of friendship may not be assimilable or subordinate to a master concept, but may rather be related by what Wittgenstein called "family resemblance." Nevertheless, one notices that the minimal conception of friendship articulated in the novel by Muñoz Molina is cast as a negation of confidentiality; in this respect it betrays its modernity.

The plan of this book is broadly chronological: the successive chapters examine friendship as it was conceived in the archaic period in Greece (from Homer through the sixth century BC); then during the flourishing of the democratic city-state under the cultural hegemony of Athens in the fifth and fourth centuries; and after that

---

[24] Oxley 1978: 100–1 describes mateship in an Australian town as "seldom very intimate" and "acted out in public."

in the Hellenistic age that begins conventionally with the death of Alexander the Great in 323 BC and continues until the Roman conquest of the Greek east, completed by the end of the first century BC, though somewhat later Greek sources are also exploited to fill out the picture. The following chapter turns to representations of friendship in Rome, concentrating chiefly on the Republic and on the early principate (first century AD) and using texts written chiefly in Latin; the final chapter deals with the later Roman Empire and looks at attitudes toward friendship among Christians and pagans in Greek and Latin literature primarily of the fourth century AD.

The organization by epoch is not intended to suggest an evolution in the nature of friendship from an early to a mature form, or to a form more closely approximating modern ideas. The functions of friendship undoubtedly respond to historical exigencies and possibilities, but it is not assumed that social changes condition a development, as opposed to inflections, in the notion of friendship. What is more, there is no guarantee of uniformity among the conceptions of friendship disseminated in a single era. Commonplaces persist for a thousand years despite vast social changes. New emphases emerge, and are the central subject of this book, but it is not necessarily the case that they conform synchronically to a reigning spirit of the times. Indeed, one theme that runs through the following chapters is the abiding image of friendship as an intimate relationship predicated on mutual affection and commitment.[25]

The terms for "friend" in the above sense are *philos* in Greek and *amicus* in Latin, and the focus of this book is accordingly on their use in the classical world over the course of its history. Some of their meanings, and those of their cognates, range beyond those attaching to the English word "friend"; other terms, for example *hetairos* and *epitēdeios* in Greek or *sodalis* and *familiaris* in Latin, overlap to some extent or in some contexts with *philos* and *amicus*. That there exists in the classical languages a vocabulary for friendship is an important index of its social role, but the concept does not depend exclusively on one locution. Related terms, which help to demarcate the semantic domain of *philos* and *amicus*, are examined in some detail where appropriate.

Accordingly, the individual chapters, despite their chronological arrangement, each address various aspects of friendship and asso-

---

[25] Evolutionary approach: cf. Fraisse 1974; periodization of cultures: Panofsky 1961; Foucault 1984 and 1984a; Golden and Toohey 1996.

ciated ideas; cross-cutting the temporal sequence is a treatment of themes and functions that are taken up more or less particularly as they become relevant at a given historical period or as the surviving evidence permits.

The chapter on the archaic age of Greece, for example, examines the syntax and semantics of the term *philos*, which as a noun has limited currency in Homeric diction, as well as the significance of the words *hetairos* and *xenos* ("guest-friend" or "stranger"), in order to establish the earliest values for these words and the social institutions – e.g. the embryonic condition of the state – to which they correspond. This chapter also examines the structure of sexual passion or *erōs*, and the ways in which it is contrasted with friendship, with particular reference to the interpretation of the bond between Achilles and Patroclus in the *Iliad*. In addition to epic narrative, archaic lyric poetry, which may have been produced largely for symposiastic occasions, is explored as a possible site for private sodalities constituted through bonds of friendship or at least comradeship (the circles addressed in Sappho's verses are treated as well); finally, I look at friendship in the context of the disruption of aristocratic rule and the ideology of heroism, as reflected primarily in the elegiac poetry of Theognis.

The chapter on the classical city presents evidence to justify the equation between *philos* and "friend." Further, it takes up the expectation of mutual assistance between friends and the connection between this pragmatic requirement and the understanding of friendship as a bond based on generosity and affection. Here are explored as well the intersections between oppositions such as friend vs. enemy, friend vs. relative, and friend vs. the wider circle of acquaintances that includes companions and fellow-citizens. I discuss these determinations of friendship, and also the ideal of equality between friends which receives special emphasis in this period, in relation to the democratic ideology of the city-state, and, more skeptically, to the conditions of economic production, which are sometimes invoked in the spirit of Evans-Pritchard's (1940: 85) dictum: "it is scarcity and not sufficiency that makes people generous." The role of friendship both in politics and in finance is reviewed critically, and argued to be far more restricted than is commonly assumed. I consider too the ways in which political and social conflicts, enacted chiefly in the struggles to establish and broaden the democracy, may have conditioned the values attaching to friendship. In some respects, as Louis Gernet (1981: 288) suggests, the revolution that "ended the nobility's power" may have served to inspire new classes with "the concept of their kind of life," and aristocratic patterns of friendship may have been generalized; but the aristocracy in turn may have appropriated archaic modes of fellowship, such as that represented by *xenia* or "guest-friendship," as enabling and expressing the kind of display proper to their class. Particular attention is given in this chapter to Aristotle's analysis of friendship in the context of his discussion of *philia* generally, since it is the most comprehensive and intelligent treatment in all antiquity.

The chapter on the Hellenistic age takes up the role of friendship in the courtly societies of the great kingdoms that succeeded upon the conquests of Alexander the Great. In Syria and Egypt, the inner circle of a king's advisers was known officially as the Friends. In this context, a new emphasis is placed on forthrightness and honesty toward superiors, for these qualities are perceived as necessary to the integrity of the ruler and the well-being of the realm. The word *parrhēsia*, which in the democratic polis had represented a political right, comes now to be understood rather as a moral virtue. At the opposite pole of the candid friend is the toady or flatterer, whose praise does harm in the measure in which the well-intentioned and tactful criticism of the true friend helps to correct the other's faults. Frank evaluation, properly applied, is also important to the moral therapies practiced in the Hellenistic philosophical schools, and I accordingly explore the connection between friendship and the common pursuit of enlightenment in these intimate societies.

In the fourth chapter, the focus shifts to Rome. Here, two questions are examined in particular detail. The first concerns the emphasis in the writings of Cicero, and in authors of the late Republic generally, on the tension between the claims of friendship and loyalty to the state. I discuss both the background of this idea in Hellenistic philosophy and the influence of the contemporary political crisis in Rome itself. The second theme is the relationship between friendship and patronage, both in the political sphere generally and more specifically in relation to the writing of poetry. The relationship between patron and client is asymmetrical rather than equal, and this has given rise to the assumption that when poets speak of friendship with their benefactors they are masking an actual relation of dependency. I argue, on the contrary, that friendship is compatible with patronage but not reducible to it. Roman friendship

even more than Greek has suffered from the modern tendency to
view it as a strictly practical arrangement, conceived openly in the
spirit in which La Rochefoucauld purports to debunk it when he
remarks that

what men have called friendship is merely association [*commerce*], respect for
each other's interests, and exchange of good offices – in fact, nothing more
than a business arrangement from which self-love is always out to draw
some profit.[26]

The last chapter, on Christian and pagan conceptions of friendship, begins by examining the way in which the triad of friendship,
frankness, and flattery appears to assume a new significance, as the
emphasis in at least certain treatises shifts from concern with the
candid criticism of others to an honest disclosure of one's own
weaknesses. Correspondingly, alongside the figure of the adulator,
who dissimulates his opinion of his friend in order to exploit him,
there seems now to emerge the type of the hypocrite, who conceals
his own debilities solely with a view to being liked. The chapter
concludes with an examination of how the ideas of brotherhood and
universal love begin to displace, at least in the writings of some
Christians in the fourth century AD, the classical ideal of friendship
predicated on the mutual respect inspired by personal virtue. In
addition, I consider the sources of the Christian notion of friendship
with God, which seems the antithesis to the classical insistence on at
least a certain minimum of equality between the partners to a
friendship.

The review of the contents of this book given above also reveals
what is not to be found in it. Many stories and anecdotes betray the
variety as well as the intensity of the sentiments that enter into
friendship and that are "part of its large untidy essence" (Strawson
1991: 5). Private letters such as Cicero's or the rich correspondence of
Symmachus, Libanius, and Gregory of Nazianzus in the fourth
century AD illuminate personal experiences of missing an absent
friend, the pain and anger that attend a falling out, or the simple
delight that two people take in each other's company that makes
these ancient figures seem young and alive. Autobiographical accounts like Augustine's *Confessions*, as well as eulogies of the dead,
bespeak a quality of grief for lost friends that is the other side of love.
There is a specificity and timelessness about these narratives and

[26] La Rochefoucauld 1964: maxim 83; cit. Silver 1996: n.52.

moments of self-revelation that speak across centuries, if one has the ear to listen to them. But it is just their timelessness, and my reluctance to mediate the sensibilities of others through my own powers of empathy, that have discouraged me from exploiting such opportunities for emotional insight in the course of this history. The book is drier for it; however, readers will be guided to many deeply moving passages in classical literature that they may savor and appreciate for themselves.

It is also in the nature of a short book to be selective, and certain topics have necessarily been neglected or treated all too briefly. For example, virtually nothing is said about *amicitia* as a term for alliances between states, although the use of *philia* in this sense is discussed, albeit succinctly. A fuller discussion of terms related to *philos* and *amicus* would also have been desirable. Again, I have neglected to contemplate – and this is perhaps a more important exclusion – what the lack of a specific term for the relationship between *philoi* may imply for the nature of friendship in classical Greece. The wide reference of the word *philia* to all kinds of affectionate associations presumably reveals something about the connection between Greek friendship and other forms of love. I hope that these and other omissions are compensated for by the relatively greater attention bestowed on some of the more controversial aspects of friendship in antiquity.

This book is the first comprehensive study in English of friendship in the classical world.[27] There are numerous specialized investigations, of course, though fewer than one might have expected of a concept so important in ancient society. Indeed, there is relatively little research on the history – properly speaking – of friendship in any culture.[28] To some extent, then, this book attempts to break new ground. I am, of course, deeply indebted to the work of colleagues. When I disagree with their views, I cite them in order to alert the reader to serious alternatives. For if there is one thing that I am certain of in connection with ancient friendship, it is that this is not the last word on the subject.

[27] For a survey in Italian, see Pizzolato 1993.
[28] But see Parekh 1994 on friendship in classical India.

CHAPTER I

Archaic Greece

THE WORLD OF HOMER

As the oldest evidence for the history of friendship in the classical world, the two epic poems attributed to Homer present a paradox. The relationship between Achilles and Patroclus in the *Iliad* is often cited in antiquity as one of three or four legendary friendships. Theocritus (29.34), for instance, calls it exemplary; Bion of Smyrna (fr. 12) lauds Achilles and Patroclus along with Theseus and Peirithous and Orestes and Pylades, and Dio Chrysostom (*Or.* 57.28) mentions the same three pairs as the only examples of true friendship in all history. Lucian (*Toxaris* 10, trans. Harmon 1936: 119) remarks on the Greek "poets, who have rehearsed in the most beautiful of epic lines and lyric verses the friendship [*philia*] of Achilles and Patroclus and the comradeship [*hetaireia*] of Theseus, Peirithous, and all the rest"; Plutarch (*On Having Many Friends* 93E) praises them; in the fourth century AD, Themistius (*Or.* 22.266b, 271a), tutor to the emperor Gratian, and Libanius (*Or.* 1.56), tutor to Julian the Apostate, are still mentioning Achilles and Patroclus as model friends.[1] Their friendship, according to William Anderson (1993: 35), "showed the way for later Greek tragedy to explore the pathos of self-sacrifice and the guilt in allowing another to take on one's own fatal danger."

Nevertheless, many modern scholars suppose that in archaic epic, friendship is conceived as a formal and non-emotional bond based on obligation rather than love. Thus Paul Millett (1991: 120–1), summarizing the influential argument of Arthur Adkins (1963), writes: "Homeric 'friendship' appears as a system of calculated cooperation, not necessarily accompanied by any feelings of affection."

---

[1] Cf. also Hyginus, *Fables* (prob. second-century AD) 257.1.

What is more, friendship, family ties, and even relations with those outside the community are seen as coalescing. Walter Donlan (1985: 300) cites the view of Julian Pitt-Rivers (1973: 90) that "non-kin amity loves to masquerade as kinship," and notes that "slurred distinctions between 'friends,' 'companions,' and kin are frequent in the epic." Or, as David Halperin (1990: 84) expresses it: "friendship is parasitic in its conceptualization on kinship relations and on sexual relations. That is, it must borrow terminology from these other spheres of human relations in order to identify and define itself." Homeric epic thus concentrates the issues concerning the nature of ancient friendship that are broached in the introduction to this book.

Before approaching the evidence for friendship in Homer, it is desirable to say something about how the poems were composed, for this bears upon the relationship between life as it is represented in heroic epic and historical Greek society. The *Iliad* and the *Odyssey* achieved their present form in or around the eighth century BC. Earlier Greek texts, dating to the second millennium BC and written in a different script, can be read, but these documents, preserved on accidentally fired clay tablets, are palace records and inventories which reveal nothing of the personal relations between friends. The etymologies of Greek terms relating to friendship are disputed, and are an unreliable basis on which to reconstruct the pre-history of the concept.

The Homeric epics indeed contain older matter extending over centuries. Before writing was reintroduced into Greece in the form of the familiar Greek alphabet, poets employed clusters of words and themes in order to produce metrically correct and coherent verses in the act of performance, varying rather than reproducing previous versions of a story. These formulaic elements tend to be conservative: to change "bronze" to "iron," for example, produces an alteration in the number of syllables that disrupts the meter of a traditional expression, and for this reason, along with a desire, typical of epic, to be faithful to tradition, Homeric warriors are clad in antique brazen armor and bear spears tipped with bronze rather than iron. It is impossible, however, to isolate chronological strata in the poems. They must therefore be taken as composite works that ceased incorporating new elements only after they were reduced to writing.[2]

The relationship of the Homeric poems to the historical world of

---

[2] Formulaic composition: Lord 1960; Parry 1971; impossibility of isolating chronological strata: Nieto Hernández 1990.

archaic Greece is thus complex and remains controversial. Recent
archaeological studies suggest that at the end of the eighth century
BC, Greek society predominantly took the form of small independent
communities of fifty families or fewer. Some scholars suppose that
these villages were ruled by chieftains or "big men" who had to
reckon with more or less powerful neighbors but enjoyed a wide
latitude for individual action.[3] With such a model in mind, Walter
Donlan (1980: 301) infers that "Sociability in the Dark Age revolved,
as it does in all village societies, around the twin axes of kinship and
neighborhood," leaving little room for an independent and voluntary
bond such as friendship.

The world portrayed in the Homeric epics, however, is by no
means so elementary: cities are quite grand, with walls, market
places and public edifices, and are at the center of extended political
units comparable to states. Whether the Homeric poems recall the
splendor of the Mycenaean palace culture, or eighth-century society
was more developed than the archaeological evidence suggests,
remains moot; no doubt a fair amount of sheer invention entered
into the image of ancient grandeur. Perhaps inconsistencies in the
epics correspond to contradictions in the contemporary world. An
understanding of Homeric friendship must depend finally upon the
poems themselves which, despite their lengthy evolution, are in large
measure internally coherent in their representation of social life.[4]

Each poem, however, is a work of literature with its own theme
and character, which affects the way friendship is represented. The
Odyssey, for example, emphasizes the integrity and autonomy of the
individual homestead. When Odysseus has succeeded in returning
home to Ithaca, he relies on the support of his father, his son, and
loyal slaves to rescue his estate from fellow-citizens who, in his
absence, have been seeking marriage with his wife Penelope.
Personal bonds among fellow-Ithacans exist, of course, but the
poem stresses the importance of the family unit in safeguarding its
own property, as well as Odysseus' implacable vengeance. No one
from outside his estate helps Odysseus materially in reasserting
control over his own domain, though he is described as having been

---

[3] See Adkins 1972: 10–21; Quiller 1981; Rihll 1986; cf. Antonaccio 1995: 254–6.
[4] Cities in Homer: van Wees 1992: 28–31, 36; Snodgrass 1980: 27; Morris 1992: 27; cf.
Raaflaub 1991: 246–7; eighth-century society more developed: Sakellariou 1989: 392; *contra*
Runciman 1982: 364–70; contradictions in contemporary world: Nimis 1986: 222; Scully
1990: 81–99; Raaflaub 1991: 250–1; internal coherence of Homeric poems: van Wees 1992:
39; cf. Raaflaub 1991: 211; Raaflaub 1993: 42–59 advises caution; *contra*: Geddes 1984.

a benign and much-loved ruler. Friendship is thus marginal to the narrative.

Early in the poem, Menelaus tells Telemachus, who has come in search of news of his father, that if Odysseus had succeeded in returning from Troy, he

would have settled a city in Argos for him, and made him a home, bringing him from Ithaka with all his possessions, his son, all his people ... And, both here, we would have seen much of each other; nothing would then have separated us two in our loving and taking pleasure [*phileonte te terpomenō te*], until the darkening cloud of death had shrouded us over. (4.174–80)[5]

This is a touching picture, but in the context of the poem, Menelaus' idea is fantastic: Odysseus' entire ambition is to return to Ithaca, not to move lock stock and barrel to Menelaus' territory. Menelaus has a vision of friendship, but it has no place within the narrative economy of the poem.

In the *Iliad*, the Achaeans are at war in a foreign land, and the poem accordingly is structured not so much around individual households as around ethnic units under the leadership of their several lords: Nestor and the men of Pylos, Idomeneus and the Cretans, Achilles and his Myrmidons, and so forth. Agamemnon, as leader of the largest contingent, the Mycenaeans, is recognized as the general commander of the Greek host at Troy, which has been assembled to avenge the abduction of Helen, the wife of Agamemnon's brother Menelaus. When Agamemnon seizes Achilles' war prize, the captive maiden Briseïs, Achilles represses the impulse to kill him and instead withdraws his forces from battle. The losses that ensue humble Agamemnon, and he offers Achilles compensation. Like Odysseus in the *Odyssey*, Achilles refuses to be reconciled, but Patroclus, dearest of the Myrmidons to Achilles, prevails upon him to let him fight in his stead, wearing Achilles' armor. When Patroclus is slain by Hector, Achilles gives over his anger at Agamemnon and returns to battle in order to avenge the death of his friend.[6]

The bond between Achilles and Patroclus is thus central to the narrative. As James Hooker (1989: 34) observes: "The plot of our *Iliad* demands that Achilles and Patroclus should share a deep, unmotivated, gratuitous affection, which flourishes outside the institutions of the social hierarchy." But the exceptional character of this relationship, which is far more intense than ordinary ties of

[5] Unless otherwise indicated, all translations are my own.
[6] Achilles like Odysseus: Seaford 1994: 24.

comradeship as represented in the poem, renders it problematic in the military society of the Greeks. For even though grief for Patroclus brings about Achilles' renewed cooperation with the army under Agamemnon, his motivation for fighting is now personal revenge rather than the justice of the collective cause. It is possible that the shift in the trajectory of the poem that occurs with the death of Patroclus was Homer's own innovation in the epic tradition – a feature, that is, of the latest stage of composition. However that may be, it produces a tension between friendship and institutionalized relationships in the world of the *Iliad*, the effects of which are considered later in this chapter.[7]

PHILOS

Turning now to the texts themselves, we may begin by observing that the vocabulary for personal relations in epic diction is different not only from modern terminology but from later Greek usage as well. As is indicated in the introduction, in classical Greek the word that most closely approximates the English "friend" is the noun *philos*. Accordingly, the substantive *philos* (as opposed to the adjective) is not normally used in the classical period of family members, for example, or fellow citizens any more than "friend" is today; rather, *philos* as a noun refers to people who associate voluntarily on the basis of mutual affection. This point is controversial, and is treated more fully in the next chapter. In the language of Homer, however, *philos* does not apply specifically to friends, and this raises a question about the description of friendship in the epics.

In epic diction, the word *philos* is used primarily as an adjective. It may modify terms for close companions or relatives, and in such contexts is naturally translated as "dear"; the adjective preserves this sense in classical and later Greek as well. In archaic or archaizing literature, *philos* is applied also to parts of the body, such as knees and hands, as well as to parts of the psyche such as the *thumos* (the seat of intense feelings). Since "dear" seems inappropriate in these connections, some scholars have taken *philos* as equivalent to a possessive adjective, "one's own," and have drawn the further conclusion that this is the primary or original significance of the word. Thus, Hélène Kakridis (1963: 3) speaks of "cases where *philos*

---

[7]   Affection between Achilles and Patroclus: cf. Zanker 1994: 14–16; Homeric innovation in the role of Patroclus: Janko 1992: 313–14.

clearly and without any doubt has a possessive sense," and Manfred Landfester (1966: 69) states flatly: "Attributive *philos* in poetry, from Homer to Hellenistic poetry, is a general reflexive-possessive pronoun."[8]

Related to this view is the idea that *philos* referred originally to anything in one's personal sphere or household; thus Millett (1991: 120-1, summarizing Adkins 1963) notes "that *philos* [according to Adkins] was applied to those persons and things on which the Homeric chief (*agathos*) was dependent for his survival in a hostile world."[9] In this same vein, Mary Scott (1982: 3) interprets both the neuter *phila* (of things) and the masculine *philoi* (of people) as denoting objects on which one can rely: heart, limbs, friends, possessions. All else, in the antagonistic world of heroic epic, is hostile. "The lack of a necessarily warm or personal content in *philos*," she writes, "can be seen also in the usage of the verb *philein*," which she defines as "treat in a relaxed, non-competitive manner" (5-6). Even in reference to sex *philein* refers to "treating a woman in a non-hostile manner": one has sex with "someone with whom one may feel relaxed" (16). Love is beside the point.

James Hooker (1987) has criticized the etymological interpretation on which *philos* always means "one's own" or "an inalienable possession," as well as the insistence on the contractual or institutional, as opposed to emotional, nature of *philia* and Adkins' view that the term refers to things that belong to one's own sphere or estate.[10] Hooker (55) lists a series of passages in which "the verb is qualified by a word or phrase of such a nature as to make it plain that an affectionate *attitude* is being described" (e.g. *Il*. 3.415, 9.485-6, 24.762, 772-5), and he proposes (64) that the basic sense of *philos* is just "dear": the meaning "one's own" is a later accretion, deriving from formulaic collocations with the possessive pronoun (cf. *Il*. 19.4: *hon philon huion*, "her own dear son"). The co-presence of *philos* and the possessive more plausibly suggests, indeed, that they were perceived as distinct, and David Robinson has argued on the basis of a meticulous examination of cases and contexts that the adjective *philos*, whether masculine, feminine, or neuter, is appropriately rendered by "beloved" virtually every time it occurs, and that "in

---

[8] Cf. (e.g.) Heubeck and Hoekstra 1989: 196.
[9] Cf. Heubeck, West and Hainsworth 1988: 257, 297.
[10] Possessive sense: cf. Rosén: 1959; institutional: Benveniste 1973.

fact *no* contexts in Homer either require or are best suited by a possessive sense" (1990: 98).

Robinson (1990: 101) notes that *philos* may have the active sense of "loving," the passive sense of "beloved," and the reciprocal or "active-and-passive" sense of "a friend." Expressions such as "dear knees," "dear heart" and the like commonly occur, he observes, in life-threatening situations when the hero is especially aware of how precious his limbs and vital organs are (the knees may have been conceived as a node in a life-line extending through the genitals to the chin; words for all three parts are etymologically related); alternatively, the adjective may indicate the loyalty or steadfastness of one's mind or spirit. Robinson's analysis renders otiose the supposition that *philos* denotes an objective possession rather than a personally cherished individual or thing.[11] In addition, it restores affection to human relations in the world of the epics.

As a noun, *philos* occurs relatively rarely in Homer, and when it does it has rather a broad reference. We may leave aside such cases as *Iliad* 2.110, where Agamemnon addresses the Achaean army: "O *philoi*, Danaan heroes, henchmen [*therapontes*] of Ares," for *philoi* here retains its adjectival sense, whether as modifier ("dear Danaan heroes") or in the sense of "my dear men."[12] In all periods, Greeks employed the vocative of *philos* (singular *phile*) as a conventional term of endearment, and the parallel use of the superlative "dearest" (*philtate*) is a reminder of its adjectival character. So too, when Telemachus appeals to his mother's suitors as *philoi* in the assembly at Ithaca (*Od.* 2.70), "my dear men" ironically underscores their hostility toward him.

But *philos* is sometimes applied substantivally to the people of one's own community. When Odysseus is abroad among distant populations such as the Cyclopes and Phaeacians, he is described in a formulaic phrase as being *philōn apo*, "distant from *philoi*" (*Od.* 7.152; cf. 19.301 *tēle philōn kai patridos aiēs*, "far from *philoi* and fatherland"; also 9.532). Although enmities may arise among townsmen, as the *Odyssey* makes all too clear, when opposed to complete strangers the people back home are "near and dear." One need not restrict *philoi* in these contexts to members of one's immediate family, even though certain scholia (marginal annotations in manuscripts often going back to ancient commentaries) to *Odyssey* 1.238 say that *philoi* are

[11] Knees, genitals, chin: Onians 1954: 174–86; personally cherished: Zanker 1994: 13–14.
[12] Ulf 1990: 136.

relatives (*oikeioi*) or those belonging to the same descent-group (*genos*), while those connected by *philia* are comrades (*hetairoi*). In the final book of the *Odyssey* (24.188) one of the dead suitors just arrived in the underworld tells the ghost of Agamemnon that the suitors' bodies are still untended in Odysseus' house, "for our *philoi* in the house of each [of us: *kata dōmat' hekastou*] do not yet know [of our deaths]." Some commentators cite this passage as evidence that *philos* has the meaning "kin," and indeed *philoi* refers here to the immediate relatives of the several deceased, but the phrase "in the house of each" is appended to *philoi* precisely in order to restrict the sense: the meaning is, "our dear ones, taken house by house." As a substantive, *philos* retains the looseness or breadth of the adjective (cf. *Od.* 13.192: *astoi te philoi te*).[13]

To sum up: contrary to the still prevailing view, *philos* in the archaic epic always suggests a positive affect, and this says much about the intensity of feeling for home and loved ones that is ascribed to the heroes. However, *philos* does not have in Homeric Greek the specific reference to friends that it acquires in classical diction.

HETAIROS

Philos is not the only term in Homer applied to associates other than kin. Another word frequently translated as "friend" is *hetairos* (in poetry also spelled *hetaros*). Christoph Ulf (1990: 129) identifies four kinds of connections to which the term *hetairos* may refer: small, ethnically related groups around a leader; larger bodies tantamount to an entire ethnic group; groups of leaders from independent social entities; and, finally, leaders and their entire following, for example the Trojans or the Achaeans as a whole. Ulf's classification may be overly precise, but none of his categories depends essentially on voluntary associations between individuals who are personally dear to one another.[14]

Odysseus and his crew in the *Odyssey*, for example, are mates or companions rather than personal friends. Odysseus may refer to them collectively as "dear" or *philos* (9.466) when he is mourning those who have perished, but hostilities flare up among them and

---

[13] *Philoi* as members of family: Dirlmeier 1931: 8; cf. Spinelli 1983–4: 55 n.15; the scholia are cited in Ebeling 1963: 2.434; cf. Landfester 1966: 71–2.

[14] On the senses of *hetairos*, cf. also Dirlmeier 1931: 22–3; H. Kakridis 1963: 51–75; less reliable: Stagakis 1975: 65–93.

there is no necessary sense of personal affection. When his shipmate
Eurylochus opposes Odysseus' authority among the *hetairoi*, Odysseus
reaches for his sword and only the appeals of the other comrades
prevent a murder (10.428–42). After the blinding of the Cyclops,
Polyphemus prays to his father Poseidon that Odysseus never reach
home; "But if it is his lot to see his *philoi* and to reach his well-built
house [*oikos*] and his fatherland, may he come late and badly, having
lost all his *hetairoi*, on a foreign ship, and may he find trouble in his
house" (9.532–5). The contrast is instructive: *hetairoi* refers to Odysseus' shipmates, while *philoi* indicates his dear ones back in Ithaca.

Some companions or *hetairoi* may be particularly dear. At *Odyssey*
8.581–6, the Phaeacian lord Alcinous, having observed that Demo-
docus' song about Troy has caused Odysseus to weep, inquires of the
hero:

Has then some relative of yours died at Ilium who had been a good man, a
son-in-law or father-in-law, who are closest kin [*kēdistoi*] after one's own
blood and family? Or perhaps some *hetairos*, a man of graciousness, and
good? For not worse than a brother is a *hetairos* who has wisdom.

Hetairos here is clearly distinguished from kin, whether by blood or
marriage.[15] But this *hetairos* is no ordinary comrade: Alcinous
wonders whether Odysseus may be grieving over an especially
intimate companion. Alcinous is wrong in this case: Odysseus has no
such friend; indeed, Jenny Strauss Clay (1983: 107) has suggested that
Homer is implicitly contrasting the loner Odysseus with the profound
bond between Achilles and Patroclus.

Achilles and Patroclus are not the only comrades who are close.
For example, we are told that Sthenelus "gave Aeneas's horses into
the care of Deïpylus, his dear companion [*hetaros philos*], whom he
honored above all of his age group" (5.325–6).[16] When Achilles
rejects Agamemnon's ambassadors' every appeal to return to battle,
Ajax complains that Achilles "cares nothing for the love [*philotēs*] of
his companions [*hetairoi*], with which we honored him by the ships
beyond the others" (*Il.* 9.630–1), and then declares directly to
Achilles: "we, out of the mass of the Danaans, share your roof, and
we have desired to be closest [*kēdistoi*] and dearest [*philtatoi*] to you
beyond all the other Achaeans" (640–2). So too Phoenix, Achilles'
aged tutor, draws a parallel between Achilles and Meleager who was

---

[15] Cf. the scholia cited in Dyck 1983: 154.
[16] Cf. *Od.* 22.208–9; on *hetairoi* as age-mates, see Aristophanes of Byzantium fr. 306–7, ed.
Slater 1986: 102.

not persuaded to return to battle even by "his *hetairoi*, those who were closest and dearest of all [*kednotatoi kai philtatoi*]" (9.585–6). But Patroclus, above all, is described as Achilles' *polu philtatos hetairos*, "dearest companion by far" (17.411, 655).

While *hetairos*, then, covers a relatively wide range of companionable relations, those *hetairoi* who are singled out as *philoi* belong to the most intimate circle of a man's companions and age-mates and may reasonably be regarded as friends.[17] *Philos* is not the only adjective to denote such a special status. Ulf (1990: 136) notes that the term *pistos*, "faithful" or "trustworthy," is reserved to describe the closest companions. Metrically, *philos* and *pistos* are complementary, and function like two formulaic epithets attaching to the same hero.[18]

Taken together, the terminological complex constituted by *hetairos* and the markers *philos* and *pistos* embraces the essential elements associated with friendship: a select relationship between non-kin grounded in mutual affection ("dearness") and loyalty or trust. The path to this conclusion has been rather laboriously philological. But scholars have minimized the role of voluntary affective bonds in the epics, and in the absence of external evidence only a close inspection of usage in the texts can reveal the clear conception of affection and personal friendship to which they testify.

XENOS

The adjective *philos* also serves to mark the bond between strangers (*xenoi* or, in epic diction, *xeinoi*) that is commonly translated as "guest-friendship." To take the best-known instance: when Diomedes and the Lycian hero Glaucus, who is allied with Troy, are about to engage in single combat, they discover that their grandfathers were connected by ties of hospitality. Diomedes plants his spear in the ground, and speaks cordially to his antagonist (*Il.* 6.224–31, trans. Lattimore 1951):

Therefore I am your friend and host [*xeinos philos*] in the heart of Argos; you are mine in Lykia, when I come to your country. Let us avoid each other's spears, even in close fighting ... But let us exchange our armour, so that these others may know how we claim to be guests and friends from the days of our fathers [*xeinoi patrōioi*].

[17] *Contra* Donlan 1989: 12, 22, who collapses the categories of *philos* and *hetairos* to signify the followers, whether kin or neighbors, of a Homeric warrior and his *oikos*.
[18] Hummel 1988.

The term *xe(i)nos*, rendered here as "friend and host" or "guest and friend," most commonly in Homer signifies a "stranger." In classical Greek, *xenos* means "foreigner," that is, an inhabitant of a different polis or country or a non-resident visitor as opposed to a fellow-citizen (*astos, sumpolitēs*).[19] The term may also designate a foreign friend; the lexicographer Hesychius (*c.* 5th century AD) defines a *xeinos* (s.v.) as "a friend [*philos*] from a foreign land [*xenē,* sc. *gē*]." Thus, in Euripides' *Alcestis*, Heracles is Admetus' *xenos* (540, 554); he may also be called his *philos* (562, 1011). Admetus' countrymen, however, are simply *philoi* (369, 935, 960; cf. *philos,* 212), never *xenoi.* "To be a polis ... a community had to distinguish formally between members and nonmembers" (Manville 1990: 82).

A stranger, however, is someone unknown, and it is paradoxical that a *xenos* in Homer should be called *philos* or "dear." Strangers should not be equated with foreigners; the epic word for someone who lives elsewhere is *allodapos* (e.g. *Od.* 3.74). In the *Iliad,* no two Achaeans are ever described as *xenoi* of one another, though they come from various and distant communities; correspondingly, only members of the same camp are called *ekhthroi* or "personal enemies." When Odysseus is in the land of the Phaeacians, however, the queen Arete, to whom he has appealed for assistance to reach Ithaca since he is suffering "far from his dear ones" (*philōn apo,* 7.152), reproaches her husband Alcinous for allowing a *xeinos* to sit neglected on the ground (7.160; cf. 162, 166). Odysseus is obviously not a local and is unknown to the royal couple.[20]

Similarly, when Telemachus and Nestor's son Pisistratus arrive at the palace of Menelaus in Sparta, Menelaus' henchman (*therapōn*) Eteoneus, who has found the pair standing in the forecourt, announces to the king the presence of two *xeinō* (dual of *xeinos*), and inquires whether to invite them in or send them on to someone else who might give them a friendly reception (*hos ke philēsei,* 4.26–9). Menelaus, with a show of irritation, bids him to summon the strangers in (4.36), since his house is rich enough to entertain guests. Homer is indulging in a bit of comedy here: the audience will recall

---

[19] For the contrast, cf. Pindar, *Isth.* 1.51; Theognidea 793–4; *Carm. Epigr.* 112, 123 Hansen; Sophocles *Oedipus at Colonus* 13, 1335; Lysias 6.17; [Anacreon] *Anth. Pal.* 143.4 = Campbell 1988: 106D; LSJ s.v. A.3; Scheid-Tissinier 1990 wrongly discerns this distinction already in the *Odyssey.*

[20] Conflation of stranger and foreigner: e.g. H. Kakridis 1963: 86; Achaeans wrongly described as *xenoi*: Belmont 1962: 35; Takabatake 1988: 450 misleadingly states that *xenos* implies non-Greek; use of *ekhthros*: Slatkin 1988: 130–1.

the last time Menelaus offered hospitality to a handsome stranger. But once the identity of the youths is known, they are no longer referred to as *xeinoi*. Nor does Homer ever describe either Nestor or Menelaus as *xeinoi*, whether of Odysseus or of Telemachus.[21] Rather, Menelaus addresses the boys from now on as *philoi* (e.g. 4.78, 204), and speaks of Telemachus as the son of a man who is "very dear" (*mala philou*, 4.169), whom he would receive lovingly (*philēsemen*, 4.171) above all the other Achaeans, and in whose company he would be pleased to spend the rest of his life sharing affection and joy (*phileonte te terpomenō te*, 4.179). Similarly, when Telemachus and Athena, who is disguised as Odysseus' foreign friend Mentes, arrive at the court of Nestor, they are greeted as *xeinoi* before they are recognized (3.34, 43, 70–1), but after their identities are disclosed, Nestor addresses Telemachus consistently as *phile*.[22]

How, then, do *xenoi* become *philoi*? One may trace the evolution of such a relationship in the case of Odysseus and the Phaeacian prince Euryalus. After the Phaeacian Laodamas suggests to his fellows (*philoi*) that they invite the stranger (*xeinos*, 8.133), that is, Odysseus, to engage in a contest, Euryalus taunts Odysseus for refusing the challenge, addressing him as *xeine* (8.159); exceptionally, in his anger, Odysseus employs the same label of Euryalus, a native in the land where he himself is the stranger (8.166). Later, when Euryalus apologizes for his discourtesy, offers a gift to Odysseus, and uses the complimentary address, "father stranger" (*pater xeine*, 8.408; cf. Laodamas' use of the formula at 145, etc.), Odysseus politely accepts the gesture of friendship and invokes the young man as *philos* (8.413).[23]

Euryalus has been accepted as a "dear stranger" (*xeinos philos*) or "guest-friend." In general, when *xenos* in the Homeric epics designates the special relationship between former strangers called *xenia*

---

[21] *Contra* Reece 1993: 64.

[22] Cf. 4.103, 184, 199, 211, 313, 352, etc.; the reference to *xeinoi* at 350 and 355 is in a generalizing context.

[23] Compare the sequence in which Penelope addresses the disguised Odysseus: 19.253–4 ("O *xeine*, you will be *philos*"); 309–10 ("O *xeine* ... you would soon recognize our *philotēs*"); culminating in 350 where she addresses him as *xeine phil'*, since, she says, he is the wisest of all the "dear far-dwelling strangers" (*xeinōn tēledapōn philiōn*) who have come to her house. Odysseus is, indeed, the quintessential stranger. Although Homeric Greek does not employ the definite article, Joseph Russo (Russo *et al.* 1992: 10 *ad* 17.10) finds an anticipation of this function "in one area only, that being the use of the word ξεῖνος." All but one case, however, are in reference to Odysseus, who is thus marked as "*the* stranger" (or "that stranger": Russo III *ad* 20.52) *par excellence*, a familiar, quasi-demonstrative use of the article form in Homer.

(*Od.* 5.91, 24.286), it is modified by another term or appears in a context that specifies the sense. Thus, in the encounter between Diomedes and Glaucus cited earlier, Diomedes explains that Glaucus is his "ancient ancestral *xeinos*" (6.215), adds that his grandfather Oineus entertained (*xeinis'*) Bellerophon and that they exchanged the gifts of hospitality (*xeinēia*), and concludes that therefore he is Glaucus' *xeinos philos* (6.224). So too, Telemachus inquires whether Mentes (Athena in disguise) is his ancestral (*patrōios*) *xeinos* (1.175–6); Mentes affirms in reply that he and Odysseus are exactly that (187; cf. *philoi xeinoi* at 313).[24]

The adjective *philos*, in particular, picks out among *xenoi* or strangers those with whom relations of hospitality are acknowledged. It thus qualifies a certain subset of *xenoi* as "dear," just as it does with *hetairoi*, and indeed with family members: though sons are normally dear, the epithet is not automatic; thus, Hera says of Sarpedon, Zeus' son by a mortal woman (*Il.* 16.450): "But if he is *philos* to you ..." This, then, is friendship between strangers: it is voluntary and affective. There is an expectation in the epics that strangers should be welcomed in a hospitable manner, and Zeus may be invoked as Xenios, "god of strangers" (*Od.* 9.270–1), but such courtesy is not obligatory. Neither is there a prescribed ceremony to establish *xenia*: in the manner of oral epic, scenes in which strangers are greeted, like other type-scenes, have broadly similar features, but there is no evidence – contrary to a widely held view – that friendships between strangers were solemnly sealed with ritual formalities.[25]

Some scholars have supposed that the continuity of stranger-friendships is proof that they were based on a rigorous and binding code. Thus, Arthur Adkins (1972: 18) writes: "these relationships [involving *philotēs*, a poetic form of *philia*] have a very objective character. Once they have been established, their existence does not depend on the inclinations of those who are involved in them." Nor, he adds, does *philotēs* "depend on the feelings or inclinations of those who inherit it, since Glaucus and Diomedes have never seen one

---

24 At *Od.* 19.239–40, it is supposed that a *xeinos* has given Odysseus a gift, since he was *philos* to many. At *Od.* 9.18, where Odysseus reveals his name to the Phaeacians "so that I may be a *xeinos* to you though I dwell in a faraway home," the dative ("to you") helps to fix the relevant sense. In Herodotus too, when the word *xenos* refers to a foreign friend, it is most often indicated by a hendiadys (e.g. *philos kai xeinos*, 3.21.1, 3.40.2; *xeinos kai summakhos*, 1.22.4), a verb such as *genomenos* (3.88.1, 6.70.1: one does not *become* a stranger), a possessive pronoun or the equivalent (7.29.2, together with *poieumai*; 7.237.3), or other marker.

25 Greeting scenes: Reece 1993; ritualized *xenia*: Herman 1987; on formal friendship, cf. Gibbs 1962; Paine 1970: 146–56; Goitein 1971; Brain 1976: 18–19, 93.

another before." Gabriel Herman (1987: 69) puts the point crisply: "a person could die, but the role of *xenos* could not." This language is too corporate. It is true that an ancient bond of hospitality can be invoked by descendants, who may then claim to be "ancestral" *xeinoi*. Friends might hope that succeeding generations would elect to renew the relationship, but nothing obliges them to do so: Diomedes' offer to exchange armor represents the voluntary resumption of the *xenia* between their forebears. So too, when Telemachus says to Nestor's son Pisistratus (*Od.* 15.196–7), "We aver that we are *xeinoi* forever out of the *philotēs* [affection] of our fathers, and we are also of the same age," he does not claim to inherit a parental bond but invokes it as one reason for initiating their own *xenia*. Analogously, in the classical period, the orator Isocrates tells the young Demonicus, with whose father he had been friends, that "it is fitting that sons inherit not only paternal estates but friendships too" (1.2); this is plainly a ploy to gain the boy's good will, not proof that the Greeks held friendship to be hereditary.

How and why a special vocabulary for friendships between strangers emerged is obscure (H. Kakridis 1963: 100–1 suggests that friends who met through hospitality kept the name of stranger). Much has been claimed for the importance of the institution of *xenia* in archaic society, but while it may occasionally have facilitated travel in a rough world innocent of international law, the Homeric epics give no evidence that such a function was primary: no one selects a destination on the grounds that he has a *xenos* there.[26] As for alliances between peoples, *philotēs* rather than *xenia* seems to be the term of art (*Il.* 3.323, 3.354). Whatever its origins, the practice of *xenia* in archaic epic has been assimilated to the ideal of a bond predicated on affection and identified, like intimate relations between comrades, by the marker *philos* or "dear."[27]

ERŌS

That the relationship between Achilles and Patroclus involves affection cannot be in doubt. But is there something more? In classical Athens, the bond between them was sometimes interpreted as one of erotic love. In Plato's *Symposium*, a work devoted to the praise of

---

[26] *Xenia* and international travel: e.g. Donlan 1980: 14.

[27] It is also possible, as in the case of the Lycian Sarpedon and Hector, to be a "*xeinos* and *hetairos* at once" (*Il.* 17.150).

erotic passion, Phaedrus observes that the gods "honored Achilles, the son of Thetis, and sent him to the Isles of the Blest, because ... he dared choose to help his lover Patroclus and avenge him, not only dying in behalf of but also in addition to the slain." Phaedrus continues:

Aeschylus talks nonsense in claiming that Achilles was the lover of Patroclus, when he was not only more beautiful than Patroclus but doubtless than all the other heroes too, and still beardless, since he was very much younger, as Homer tells'. (179d-180a, trans. Allen 1991: 119–20).

The idea was common enough for the Alexandrian commentator Zenodotus to have supposed that a particularly intense expression of Achilles' love for Patroclus had been interpolated by someone who wished to represent their relationship as erotic (scholia to *Il.* 16.97–100).

The view seems to have gone out of fashion after the fourth century BC, though Virgil perhaps alludes to it in his portrait of Nisus and his boyish friend Euryalus in *Aeneid* 9. There are smirking references to an erotic connection between the heroes in Plutarch (*Amatorius* 751c), Martial (11.43.9–10), the epigrammatic poet Strato of Lampsacus, and Lucian (*Amores* 54), though it is clear that their interpretations run contrary to sober opinion. Thus Martial: "However much Briseïs may have turned her back to him in bed, his hairless friend was closer to Achilles." In one of the epistles to Lucilius (88.6), Seneca mentions the relative ages of Achilles and Patroclus as a popular conundrum; this may have referred to the problem of who was lover and who beloved. Modern scholarship has resurrected the topic: W.M. Clarke (1978: 395) insists that "Achilles and Patroclus are not Homeric 'friends' but are lovers from their hearts," irrespective of whether they practiced sodomy.[28]

The matter of a sexual connection could be dismissed as irrelevant to the question of Achilles' and Patroclus' friendship were it not that in classical Greece erotic love and friendship were understood normally to be incompatible relationships. In friendship, roles are symmetrical: all parties are designated by the single term *philos*. *Erōs*, on the contrary, involves complementary roles: the active or dominant partner is the lover or *erastēs*, while the passive or subordinate partner is the beloved (masc. *erōmenos*; fem. *erōmenē*). Thus, in defining

[28] Nisus and Euryalus: La Penna 1983: 308, 313; Achilles and Patroclus as lovers: cf. Hutter 1978: 67–8; *contra* Barrett 1981: 91.

the connection between Achilles and Patroclus as an erotic bond, Plato naturally represents it as asymmetrical: that is why it is important to him to distinguish lover and beloved. Erotic relations between men were imagined on the model of pederasty, in which the lover was an older male attracted by the comeliness of a youth, whose appearance was thought to resemble that of a woman – hence the mention of hairlessness in Martial's coarse couplet. The beloved in turn was thought to respond to the care and attention of the older man, rather than to feel an active desire of the sort inspired by physical beauty. Whereas the lover, says Plato (*Phaedrus* 255d), experiences passionate desire or *erōs*, the beloved is expected to feel affection or *philia*; or, as Aristotle puts it, friends "must not be like the erotic lover and the boy he loves. For these do not take pleasure in the same things; the lover takes pleasure in seeing his beloved, while the beloved takes pleasure in being courted by his lover" (*EN* 8.4, 1157a6–9, trans. Irwin 1985; cf. *EE* 7.3, 1238b36–9; Alexis fr. 70 K-A; Theocritus 29. 22–34). Friendship, on the contrary, depends on mutuality and equality, as reflected in the jingle *philotēs isotēs*, "amity is parity," (Aristotle *EN* 8.5, 1157b36; *EE* 7.8, 1241b13).[29]

It is easy to reject the classical view of an erotic connection between Achilles and Patroclus as a projection upon the *Iliad* of a later practice. There is no secure evidence that the Greek institution of pederasty predates the Homeric epics, although some scholars believe that the bond between Achilles and Patroclus is a sanitized version of an initiation ritual. A perceived ambiguity between erotic and friendly affection may be a consequence simply of the poem's emphasis on Achilles' passion – a fervent complex of love, guilt, and grief – rather than on common expectations of a friend's obligations. In medieval Europe, where intense bonds between men were sometimes sanctioned as fictive brotherhood, they were similarly exposed to an erotic description, and might evoke, even then, memories of Achilles and Patroclus along with David and Jonathan.[30]

---

[29] Love and friendship mutually exclusive: Dirlmeier 1931: 59–61; Konstan 1993; *contra* (with weak arguments) Boswell 1994: 76–80; friendship symmetrical: Leach 1968: 57; Paine 1969a: 507; Hutter 1978: 6; erotic roles complementary: Halperin 1990: 30; cf. Skinner 1979: 142; Richlin 1983: 140, 212; Richlin 1991: 173; for an analogous complementarity in homoerotic love in a contemporary society, see Alonso and Koreck 1993; Almaguer 1993; cf. Carrier 1985; Lancaster 1988.

[30] Absence of pederasty in Homer: Buffière 1980: 367–74; cf. Sergent 1986: 250–8; Bremmer 1980; Achilles' guilt: Arieti 1985; cf. Shay 1994: 23–55; medieval Europe: Chaplais 1994: 5–14, 110–11; cf. Bray 1990; Jaeger 1991; Sinfield 1994: 14–15.

THERAPŌN

The evident disparity between Achilles and Patroclus, however, may
also have supported an erotic interpretation. Patroclus is described
as the *therapōn* of Achilles, a word that may be rendered as "squire"
or "henchman," although it does not necessarily indicate lower
social status; Glaucus occupies a similar role in respect to Sarpedon,
as Sthenelus does to Diomedes (for Sthenelus and Diomedes as
friends, see Themistius *Or.* 22.271b). Like them, Patroclus is at the
service of his lord. Prior to the departure for Troy, Patroclus' father
had instructed him, Nestor says, to offer good counsel to Achilles, for
Achilles, though the younger man, is his superior in lineage (*geneē*) as
well as in strength (*Il.* 11.785–8). Achilles' father had adopted
Patroclus into his household as *therapōn* to Achilles after Patroclus
had slain a fellow youth in his home country (23.89–90).[31]

Patroclus has the duty or privilege of waiting on Achilles in various
ways, such as setting the table. When, for example, Odysseus, Ajax,
and Phoenix arrive at Achilles' tent, Achilles calls to Patroclus to "set
up a mixing-bowl that is bigger, and mix us stronger drink, and make
ready a cup for each man, since these who have come beneath my
roof are the dearest of men" (*philtatoi andres*, 9.202–4, trans. Lattimore
1951, modified). When Achilles judges that it is time for the ambassadors to leave, he nods to Patroclus to make up a bed for Phoenix, so
that the others may "think of going home from his shelter" (9.620–2).
The affection between the heroes is embedded in a hierarchical
structure that involves an element of deference and even of fear, as
when Patroclus resists Nestor's effort to detain him: "You know
yourself, aged sir beloved of Zeus, how *he* is; a dangerous man; he
might even be angry with one who is guiltless" (11.651–3, trans.
Lattimore). At the same time, Patroclus is frankly critical of Achilles'
behavior (16.21–45), indicating that the intimacy between the two
overrides the difference in station, although Plutarch, in his essay
"How to Distinguish a Flatterer from a Friend" (67a), takes note of
Patroclus' tact. A *therapōn* may be singled out as especially dear or
philos (*Il.* 7.149 of Ereuthalion, squire of Lycurgus). It is significant
that in Patroclus' case, however, the adjective attaches rather to his
status as *hetairos*.[32]

---

[31] Status of *therapōn*: H. Kakridis 1963: 85; Stein-Hölkeskamp 1989: 27–8; cf. Shay 1994: 42.
[32] Achilles' anger: cf. Van Wees 1992: 76–7; David Sider suggests to me that Patroclus may

PATROCLUS AND ACHILLES

In a world characterized by various ties of affection, whether lateral between comrades and strangers or embedded within hierarchical relations such as that of lord and squire, Achilles' love for Patroclus overshadows all other friendships. When he learns of Patroclus' death, Achilles says to his mother Thetis: "my dear comrade [*philos hetairos*] has perished, Patroclus, whom I honored beyond all other comrades, as well as my own life" (18.80–2, trans. Lattimore 1951, modified). Later, he declares: "there is nothing worse than this I could suffer, not even if I were to hear of the death of my father ... or of the death of my dear son" (19.321–2, 326, trans. Lattimore). Most striking of all is the prayer Achilles utters as he prepares to send Patroclus into battle in his stead: "Father Zeus, Athene and Apollo, if only not one of all the Trojans could escape destruction, not one of the Argives, but you and I could emerge from the slaughter so that we two alone could break Troy's hallowed coronal" (16.97–100, trans. Lattimore). This is the passage that Zenodotus marked as an interpolation motivated by a homoerotic reading of Achilles' relation with Patroclus.

As part of the three-man embassy sent by Agamemnon to convey gifts and reconcile Achilles, Phoenix narrates the story of Meleager, who also withdrew from battle and did not return until it was too late. Meleager's fellow citizens tried to change his mind; then his parents pleaded with him; next came his closest friends; finally his wife, Cleopatra, persuaded him. Now, Odysseus, in the petition to Achilles, can be seen as representing the Greek army as a whole; Phoenix, who raised Achilles from infancy, stands *in loco parentis*; lastly, Ajax, in his appeal to his personal bond with Achilles, is comparable to the intimate friends of Meleager. The embassy, of course, fails in its purpose, and Achilles does not begin to yield until Patroclus himself pleads with him (book 16). It has been suggested that Patroclus thus occupies the place of the wife in the Meleager story: her name, Cleopatra, puns on Patroclus by reversing the roots *patēr*, "father," and *kleos*, "fame."[33]

Patroclus dies in the armor of Achilles, and there are hints in the *Iliad* that the two are symbolically identified as alter egos: both are

---

exaggerate his fear in order to escape the garrulous Nestor; Patroclus' frankness: Bruce Heiden, personal communication.

[33] J.T. Kakridis 1949: 21–4; Nagy 1979: 104–8.

called "best of the Achaeans," both are said to be "equal to Ares," and the lamentation over the body of Patroclus prefigures that for Achilles himself; the metaphorical assimilation calls to mind Aristotle's image of a friend as another self.[34]

The bond between Achilles and Patroclus occupies an extreme position on the spectrum of friendships, and the rich artistic resources of epic poetry are exploited to indicate its depth of feeling. Its exceptional character, which derives from Achilles' ardent temperament and the special circumstances in which Patroclus dies in his place, makes it the model of an exclusive dyadic relationship that appears to transcend the normal order of things. Achilles' private motive for returning to battle is a sign of the potentially anti-social character of his passion for Patroclus, and points to a latent tension in the ancient conception of friendship that in later times takes the form of a conflict between loyalty to friends and duty to others.[35]

THE WORLD OF HESIOD

The *Works and Days* of Hesiod introduces a world very different from that of the Homeric epics. It is, as Paul Millett (1984: 85) observes, "a peasant society," which is to say a society of farmers who depend to a substantial degree on their own labor though they may possess slaves and hire help, who own their property or *oikos*, and who are subordinate to a class that has a disproportionate control of power, like the princely aristocracy of whom Hesiod complains. Cooperation is an important value, but it is to be treated with caution and an eye to one's own advantage: "welcome him who welcomes you [*ton phileonta philein*], meet him who meets you, give if he gives, give not if he gives not" (*Works and Days* 353-4). The context suggests that *philein* here means "receive hospitably," a common signification in Homer (e.g. *Od.* 4.29). Similarly, Hesiod advises that we summon to dinner one who welcomes or is well-disposed toward us (*ton phileonta*, 342), but leave an enemy (*ekhthros*) alone. He goes on to specify that it is best to invite whoever lives nearest, "for if any local trouble should

[34] Alter egos: Sinos 1980: 55; common epithets: Nagy 1979: 32–3, 292–4; lamentation: J.T. Kakridis 1949: 67–8; Nagy 1979: 113; Schein 1984: 129–32; Seaford 1994: 166–72. It has been suggested that the non-Greek root of *therapōn* signified "ritual substitute," and that this idea informs the narrative by which Patroclus dies in the role of Achilles (Nagy 1979: 292; cf. Van Brock 1959).

[35] On the "buddy" ideal, cf. Black 1980: 53; on the tension between loyalty to friends and social responsibility, cf. pp. 116, 131–5.

arise, neighbors [*geitones*] come as they are, while relatives get dressed: a bad neighbor [*geitōn*] is as much a disaster as a good one is a blessing" (344–6). This practical counsel thus looks to the cultivation not of friendship as such but of neighborliness, the value of which is recognized in any village society.[36]

There is, however, one passage in which Hesiod seems clearly to be speaking about friendship:

> Do not make a *hetairos* equal to a brother [*kasignētos*], but if you do, be not first to wrong him or lie with your tongue. If he begins by saying or doing something offensive, remember to pay him back double. If he accepts you again into his affection [*philotēs*] and is willing to pay the penalty, receive him: base is the man who makes now one *philos*, now another. (707–13)

The term *philos* here, which occurs in the usual formula for making friends (with *poieisthai*), is likely to be substantival rather than adjectival;[37] the context, moreover, suggests the deliberate acknowledgement of a special bond that can be broken for cause but must otherwise be cherished and respected. The friend here is in a category distinct from that of relative, neighbor, or comrade in general. To have made a friend of someone involves not just warm feelings but a sense of commitment to a relationship.

In the following verses, Hesiod warns against being known either for having too many *xeinoi* (that is, being *poluxeinos*) or none at all (*axeinos*); one must not be a *hetairos*, he adds, of bad men or pick fights with good (715–6). In these compounds, *xeinos* apparently means "companion" or "comrade"; a moment later Hesiod speaks of a communal feast as *poluxeinos* (722). The dinner or feast (*dais*) is evidently an important locus where comrades meet, and the closest among them may become *philoi*.[38]

The circle of friends, then, occupies a social space within the larger community of people (*laos, dēmos*) who are residents (*endēmoi*) of the polis, as opposed to outsiders (*xeinoi*, 225–7). The townspeople are imagined chiefly as independent proprietors, each the head of his own household or estate. Disputes over property or inheritance may be heard in the market area or *agora* (30) and are subject to the judgment of a class of princes (*basileis*, 261) who have a certain

---

[36] On the definition of "peasant," cf. Redfield 1956: 26–31; Magagna 1991: 2–19; neighborliness: cf. Anderson 1971: 103–6, 147–8, 167–9.

[37] Contrast adjective at 120, 184, 306, 309, and 520, all with dative = "dear to"; in 370 and 608, *philos* modifies a noun.

[38] Cf. Van Wees 1992: 55.

reputation for bribe-taking (cf. 221). Neighbors are competitive and vie with one another to accumulate wealth (23), but they may also assemble for meals as comrades. Beyond the family and among companions of one's own class and community, friendship affords a special tie of affection and trust.[39]

These are the elements that will provide the context for personal friendship in the classical city-state: the articulation of a sphere between individual household and civic society at large, regulated by conventions of sentiment rather than by the law of property and political rights, and betraying, at least in the early stages, a particular connection with class identity articulated around the collective feast or symposium. Nor is it entirely surprising that Hesiod's peasant world should seem to anticipate the society of the polis. Remains of early urban structures such as temples or sanctuaries suggest a progressive culture on the island of Euboea, for example, whither Hesiod traveled by ferry to compete in a poetry contest at Chalcis (650-9).[40]

LYRIC POETRY AND THE SYMPOSIUM

Internal evidence from archaic Greek lyric, elegiac, and iambic poetry (the three types are distinguished by meter and musical accompaniment), as well as a variety of later testimonies, suggest a continuing connection between friendship and symposiastic contexts in the sixth and fifth centuries BC. Technically, the symposium is said to be the second part of a feast of any kind, when dishes were removed and the drinking commenced. In Athens of the fifth century BC, however, drinking parties were regarded as an aristocratic style of entertainment, devoted to reveling, eroticism, display of wealth, and the cultivation of excellence at the lyre and poetic recitation. They may have provided a special venue for clubs or groups (*hetaireiai*) of high-born companions (*hetairoi*) which were a locus of anti-democratic sentiment and occasional political activism. Because the Athenian songs provide the clearest evidence of a relationship

---

[39] Bribe-taking princes: cf. Drews 1983: 105-6, 114.

[40] On the continuity between the archaic *dais* and the classical symposium, cf. Dentzer 1982: 126, 152, 445; Clay 1994: 38; Hesiod and the polis: Donlan 1989: 6; Euboea: Coldstream 1984: 11; more cautious: Snodgrass 1983; on Hesiod's home town of Ascra, see Snodgrass 1990: 132-3.

between symposia and friendship, it is worth considering them briefly before examining more archaic compositions.[41]

One of the lyric drinking songs or *skolia* that were sung at Athenian symposia announces: "He who does not betray a man who is his friend [*andra philon*] has great honor among mortals and gods, in my judgment" (908).[42] The hint of political treachery and civil strife is not atypical; in a song that takes the form of a prayer to Athena we read: "Restore this city and its citizens without pain and civil war [*stasis*]" (884). Another runs: "If only it were possible to know without being deceived about each man who is a friend [*andra philon*] what he is like, cutting open his chest, looking into his heart, and locking it up again" (889). Compare the advice on *hetairoi* (892): "a comrade should be straightforward and not think crooked thoughts [*skolia*]," punning on *skolia*, the name of the genre. A fragment of a drinking song quoted in Aristophanes' *Wasps* (1239–40) insists, "It is not possible ... to be a friend [*philon*] to both" (912) – a warning about conflicting loyalties and the necessity of taking sides.

Harmodius and Aristogeiton, the tyrant-slayers memorialized as lover and beloved who liberated Athens from the autocracy of the Peisistratid family, were a popular subject at Athens (893–6); in two *skolia* (894, 896) Harmodius is apostrophized as "dearest" (*philtate*), symbolically embracing him in the symposiastic company. One song (897) urges a comrade (*hetairos*) to favor worthy men and avoid the cowardly, another (903) to beware the scorpion under the rock – again the suggestion of social conflict and betrayal (these two are attributed also to the poetess Praxilla = 749–50). The *skolia* recall fondly the camaraderie among youths: one praises health, looks, wealth, "and fourth, to be young among friends" (890; cf. 892, 902).

According to an increasingly popular view among scholars, symposia provided the context for the performance of almost all of lyric and related genres of short verse. One authority (Rossi 1983: 49) affirms: "The symposium is the site of *all* monodic [non-choral] poetry ...: the history of lyric is the history of the symposium." The social character of the symposium in the period prior to the Athenian democracy is not easy to assess, but it is commonly supposed that as

[41] Later testimonies: Cooper and Morris 1990: 79; symposium as second part of feast: Schmitt-Pantel 1992: 4–6, 32, 46; aristocratic symposia: Aristophanes *Wasps* 1208–20; Plato *Republic* 420e; Dentzer 1982: 448; Cooper and Morris 1990: 77–8.

[42] Lyric poets (except for Alcaeus and Sappho) cited according to Page 1962; this is one of a series of *skolia* preserved by the antiquarian Athenaeus in his table-talk compendium *Wise Men at Dinner* 15.694c–696a.

an institution it was sustained chiefly by *hetaireiai*, fellowships or leagues of elite comrades, and that it was "the center of social and cultural life of the upper class in the archaic period" (Stein-Hölkeskamp 1989: 112; cf. 86). Thus one scholar (Pellizer 1990: 180) observes that "almost all elegiac and iambic poetry from Archilochus onwards ... finds its natural focus in the *symposion* of the *hetaireia* or the *symposion* of the tyrant"; another remarks crisply (Rösler 1980: 40): "Without *hetaireia*, no lyric poet Alcaeus."[43] The *hetaireiai* are presumed also to have been politically engaged: "To be sure, the primary function of a *hetaireia*, at all events in connection with the upheavals of the seventh and sixth centuries and often later as well, is a political one" (Rösler 1980: 33–4). The private character of the symposium made it a natural place for the hatching of conspiracies among the elite; Walter Burkert (1991: 18) comments: "The symposium as the ritual that constituted the closed club of *hetairoi* was in fact in opposition to the public sacrificial feast at the temple of the *polis*." Some scholars suppose that symposia were originally instituted as warriors' fraternities (perhaps also as scenes of initiatory rites), and were reduced to drinking parties only when archaic military heroism such as that celebrated in the Homeric epics gave way to the less aristocratic phalanx or lock-step formation of heavy-armed infantry. However that may be, archaic poetry is seen as wholly implicated in ceremonies in which men bond with each other; friendship thus becomes poetry's function, poetry friendship's vehicle.[44]

The lyric poetry that survives, however, offers surprisingly little insight into friendship. There is an apparent reference to young friends and some kind of invocation of friends in the Spartan poet Alcman (frs. 10b, 70). Anacreon, originally from Teos, mourns the premature death of a young *philos* who died in defense of his country (fr. 419). The Leucadian Philoxenus, who wrote a poem entitled "Dinner" (*Deipnon*), addresses a friend (fr. 836b.16, as emended), and in the same poem (it appears) mentions *hetairoi* having their fill of food and drink (v. 39); "comrades" here, as in Hesiod, perhaps refers to all the diners while *philos* picks out a special friend.

Alcaeus of Lesbos addresses a poem to a former friend he once could invite "for kid and pork" (fr. 71 Campbell); a scholiast suggests

---

[43] Cf. also Rösler 1990: 230; Schmitt-Pantel 1990: 20–2; Schmitt Pantel 1992: 32–42; Stehle 1994; martial elegy at symposia: Bowie 1990; Murray 1991: 96–8.

[44] Symposium vs. public feast: cf. Dentzer 1982: 448–89; warriors' fraternities: Murray 1983, 1983a; Bremmer 1990; cf. Schmitt-Pantel 1992: 45–52.

that the addressee is an *erōmenos* or boy love, which does not necessarily exclude a symposiastic context; in a drinking song, he addresses an *aitēs*, a Doric or Thessalian term for friend or beloved (cf. Alcman fr. 34). In another poem he appears to reproach friends who fail him (fr. 130a); writing, perhaps, from exile, he adapts the Homeric formula, "far from dear ones" (*pēle tōn philōn*, fr. 148, as restored). Alcaeus twice mentions *hetairoi* in the context of war (129.16; cf. 150.3–4).[45] On the evidence of these fragments, men had friends, drank with buddies, and were close to comrades-in-arms, which is not astonishing news. Larger claims about the political role of male bonding are moot.

SAPPHO AND WOMEN'S FRIENDSHIPS

Sappho, the other poet from the island of Lesbos and best known for her love poetry, addresses some women as *philai* and *hetairai*; while the word *hetaira* in classical Greek had acquired the derogatory sense of "courtesan," Athenaeus (13.571d) explains that "free women and maidens even now call their companions and friends *hetairai*, as does Sappho," and cites two instances (frs. 142, 160 Campbell); one may compare, in the classical period, Aristophanes, *Ecclesiazusae* 528–9, where Praxagora, the heroine, explains that she left the house early in the morning because a *hetaira* and *philē* was in labor and had summoned her. So too, the Byzantine dictionary known as the Suda (Σ 107) speaks of Sappho's "comrades and friends" (test. 2 Campbell; cf. also fr. 126).

Sappho's relation to the women in her circle is highly controversial. Some poems to women are erotic, and the analogy of male pederasty has suggested that Sappho's beloveds were younger women; certain fragments and testimonies lend support to this view.[46] But perhaps the contrast between relations of domination and subordination, typical of male eroticism, and ties of friendship characterized by equality and symmetry of roles was not so marked among women as it was among men, and the vocabulary of comradeship was, accordingly, more compatible with that of amorous passion in women's poetry. If indeed the structure of female homoeroticism

---

[45] Boys at symposia: Bremmer 1990.
[46] E.g. *parthenos*, "maiden," in fr. 153; *pais*, "girl" but perhaps = "daughter," in frs. 155, 164, 157d (dubiously attributed to Sappho); cf. the description of Sappho as an educator in a papyrus commentary, cited in fr. 214b; full evidence presented in Lardinois 1994.

differed from male pederasty, then Sappho's poetry may open a
window upon an erotic construction of friendship distinct from
masculine conventions. To be sure, Sappho's poetry originated in a
particular region of the northern Aegean Sea in the sixth century BC,
where social conditions need not have resembled those in Athens a
century or more later and may even have been exceptional in the
Greek world. But Sappho's poetry continued to be sung in later
times, very possibly in symposia in Athens and elsewhere, thus
preserving and representing an image of women's friendship different from that obtaining among men. It is unfortunate that the
condition of the sources does not permit a more secure and elaborate
investigation of this tantalizing possibility.[47]

IAMBIC AND ELEGIAC POETRY

Turning to iambic and elegiac poetry, Archilochus of Paros (and
later Thasos) addresses a poem to a guest who, unlike a friend, has
come uninvited – one presumes to a feast or symposium (fr. 124b);
other fragments speak of pain suffered at the hands of friends (129)
and (if the text is secure) of a friend offering assistance in battle (15).[48]
Elsewhere, Archilochus apostrophizes friends and comrades (13.6,
196; cf. *polu philtat' hetairōn*, "much the dearest of my comrades,"
168.3). Nagy (1979: 251) suggests that the insults that Archilochus
notoriously heaped on Lycambes, driving him to suicide, "are in all
likelihood framed for a general audience of receptive *philoi*," and sees
such blame poetry as "an affirmation of *philotēs* in the community."
The poems themselves, however, offer little support for such a
hypothesis. Hipponax of Ephesus, the other poet famous for invec-
tive, mentions a former comrade who, spurning his oath, treated him
unjustly (fr. 115.15–16).

An anonymous elegiac poem speaks explicitly of fellow symposiasts
as friends (adesp. eleg. 27); other poets such as Simonides of Ceos (fr.
25.6) and Dionysius Chalcus (probably mid-fifth century: frs. 4.2, 5.3)
also associate drink with friendship. An anonymous iambic poem
evokes the danger of wronging one's friends (adesp. iamb. 35.11), but
it is Solon of Athens who first associates mistreatment of friends with

---

[47] Contrast between women's love and friendship less marked: Parker 1993; Greene 1994; cf.
   also DuBois 1995: 10–18; vocabularies compatible: Konstan 1995: 57–9; Sappho's poetry
   and symposia: Skinner 1993: 136–7.
[48] Iambic and elegiac poetry cited according to West 1989, 1992.

civil dissension (fr. 4.21–2), and he too who articulates for the first time the ideal of being sweet to one's friends and bitter to one's enemies (13.5). Solon wishes to die among his *philoi* (21) and to be befriended by the powerful (37.5); he also deems happy a man who has, in addition to children, dogs, and horses, a foreign friend (fr. 23.2).

The evidence so far presented, thin as it is, suggests that common meals and drinking occasions were at least one matrix for friendship, and that private festivities may have provided opportunities for enhancing solidarity among fellow soldiers, age-mates, neighbors, or comrades generally. At such parties, which in classical times at least might involve a master of ceremonies (*arkhōn*), special games, and other ritualized practices, the closest companions may have been singled out as *philoi*. To the extent that archaic poetry was symposiastic, which remains highly uncertain, it may be seen as extolling bonds among men belonging to recognized circles of friends and acquaintances. Such institutionalized liaisons, moreover, may have emerged as a social practice especially among the aristocracy, articulated perhaps in response to popular unrest. It has been suggested, however, that Solon, who is associated with various democratic reforms in Athens in the first half of the sixth century and wrote poems of a self-consciously political nature, sought to widen the sphere of *philoi* in reaction against the traditional exclusivism of occasional poetry.[49]

THEOGNIS: FRIENDSHIP AND CLASS CONFLICT

Given the paucity of the sources, none of the above inferences is beyond criticism. But the epigrams assembled under the name of Theognis – Theognis himself lived in Megara, a small polis in the Peloponnese not far from Athens, in the seventh or sixth century BC, but verses similar in tone and form tended to migrate into the collection – represent a substantial corpus of poetry that is intensely preoccupied with class conflict and the distinction between friends and enemies. The Theognidean elegiacs project a situation of social instability (*stasis*, 51, 1081), in which a traditional aristocracy, designated as "good" (*agathos* or *esthlos*), has been displaced by a base class (*kakos*, *deilos*) that relies on wealth rather than birth: "Who could

---

[49] Symposiastic rituals: Lissarrague 1990; Solon expanding the range of *philoi*: Anhalt 1993: 147.

endure to see the good deprived of honors, the worse attaining them?" (1110–1; *timē* means both moral honor and public office; cf. 35–8). Because the categories of good and bad refer both to character and status, the newly dominant order appears the better; at the same time poverty corrupts the manners of the former nobility, rendering it ethically as well as socially inferior.[50] These ambiguities generate the ironic tension that gives Theognis' poetry its energy: "Those who used to be good are now base [*deilos*]" (57–8); "O Wealth, finest and most desired of all the gods – with you even a man who is base [*kakos*] becomes good" (1117–18). Intermarriage between the orders compounds the perversity (185–8, 1112).

A consequence of the perturbation of class relations is that the solidarity within the old aristocracy is disrupted, and this gives rise to reflections on the unreliability of friendship. On the one hand, it is best to treat the populace in general with suspicion and reserve: "Make no heart-felt friend from among *these* citizens [*astoi*], son of Polypaus, no matter what the necessity; appear a friend to all in word, but do not entrust any serious business to any" (61–5; cf. 283–4). Again: "never make a base man your *philos hetairos*" (113; cf. 1080); the advice has a self-evident character because Theognis' vocabulary amalgamates ethical and class connotations. But ties within the nobility are also undermined: "You will find few men, son of Polypaus, who prove trustworthy comrades [*pistoi hetairoi*] in difficult circumstances" (79–80; cf. 73–4, 209, 322a, 415–16, 529, 575, 645, 697–8, 813–14, 861). As John Lewis (1985: 207) observes: "A majority of the passages in the corpus dealing with *philoi* turn out to have as their subject persons who are no *philoi* at all." Wealth attracts many friends, poverty few (929–39). Symposiastic camaraderie is no sure test, for "many become *philoi hetairoi* round the wine jug, few in a serious situation" (643–4). A person who conceals his thoughts is "a base *hetairos*, better as an enemy than as a friend" (91–2; cf. 95–6, 979); correspondingly, it is easier to deceive a friend than an enemy (1219–20).[51] Even with regard to his own class, apparently, Theognis exhorts his spirit to "twist your character adaptably toward all friends, mixing in the traits that each one has" and camouflaging its color like an octopus on a rock (213–16). His suspiciousness leads him to encourage the very behavior he has condemned.

In the hostile and competitive world of the Theognidean poems,

[50] Cf. Cerri 1968; Legon 1981: 111–15; Donlan 1985: 239–42.
[51] Cf. Donlan 1985: 230–4.

loyal friendship obtains among the few *hetairoi* or comrades who may be called *pistos*, "trustworthy," and *philos*, "dear"; with these alone is it safe to be friends (*philoi*, noun). By nature, these should include all who belong to the better ranks – the *agathoi* or *esthloi* – but with their decline friendship has been corrupted, and is now largely defensive in function, practiced honestly only by the small minority of aristocrats who abide in the antique values.[52] While lamenting its deterioration, the corpus thus simultaneously claims friendship as the specific virtue of an embattled upper class which is imagined as having inherited it from an earlier epoch of organic solidarity among the elite.

Walter Donlan (1985: 226; cf. 243) concludes that "historically, the institution of friendship had changed." More specifically (225): "What appears in Theognis is a form of friendship that is qualitatively different from the traditional ideal: wary, suspicious, even hostile; loyalty and fidelity are no longer automatic reflexes." This is to endorse a Theognidean nostalgia for a bygone world of honor and good faith. Theognis' verses testify not so much to a memory of former integrity as to the vision of a dispossessed class which projects its own forms of solidarity – coteries of faithful comrades bound by personal ties – onto an idealized past. Neither is it the case that "the poet is speaking to an ostensibly integral community of *philoi* that is the *polis* of Megara" (Nagy 1985: 27). There is no city constituted out of *philoi*; the circles of friends memorialized by Theognis are a product of faction and defensiveness. The ethos of intimacy and trust among close companions is not the vestige of an archaic order in which "personal friendship and political friendship are not to be distinguished" (Donlan 1985: 230); it is rather a new politicization of friendship on the part of a class that has lost some of its former prerogatives.

The Theognidean verses, which have much in common with the Attic *skolia*, testify to the emergence of friendship as a social practice associated with the milieu of a reduced nobility. This is novel. Homeric warriors did not self-consciously cultivate partisan friendships; when Odysseus ran into trouble, he relied on family, not friends. Among the struggling farmers addressed by Hesiod's didactic poetry, good neighbors count for more than friends, although one must not neglect trustworthy companions. In Theognis' poetry,

---

[52] Cf. Stein-Hölkeskamp 1989: 91.

however, friendship is represented as a bond that potentially unites companies of right-thinking people. It is still predicated on personal affection and trust, but these dispositions are now identified as the virtues of a specific class.

It is plausible that Theognis' verses, and Solon's too, reflect the social conflicts that attended the emergence of the classical city-states. But one cannot entirely dismiss the possibility that the audiences who enjoyed the *Iliad* and *Odyssey* when they first assumed the form in which we know them also sang, on other occasions, personal poetry not very different from that which survives from the archaic period. The several genres may well have been contemporaneous and complementary, rather than sequential. Rather than posit a progression in the characterization of friendship from Homer to Hesiod and lyric poetry, or imagine in a neo-Kantian spirit that private poetry signifies the nascence of the modern self as it awakened from the collective identity of heroic epic, it is best to take archaic literature in its entirety as the variegated expression of the civic and military culture that preceded the rise of the democratic polis.[53]

[53] Contemporaneity of genres: Dover 1964; neo-Kantian interpretation: Snell 1953; cf. Cassirer 1953.

CHAPTER 2

The classical city

THE GREEK WORD FOR "FRIEND"

The poems of Solon bear witness to a period of class tension in sixth-century BC Athens, which was followed by nearly half a century of autocratic rule by Pisistratus and his sons. At the end of the century, a revolution installed a direct democracy that was ultimately to bestow political rights on all adult male citizens, including the poorest. The elite families did not completely abandon aspirations to power, and twice in the fifth century succeeded in instating oligarchical regimes of brief duration, but the broadly based democracy endured until the Macedonian hegemony curtailed the independence of the autonomous city-states. The epoch beginning with the democratic reforms in Athens and ending with the death of Alexander the Great in 323 BC is conventionally called classical or Hellenic.

Documents from the democratic era are relatively copious, and the regular term for "friend" in classical (and later) Greek is *philos*. It designates a party to a voluntary bond of affection and good will, and normally excludes both close kin and more distant acquaintances, whether neighbors or fellow-citizens.

Evidence for the restricted range of the noun *philos* is abundant. Plato, for example, writes (*Meno* 91c1–3): "May such a madness never seize any of my relations or friends [*mēte oikeiōn mēte philōn*], nor a fellow citizen or foreigner" (cf. Plato, *Ep.* 7.334c). Lysias, in his speech on the impiety of Andocides, points out that the latter gave testimony against his *sungeneis* ("relatives") and *philoi* (6.23; cf. 6.2); Lysias resoundingly inquires: "Who could endure such things, what *philos*, what *sungenēs*, what demesman (*dēmotēs*: member of the same village or borough) could show favor to this man in private while openly offending the gods?" (6.53; for "friends and demesmen," cf.

53

Lys. 27.12; Aristoph. *Eccles.* 1023–4). The speaker in another of
Lysias' orations (19.12) states:

First of all I shall explain to you how they became in-laws of ours. When
Conon was serving as general in the Peloponnese, he became friendly
[*philos*] long ago toward my father, who was in charge of a warship, and
asked that he give my sister in marriage to the son of Nicophemus, who was
suing for her hand.

Friendship is one thing, relationship by marriage another (cf. Lys.
5.1). The defendant in Isaeus' speech, "On the Property of Menecles," explains to the jury that his father had been a friend and
associate (*philos kai epitēdeios*) of one Menecles, with whom he had
been close (*ekhrēto oikeiōs*); when Menecles lost his first wife, he
requested the hand of the speaker's sister in marriage, alluding to the
philia that had obtained between their father and himself: "and in
this way we, who had formerly been his *philoi*, became his in-laws
[*oikeioi*]" (2.3–5).

In Xenophon's *Symposium* (4.51), Niceratos says his friends avoid
him when they are well off, but should they suffer some misfortune
they produce genealogies to establish kinship. In his *Memorabilia*
(1.2.51–2), Xenophon records that Socrates was accused of inducing
his associates to dishonor "not only their fathers but also their other
relatives," and that he disparaged the good will "of friends too" (*kai
peri tōn philōn*). Some centuries later, the neo-Pythagorean writer
Callicratidas, in his treatise "On the Well-Being of the Household,"
observes that "the good that derives from friends contributes to the
household, for thus it becomes greater and more distinguished, not
just by property or being numerous in kin [*sungeneia*], but also by an
abundance of *philoi*."[1]

Alongside the polarity between *philoi* and kin, there is a three-way
distinction between relatives, friends, and fellow-citizens. Isocrates,
in a pamphlet written to defend his career as a teacher, intones
(15.99: "Antidosis"): "if any of the men who have associated with me
have become good in respect to the polis and their *philoi* and their
individual household (*idios oikos*), I think it is right that you laud them
and entertain no gratitude toward me." Xenophon, in his romantic

---

[1] Stobaeus, *Ecl.* 4.28.16 = Thesleff 1965: 104.19–24; cf. also Aristophanes, *Wealth* 828–38;
Demosthenes 37.15; Isocrates 19.10; Isaeus 1.5–7; numerous examples in later writers, e.g.
Appian (second century AD), *Civil Wars* 1, prol. 5, of the Roman factions in 43 BC which
did not spare "friends and brothers ... so much did contentiousness overpower good will
toward one's own [*oikeia*, neut.]"; also Josephus (first century AD): see Rengstorf 1983: s.v.
philos.

biography of Cyrus, the founder of the Persian Empire in the sixth century BC, tells us that as boys, the Persians were taught to hate ingratitude: "for they believe that those who are ungrateful would also be most neglectful of the gods and their parents and country and *philoi*" (*Cyr.* 1.2.6; *philoi* are not peers in general, for which the term is "age-mates," *hēlikes* or *hēlikiōtai*, 1.4.4, 1.4.10, 1.4.26). At the end of the book, the aged Cyrus prays to the gods: "I beg you to bestow now happiness upon my children and wife and friends and country [*patris*]" (*Cyr.* 8.7.3; cf. 8.7.6, 8; [Plato] *Ep.* 9, 358a). Plutarch, in his attack on Democritean and Epicurean detachment from political life, disavows the kind of tranquillity that amounts to "a betrayal of friends, relatives, and country" (*philōn kai oikeiōn kai patridos*).[2]

Philoi, then, occupy an intermediate zone between kin and country. The relationship between *philoi* is voluntary or achieved as opposed to an ascribed connection grounded in status such as common membership in a family or community. One is born into a family and a city, but one makes friends: the Greek verb is *poieisthai* (middle = "make for oneself"), which is employed also in the sense of "adopt." Relationships that are made can be broken; although the Greeks placed a high value on loyalty to friends, they recognized that the relationship is mutable. Demosthenes (23.122) does not hesitate to explain before a court:

For it is not the part of healthy men, I believe, either to trust someone whom they take to be a friend so much that they deprive themselves of defense if he should try to wrong them, nor again to hate so much that, if he should cease [his enmity] and wish to be a friend, they make it impossible for him to do it. But one ought to love and to hate, I believe, just so far as not to overshoot the occasion of either.[3]

If I have dwelled on the specificity of Greek friendship, the reason is that many, perhaps most, scholars today suppose that the range of *philos* is much wider than the English "friend," and may include both kin and countrymen.[4] This view is in part due to a confusion between the extension of the concrete noun *philos*, which means "friend," and that of related terms such as the verb *philein*, which

---

[2] *De tranquil. animi* 465c; cf. Diogenes Laertius 7.33: *politas kai philous kai oikeious*; Epictetus, *Discourses* 2.22.18; Konstan 1996.

[3] Cf. Sophocles, *Ajax* 678–82, 1376–7; Aristotle, *Rhetoric* 2.21; *EN* 9.3; Dionysius Comicus, fr. 6 Kassel-Austin; among later sources, the neo-Pythagorean Zaleucus, "Preamble to the Laws," Thesleff 1965: 226.18–21, preserved in Diodorus Siculus 12.20.3; Philo, *Virt.* 152; Diog. Laert. 1.87, 8.23; *contra*: Plutarch, *On Having Many Friends* 95f.

[4] See above, pp. 1–3; Konstan 1996.

signifies various kinds of love and affection, and the abstract noun
philia, which has much the same scope as the verb. The adjective
philos, moreover, retains the broad sense of "dear," which may be
applied to family members (e.g. Aeschylus, *Agamemnon* 326–9) and to
inanimate objects: thus Aristotle, in the *Eudemian Ethics* (7.2,
1136b3–5), observes that "what is loved [neut.] is dear [*philon*] to the
one who loves, but one who is loved [masc.] and loves in return is a
friend [*philos*]." Despite the resemblance between the forms, the
substantival and adjectival uses are rarely confounded. Thus, *philos*
with the dative case in general signifies "dear to," while "friend of"
more commonly takes the genitive; again, the definite article commonly indicates the substantive. The superlative is adjectival and
means "dearest," not "best friend." Context normally disambiguates
the sense. That the noun *philos* should have acquired a restricted
meaning is not in itself surprising; in English, for example, we readily
recognize a difference between the extensions of the words "love"
and "lover."[5]

HELPING FRIENDS

One sign of friendship is a disposition to come to the other's
assistance. Failure to provide help in a crisis is correspondingly
understood to indicate a lack of the good will that characterizes true
friendship. In this way, friendship may be said to depend not only on
sentiments and intentions but on deeds: what counts is what one does
for a friend, for that is the surest evidence of devotion. In one of the
few passages outside of philosophical or didactic treatises that
provides something approximating a definition of friendship, Demosthenes ("Against Aristocrates": 23.56) explains why no one,
however useful to the state, can legally be declared exempt from
retribution irrespective of the crime: the law of Draco, he argues,
permits men to avenge the abuse of their wives, mothers, sisters, and
daughters – those "in whose behalf," Demosthenes says, "we fight
our enemies [*polemioi*]." Demosthenes adds the gloss that retaliation
is allowed even against those who are friendly (adjective *philioi*),

since there is no class [or family: *genos*] of those who are friendly and hostile

---

[5] On *philos* with the genitive vs. dative, cf. England 1921 *ad* Plato *Laws* 8.837a7; for differences
in sense among words that have a common root, cf. Dover 1971: 204; Carney 1995: 373;
Nagy 1985: 26 warns against simply rendering the adjective as "dear" and the noun as
"friend," but the greater peril is in ignoring the distinction.

[*philioi kai polemioi*], but rather what they do renders each of them so, and the law has granted punishment of those who do inimical acts as having the status of enemy [*ekhthros*].

The contrast is between those who earn, and can lose, the name of friend by their actions, and members of the household, who are by definition those whom one defends (cf. Isocrates, *Ep.* 2.4 on the obligation to fight in behalf of country, parents and children). Kin belong to a single *genos*, whereas enemies and friends are not predetermined categories but depend on behavior.

By constituting friends, as opposed to family, on the basis of actions, Demosthenes exhibits a practical concern with help and harm that finds frequent expression in ancient texts. For example, in his *Memorabilia* (2.9.8), Xenophon represents Socrates as recommending friendships in which one "receives services [*euergetoumenon*] from worthy men and performs services in return [*anteuergetounta*]." In a fictive contest between Menander and a comic playwright called Philistion, the section subtitled "On a Friend" includes the aphorism: "Gold can be put to the proof by fire, but good will among friends is tested by circumstances" (83–4 Jaekel; cf. Democritus frs. 101, 106 D-K). Among the sentences attributed to the Pythagorean Clitarchus is the observation, "reversals test friends."[6]

Encapsulating the popular Greek conception, Paul Millett (1991: 118) puts the emphasis squarely on the utility of friends: "In choosing friends, primary considerations were willingness and ability to repay services in full." The Greeks, however, saw helpfulness as confirmation of kindly intentions: to be a friend is to afford help when it is needed. This may seem like a distinction without a difference: either way, services are expected of friends. But in general, gnomic phrases such as those attributed to Menander strike a less calculating note: "a worthy friend is a physician to your pain" (456) and "there is no possession lovelier than a friend" (575) exploit metaphors of succor and riches to exalt, not reduce, the sense of an unselfish relationship. "Be just to your friends and foreign friends" (v. 208) and "honor your friends as you would a god" (v. 357) insist on decency, even if the idea of fair return lurks between the lines.[7]

Failure to provide assistance when required was a breach of

---

[6] Chadwick 1959: no. 92; cf. Ennius tragic fr. 351 Jocelyn 1969: "a sure friend shows in things unsure" (*amicus certus in re incerta cernitur*).

[7] Menander's "Sentences" are cited according to Jaekel 1964; on respect for friends, cf. also Sophocles, *Philoctetes* 673; Euripides *Iphigeneia in Tauris* 605–10, 708–18; Connor 1971: 46.

friendship, and a friend so heedless of loyalty might be considered a
personal enemy or *ekhthros*: the disjunction "friend or foe" was
congenial to the Greek habit of thinking in polarities.[8] Not only
friends, of course, were counted on for support. Mention has been
made of Xenophon's view (*Cyr.* 1.2.6) that the Persians loathed
ingratitude because it leads to neglect of gods, country, parents, and
friends; the unstated premise is that one is obliged to all of these for
services rendered. The association between friendship and aid in
adversity was such that relatives, too, who withheld their backing in
a crisis were naturally thought of as enemies; in contrast with such
betrayal, those kinsmen who faithfully tendered support might be
described as friends.

The multiple axes that subtend friendship thus generate an
apparent contradiction: friends are defined by good will rather than
a pre-existing tie of blood or ethnicity; good will is manifested in
beneficial actions, and failure to help, like active animosity, may be a
sign of enmity. Relatives too who let one down are considered
enemies and, contrariwise, family members (and others) who offer
help when needed may be described as friends. This circle does not
collapse the distinction between friends and family or fellow-citizens;
English, after all, offers analogous cases ("my brother proved a true
friend"). It is in the nature of social categories to be overdetermined,
and a certain latitude is to be expected.

Euripides' tragedy *Orestes* illustrates the complex of elements that
condition the idea of friendship in a setting charged with issues of
perfidy and fidelity. When the action begins, Orestes, maddened by
Furies, has been condemned to death by the Argives for the murder
of his mother. His uncle Menelaus balks at defending him, but
suddenly Pylades arrives on the scene, having been banished from his
home in Phocis. "Dearest of men," Orestes exclaims, "trusty [*pistos*]
amid troubles" (725, 727). Launching on a musical duet, Pylades
salutes his friend in turn: "dearest to me of age-mates and *philoi* and
kin [*sungeneia*]; for you are all of these to me" (732–3): as well as being
philoi, Pylades and Orestes are second cousins, and had been raised
together as children (hence, "age-mates") after the death of Orestes'
father, Agamemnon, at the hands of his wife Clytemnestra. The duet
concludes with Orestes' exclamation: "This proves the proverb:

[8] Pindar, *Paean* 2.20–1; Lysias 30.33; Plato, *Epistle* 8.352e; the enemy of an enemy is a friend:
Sophocles, *Philoctetes* 585–6; cf. Lloyd 1966; on the conventional pairing of love and hate,
Joly 1968: 16, 30.

'Have comrades [*hetairoi*], not just kin [*to sungenes*]!' For a man, though an outsider [*thuraios*], who is conjoined by character is a better *philos* for a man to have than ten thousand of his own blood" (804–6). Orestes' thought is: reliability is the test of a *philos*; for someone who will stand by you – that is, be a *philos* – choose a *hetairos*, not a relative, though in theory a kinsman might qualify.

Earlier, Orestes had reminded Menelaus that Agamemnon gave his life for his brother's sake, "as *philoi* should for *philoi*" (652), and he drew the point that "*philoi* should aid *philoi* in trouble; when fortune is generous, what need is there of *philoi*?" (665–7). Menelaus, however, in failing to assist his *philoi* (719), stands revealed as false toward them (740); his caution represents "what bad friends do for friends" (748). Throughout the tragedy, unhesitating support is treated as the essential criterion of friendship, thereby honing the contrast between the circumspection of Menelaus and Pylades' selfless devotion. For Pylades, "friends share everything" (735); he will tend Orestes in his illness, for "trepidation among *philoi* is a great evil" (794); "where else shall I show myself a friend," he asks, "if I do not defend you in dire misfortune?" (802–3). Clytemnestra, who slew Agamemnon and banished Orestes, is an outright enemy (*polemia*, 798).

Given the high expectations of mutual assistance from *philoi*, the ideal of friendship serves as a touchstone for fidelity. Thus, Orestes casts Agamemnon's resolute action in recovering Helen for Menelaus, despite the injustice of the cause (647–8), not as a show of brotherly affection but rather as an example of the allegiance due to friends. The point is not that kin were normally included among one's *philoi*, but that some relatives live up to the commitment demanded of friends while others, like Menelaus, fall short of it.

In these verses, *philos* has roughly the sense of ally or one who offers help in a predicament. Similarly, in Euripides' *Electra*, the heroine asserts that "women are their husbands', not their children's friends [*philai*]" (265). Relatives may be loyal friends but that does not mean that the noun *philos* normally includes kin. When Sally Humphreys (1986: 85 n. 38) remarks: "*Philos* can refer both to kin and to friends," it must be understood that one is not a *philos* on the basis of kinship as such; there is no such thing as an "objective state of being *philoi* . . . by virtue of blood ties."[9]

---

[9] Else 1963: 349; cf. Dirlmeier 1931: 11–13; Goldhill 1986: 93–4; Heath 1987: 73–4.

FRIENDSHIP AND POLITICS

Orestes was produced in 408 BC, following the overthrow of the first
oligarchic revolution, and the tense plot seems to reflect the crisis in
values engendered by the strains of the Peloponnesian War and by
civic instability. The murderous plan by which Orestes and Pylades
will attempt to kill Helen, Orestes' aunt, in the wake of matricide,
take hostage the innocent daughter of Menelaus, and set the palace
of Argos on fire exposes the dark side of their unconditional alliance:
anything is fair against those who lend less than total support.
Euripides appears to be exploring the pathological violence that
ensues when personal loyalty is elevated over all other ties and
obligations.

Thucydides, in his memorable account of the consequences of the
revolution at Corcyra (3.82.4–6), observes:

Foolish daring was regarded as bravery and loyalty to comrades [*andreia
philetairos*], and prudent hesitation as cowardice in disguise ... Even kinship
became less close than comradeship [*tou hetairikou*] because of the latter's
greater readiness for daring without justification ... They confirmed their
trust in each other not so much by sacred oaths as by companionship in
crime. (trans. West 1987: 36–7; words in brackets added)

A number of critics have taken these words as a gloss on the extreme
to which friendship is taken in *Orestes*. Thucydides, however, employs
the language of comradeship rather than friendship, in line with the
common use of the term *hetaireia* to designate the aristocratic clubs
that were politically active in Athens during the tumultuous years of
the war with Sparta in the late fifth century BC. Barry Strauss (1986:
20) provides a crisp summary of the evolution of these societies:

In origin, these were primarily social institutions, lasting associations
formed in youth between boys of similar age and class ... By the fifth
century they had taken on an important political role, becoming, as
Thucydides (8.73.3) says, "associations for the management of lawsuits and
elections." In the late fifth century they seem to have been primarily
oligarchic, groups of *gnorimoi*, "notables," as Aristotle says (*Ath. Pol.* 34.3),
and they organized conspiracies in 411 and 404. After 403 they continued to
play a political role, but rarely a secret or subversive one.

Along with the specialized sense of *hetaireia* in Athens, the concrete
noun *hetairos* acquired in particular contexts (e.g. Lys. 12.43) the
connotation of political accomplice or one engaged in secret plots.
But Greek had available other terms for conspirator (e.g. *sunōmotēs*;

sustasiōtēs from *stasis*, "revolution"), and *hetairos* normally retains the elementary sense of "companion," as in the formulaic expression "friends and comrades" (e.g. Isocrates 8.112, 15.96, *Ep.* 9.13–4). Nothing suggests, then, that the bond between *philoi* represented in *Orestes* alludes to organized and secret activities of oligarchic factions, though the struggle between the young aristocrats and the *dēmos* manipulated by cynical demagogues may well be Euripides' comment on the contemporary political climate at Athens.[10]

Apart from the matter of conspiratorial aristocratic clubs, however, it has been argued that Athenian politics was normally conducted through informal personal networks among *philoi*. Thus, Robert Connor (1971: 41) writes: "political groups in fifth century Athens were largely groups of *philoi*." Connor observes further (64–5) that "*Philia* created political groups and held them together," for "personal ties and loyalties" rather than class interests or national policy were the foundation of political activity and success. Hutter (1978: 25) affirms that "The entire free citizenry of the *polis* was held to be related in the manner of a friendship. Politics came thus to be seen as the means for the exercise of friendship."[11]

According to Connor, the personal style was characteristic of Athenian politics until the supremacy of Cleon during the Peloponnesian War, who went so far as to renounce the support of his peers, or friends, in an effort to cultivate influence among the lower orders, a practice that earned him the hostile title of demagogue among more conservative figures such as Aristophanes. Circles of loyal friends abided as a political force, however, alongside the strategy of the new politicians, as Connor dubs them, to represent themselves as the lovers or intimates of the people at large: thus, Isocrates (16.28) mentions Alcibiades' *philia* toward the *dēmos*, which is said by his son to be ancestral in his family; so too Demosthenes (58.30) reports that Theocrines, a corrupt politician, claims to love the populace (*humas* = the jurors) next after his own *oikeioi*.[12]

Philia or affection, as we have seen, is not the same thing as being

---

[10] Euripides in relation to Thucydides: cf. Willink 1986: xxiv; *contra* West 1987: 33–7; Porter 1994: 327–32; *hetaireiai*: Sartori 1967: 129–43, 153; cf. Lysias 12.55; Isocrates 16.6 on the charge that Alcibiades was assembling "a *hetaireia* for revolutionary business"; Hutter 1978: 26–55 indiscriminately lumps various kinds of association under the title "hetaery"; terms for conspirator: Ghinatti 1970: 13–14, 55–8; *philoi* in *Orestes* as oligarchic factions: Hall 1993: 269–70; aristocrats vs. demagogues: West 1987: 36; Hall 1993: 265–8.

[11] Cf. also Gehrke 1984; Ober 1989: 85.

[12] Personal style of politics: Connor 1971: 36–44; on Cleon, 91–110.

friends, and the evidence that politicians in classical Athens relied for support chiefly on personal *philoi* is in fact quite thin. Mogens Hansen (1991: 283) sums up the situation thus:

we find plenty of philosophical discussion of *philia* in Xenophon and Plato and Aristotle but no sign, either there or in the historians or the orators, that it was an important political concept – unless we go round about and assert that *philoi* were the same as *hetairoi*, and come back to *hetaireiai* as political groupings. But then we are up against the fact that in the fourth century the *hetaireiai* do not seem to have been political clubs.[13]

Nevertheless, a few references in contemporary sources to the role of *philoi* in politics invite closer inspection.

Euripides' *Electra* dramatizes an earlier moment in the dynastic struggle between the children of Agamemnon and their mother Clytemnestra, who, after slaying her husband, took as her consort Agamemnon's cousin, Aegisthus. The action begins with Orestes' stealthy return from exile, accompanied by Pylades, whom he salutes as "faithful *philos* and *xenos*" (82). After he has revealed his identity to Electra, Orestes inquires about the political situation: "Do I have the good will of *philoi* in Argos, or am I like my luck – stripped of everything? With whom can I collaborate? By night or in daylight? By what road shall we turn upon our enemies [*ekhthroi*]?" (601–4). Orestes' old tutor, who had remained in Argos, replies: "Son, you have no friend in ill luck, for this is a real find – someone to share good and bad alike" (605–7). In fact, however, the humble farmer whom Electra has been forced to marry welcomes any friend of Orestes as a friend of his (300–2), and Electra declares the chorus of Mycenaean women to be trustworthy friends (272–3). Orestes has some local support, evidently indicated in the language of friendship.

When a cry is heard from within the palace, Electra asks: "Was the groan Argive or that of friends?" (755). Electra momentarily imagines Argos as a foreign power – the foe, as opposed to her allies. A messenger relieves the suspense: "To all friends I declare that Orestes has conquered" (762). *Philoi* include all who are sympathetic to the young rebels. In the atmosphere of civil war, in which fugitives return to overthrow the upstart regime, relations are polarized between friends and foe and *philoi* are equivalent to partisans. After the matricide, Electra sings over the corpse of her mother: "*phila* yet

---

[13] Cf. Arnheim 1977: 142–5; Rhodes 1986: 138–9; Sinclair 1988: 141–2.

not *phila*, we drape you in this cloak" (1230–1). Though dear as a mother, Clytemnestra is an enemy.[14]

Electra was written some years prior to *Orestes*, but the initial situation resembles an event contemporary with the later tragedy. In 407 BC, Alcibiades, who, like Orestes, had been in exile from his homeland, sailed to Laconia with twenty ships in order to determine "how the city [Athens] stood with regard to him" (Xen. *Hell.* 1.4.11). Xenophon writes (1.4.12–3): "When he saw that it was well disposed toward him and that they would elect him general and that his companions [*epitēdeioi*] had been privately summoned, he sailed into the Piraeus ... The crowd [*okhlos*] from the city gathered about the ships." Some believed, says Xenophon, that Alcibiades had been treated unjustly; others that he was responsible for all the ills of Athens.

Alcibiades, anchoring off shore, did not immediately disembark, fearing his enemies. Standing on the deck he looked to see whether his *epitēdeioi* were on hand. Noticing his cousin Euryptolemus the son of Peisianax and other kinsmen [*oikeioi*] and *philoi* with them, he then disembarked and proceeded up to the city with those who were prepared not to allow anyone to touch him. (1.4.18–9)

In the assembly, Alcibiades is awarded plenipotentiary powers.

Barry Strauss cites this passage to illustrate the responsibilities of friends: "At every crucial moment one's *philoi* were expected to be at hand" (23). Alcibiades' friends, according to Strauss, are a retinue of partisans who were the usual instruments of personal politics in Athens. Strauss emphasizes that the "friends" of Athenian leaders were different from the "companions" (*hetairoi*) who were members of a *hetaireia*; the clubs were based on reciprocal ties, while the followers of prominent politicians were organized principally around loyalty to the leader: "That the leader was essential to the group, that its members felt a personal loyalty to him rather than to a corporate entity, is strongly suggested by ancient terminology, which prefers to any corporate title such names as 'the friends of Pericles' (Plut. *Per.* 10.1–2)," and similar locutions (1986: 19). Wider associations were possible: "A man with *philoi* could assume that his *philoi* each had other *philoi*, upon whose support he could sometimes rely" (29).

Let us return to Alcibiades. Xenophon says that Alcibiades looked

---

[14] The political overtone is missing in Sophocles' *Electra* 1154: "mother but no mother" (*mētēr amētōr*); cf. Euripides *Phoenissae* 1446; for fuller discussion of Euripides' *Electra*, see Konstan 1985.

to see whether his *epitēdeioi* were present (1.4.18). Like *philos, epitēdeios* is employed both as an adjective and a substantive. As a noun, it is often little more than a synonym of *philos* (e.g. Lys. 1.22; Demosth. 35.6, 36.1; Isocr. 15.102), but it preserves the sense of advantageousness or serviceability which is basic to the adjective; thus Lysias speaks punningly of men who seem useless (*anepitēdeioi*) to their *epitēdeioi* (8.1; of the Athenians as allies, Thuc. 1.57). Who, then, are Alcibiades' *epitēdeioi*? Not the mass of citizens, who are represented by the crowd or *okhlos* gathered at the Piraeus. Alcibiades has already determined that these, in their majority, are sympathetic to him. His companions or *epitēdeioi* consist of relatives (*oikeioi*) and *philoi*, who have been mustered for the specific purpose of acting as a bodyguard on the trek from the harbor at Piraeus to the city itself. For this, Alcibiades wants his closest associates, whom he draws from among his kin and personal friends. They are not a claque.[15]

In discussing whether it is a good thing to have many friends, Aristotle notes that it is impossible to distribute oneself among a large number, or to rejoice and condole with many at once (*EN* 9.10, 1171a2–7); *philia* between *hetairoi* does not involve a large number of friends, and those friendships memorialized by the poets are generally between pairs (1171a14–15). Aristotle then adds:

Those who are friends to many [*poluphiloi*] and treat everyone in an intimate manner do not seem friends to anyone, except in the political sense [*politikōs*]; they also call them ingratiating [*areskoi*]. Now, it is possible to be a friend to many in the political sense and not be ingratiating, but truly decent [*epieikēs*]. (*EN* 9.10,1171a15–19)

Aristotle thus acknowledges a latitudinarian sense of "friend" in public life, where people curry favor with constituencies (this is

---

[15] Note *epitēdeioi* at Demosth. 48.2, which at 48.40 becomes *tois oikeiois kai tois epitēdeiois tois heautou kai tois emois*, indicating friends and kin; on *epitēdeios*, cf. Eernstman 1932: 134. *Oikeios* as a noun means "relative," often by marriage; it does not normally mean "friend" (cf. Aristophanes of Byzantium, fr. 263 Slater [1986]; Eernstman 1932: 132; Treu 1972: 419; Sissa 1988: 191), nor, correspondingly, does *philos* ordinarily embrace *oikeioi* (*contra* Eernstman 1932: 83, 134). [Plato], *Ep.* 7 is addressed to *oikeioi te kai hetairoi* (323a): at 324d Plato says that some of the thirty tyrants were his *gnōrimoi* and *oikeioi*, the latter a reference to his cousin Critias; by contrast, Socrates is *philon andra*; cf. also Demosth. 49.37–8; 31.11; 57.68. As an adjective, *oikeios* can mean "friendly," "well-disposed" ([Plato] *Ep.* 13, 363a: *anēr pasin hēmin oikeios te kai eunous*). The adverb *oikeiōs* with *khraomai* means to treat someone kindly. Cartledge 1987: 151 suggests that *hoi khrōmenoi* (cf. Xenophon, *Agesilaos* 6.4, 11.13) may represent a narrower circle than *philoi*; I infer rather that the *philoi* are those among the *hetairoi* who became Agesilaos' true intimates. The abstract noun *oikeiotēs* may denote intimacy outside the family as well: Thucydides 4.19.1; Plato, *Symp.* 197d; so too the adjective *oikeios* (cf. the superlative, coupled with *hetairotatos*, at Plato, *Phaedrus* 89e).

different from what Aristotle calls *politikē philia*, which will be discussed shortly). He does not say that the word *philos* has the distinct meaning of "partisan" or "backer" in the civic realm, only that statesmen, even upright ones, tend to form numerous superficial friendships.[16]

In political life, friendship tends to be parasitical on the private relationship, suggesting an intimacy where in reality there is none. It may be rhetorically effective to blur the boundaries between friends and followers, as when Mark Antony addresses the company at Julius Caesar's funeral as "Friends, Romans, countrymen" (*Julius Caesar* III.ii). In this spirit, Xenophon's Cyrus invokes his troops as *andres philoi* (*Cyr.* 1.5.7), as does Abradatas when he leads Cyrus' chariots into battle against the Egyptians. In the latter case, Xenophon reanimates the conventional formula, commenting that the strongest phalanx is composed of fellow fighters who are personally dear to one another (*philoi summakhoi*); but he notes that only Abradatas' own *hetairoi* and table-mates (*homotrapezoi*) joined him in the fatal charge (*Cyr.* 7.30).

Doubtless, intimates often stuck together in politics, but this is not tantamount to the claim that networks of close friends were the basis of political activity in the democracy. Neither was the extension of the term *philos* so wide as to include all those who lent their backing at a given moment to a particular leader. Friends normally constituted a small circle of trusted companions, however much candidates for office might seek to stretch the term. It was the Athenian majority, whom Xenophon disparagingly labels the mob (*okhlos*), that was decisive in Alcibiades' successful return to Athens. His personal friends and relatives were on hand mainly to provide protection.

The Athenian *skolia* or drinking songs, which were surveyed in the preceding chapter, very likely reflect the culture of aristocratic youths in the decades following the defeat of the Persian invaders early in the fifth century, when symposiastic entertainments seem to have become more lavish. Signs of anxiety over class conflict (*stasis*, 884; cf. 889, 912) perhaps point to the increasingly radical climate of opinion leading up to the democratic reforms of Ephialtes in 462/1, when confrontations between the populace and the upper class differed from civil war "only because blood did not flow, though, indeed, Ephialtes fell victim to an assassin and the threat of counter-

---

[16] On "the importance of the pair, the twosome, for friendship," cf. Little 1993: 33; on the wider sense of "friend," cf. below, pp. 124–5.

revolution turned serious" (Fornara and Samons 1991: 66). In these circumstances, coteries of young men from distinguished families may have celebrated personal loyalties as a form of social solidarity. Plutarch (*Pericles* 10; *Cimon* 17) alleges that a hundred *hetairoi* (not *philoi*) died fighting at Tanagra in order to clear Cimon of the charge of Laconizing – a spectacular instance, if true, of the cohesion nurtured partly, no doubt, in symposiastic festivities. In any case, the cultivation of comradeship may have been particularly associated in this period with the sodalities and values of the nobility.[17]

Aeschylus' *Oresteia* was performed in 458 BC, shortly after the crisis involving Ephialtes. When Orestes, in disguise, reports the invented story of his own death to his mother, Clytemnestra laments: "You strip me, all-wretched, of my *philoi*" (*Choeph.* 695). Her lines have been taken as a testimony to the ties of kinship, which are not cancelled by the mortal conflict with her son that has resulted from the murder of Agamemnon. Richard Seaford (1989) has challenged on dramatic grounds the attribution of these verses to Clytemnestra and reassigned them (with nineteenth-century editions) to Electra, assuming that she has emerged from the palace and is at her mother's side (though unannounced, she can be recognized by the audience from her earlier appearance on stage). Feigning belief in the false story, it is Electra, then, who declares herself bereft of all support. This makes sense: moments later, Clytemnestra boasts that she and Aegisthus are not wanting for friends (717), whereas Electra perceives her isolation and helplessness. The usurpers count on having *philoi*. Perhaps Aeschylus, who in this trilogy celebrated the overthrow of tyrannical rule and the inauguration of democracy, chose to represent reliance on personal friends as a feature of autocratic power, thus undermining the aristocratic style in politics.

In Sophocles' *Antigone* (probably *c.* 442), the newly enthroned Creon is suspicious that friends of Polyneices, who attacked the city in an effort to gain the kingship, may try to keep his cause alive and stir up trouble in Thebes; this is his chief motive for prohibiting the burial of Polyneices' body. He thus declares (182–3, 187–90): "Whoever thinks a friend is greater, rather than his country [*patra*], I declare him nowhere ... Nor would I deem a man hostile to the land a friend to me, since I know that it is she that saves us and as we sail upon her if she is right we make friends." Creon never imagined,

---

[17] Lavishness of symposia: Vickers 1990; Plutarch on the hundred *hetairoi*: Connor 1971: 59–60.

when he promulgated his decree, that his niece Antigone, Polyneices' sister, would be the one to defy the ban; it is not her relationship to Polyneices that he is thinking of when he refers to the dangers of alliances among friends, but secret associations hostile to his authority.[18]

Connor (1971: 53; cf. 47) comments: "Friends and city could and did come into conflict, and, as in the *Antigone*, there was no ready resolution." The tragedy, however, cannot be taken as evidence that pockets of *philoi* were politically active under the democracy. On the contrary, Creon's fear of conspiracies among groups of friends characterizes him as a tyrant. In the civic discourse of Athens, friendship is regarded as a virtue (cf. Aristotle, *EN* 8.1,1155a2), not a threat, and never is loyalty to friends treated as potentially subversive.[19]

Whether or not friendship served to consolidate small circles of aristocrats, its role in the politics of the Athenian democracy seems to have been marginal. Relations among *philoi* were in principle separate from public life.

ARISTOTLE ON THE KINDS OF *PHILIA*

The most extended treatment of *philia* is to be found in the writings of Aristotle, especially in his two treatises on ethics – *Nicomachean Ethics* and *Eudemian Ethics* – and in the *Magna Moralia*, a collection of notes probably assembled after Aristotle's death. As a window onto Greek ideas of friendship, this material is invaluable, but it has also been the cause of misunderstanding. The reason lies not in the distance between a professional philosopher's doctrines and popular attitudes, but rather in the fact that Aristotle is not, in the first instance, interested so much in friendship itself as in the nature of affectionate ties or relations in general. The name for such bonds, whether between friends or kin or fellow citizens or any other association, is *philia*, and Aristotle investigates the several varieties of *philia* in turn. This is a reasonable procedure and should not be cause for confusion, but the inveterate custom of translating *philia* as

---

[18] On Creon's fear of *stasis*, cf. Konstan 1994: 50–3; on secret associations as opposed to friends: Konstan 1996: 89–91; *contra* Connor 1971: 50–1.

[19] The tyrant's fear of friendships: cf. *Prometheus Bound* 224–5; Hutter 1978: 9: "Every dictator ... is aware of the potential threat of friendship"; Rosivach 1988; the tyrant as friendless: Xenophon, *Hiero* 3.8; [Plato] *Ep.* 1, 309b–310a; loyalty to friends not subversive: Konstan 1994/5.

"friendship" rather than "love" or "loving relationship" has produced some awkwardnesses in English versions of the ethical treatises and, on occasion, error as well.

Chief among the errors is the widespread supposition that Aristotle has no notion comparable to that of friendship in English, since for him *philia* covers so wide a range of relations as to be effectively a different concept. Indeed, it is. But one type of *philia* corresponds closely to friendship, namely, the affection that obtains between *philoi* or friends. Aristotle is careful to distinguish this kind or *eidos* from other species of love. In particular, he reserves the noun *philos* for the category of friends, in accord with ordinary Greek usage; when he speaks of other kinds of *philia*, for example that between parents and children, he does not mention *philoi*. Of course, he employs the verb *philein*, "to love," in such contexts, since the verb has the same broad extension as the abstract substantive *philia*. In general, Aristotle simply takes for granted this point of Greek diction. In one passage, however, he makes it explicit. In the *Eudemian Ethics* (7.4.1–2, 1239a1–7) he writes: "it would be absurd for a father to be a friend [*philos*] to his child, but of course he loves [*philei*] him and is loved [*phileitai*] by him." The context for this observation is the nature of *philia* between people of unequal station; Aristotle's thesis is that beyond a certain degree of difference, such individuals cannot be thought of as friends, even though mutual affection may obtain between them. In English too, of course, it is not customary to speak of an adult and a small child as friends.[20]

Once the Greek usage is recognized, certain paradoxes in Aristotle's treatment of friendship evanesce. For example, Aristotle defines the relationship between *philoi* as follows:

They say that one must wish good things for a friend for his sake, and they call those who wish good things in this way well-disposed [*eunous*], even if the same does not arise on the part of the other; for good will in those who feel it mutually is *philia*. We must add that it must not escape notice, for many are well-disposed toward people they have not seen, but believe that they are decent and worthy, and one of them might feel the same thing toward him. These then would seem to be well-disposed toward each other, but how might one call them friends if they escaped [the other's] notice of how they were disposed toward one another? It is necessary, then, that they be well-disposed toward one another and wish good things, not escaping [the other's] notice, in regard to some one of the abovementioned kinds [i.e., usefulness, pleasure, or goodness]. (*EN* 8.2, 1155b31–56a5)

[20] See further Konstan 1996: 74–8.

Not long after this passage, Aristotle provides an extraordinary illustration of what he calls the most natural kind of *philia*, namely, that between mother and child:

For some [mothers] give out their own children to be raised, and they love [*philousi*] and know them, but they do not seek to be loved in return [*antiphileisthai*], if both [loving and being loved] are not possible; but it seems to them to suffice if they see them [i.e., their children] doing well, and they love them even if they, as a result of their ignorance, provide in return none of the things that are due a mother. (8.8, 1159a28–33)

It is obvious that this example of maternal love does not fit the definition of *philia* provided earlier, and critics since antiquity have sought to resolve the discrepancy. Thus Aspasius, a Greek commentator on Aristotle writing in the second century AD, explains:

There is *philia* in loving [*philein*] and in being loved, but more, it seems, in loving than in being loved ... He offers as a sign of this that mothers take delight in loving even if they are not loved. For sometimes, if [their children] are given for rearing to other women, though they themselves are not loved, it is enough for them if they see them doing well. But [Aristotle] has [here] assumed not *philia*, but rather *philēsis* [the feeling of love]. For *philia* is in those who love mutually [*antiphilein*]. But nevertheless the [love] of parents for their children is a trace of *philia*. I say "a trace," because sometimes sons do not love in return. But it strongly resembles *philia*, because parents wish good things for their sons for their sakes. (179.28–180.5 Heylbut)

In fact, no such contorted ingenuity is required. The initial definition pertains to *philia* between *philoi*, that is, to friendship proper, which is a loving bond of a particular kind, involving altruism, reciprocity, and mutual recognition. The love – *philia* – that a mother bears for her child is a different kind, and does not depend upon requital or appreciation. This is love in its most elementary and natural form, and Aristotle esteems it as such.[21] But it is not the same as the affection that constitutes the bond between *philoi*, which answers to more narrow criteria.

Just as maternal love is different from that between friends, not insofar as it is love but in the conditions that constitute it as a particular kind of bond, so too Aristotle recognizes other forms of *philia*, for example that among fellow-citizens or *politai*, which he

---

[21] The Epicureans disagreed: "love [*storgē*] toward children is not by nature, since people do not necessarily love their offspring; for involuntariness is a characteristic of things that happen by necessity, and a consequence of involuntariness is resistance, which is obviously absent from the love of children" (Demetrius Lacon, *Puzzles* 17.67–8 = Puglia 1988: 182–3).

accordingly labels *politikē philia*, and that between *hetairoi*, which he calls *hetairikē philia*, "comradely affection" (e.g. *EN* 8.11, 1161a25–6, where it is compared to the *philia* between brothers). Affection, according to Aristotle, arises whenever there is communality or shared purpose. As he explains: "All *philia*, then, is in partnership [*koinōnia*], as has been said."[22] He goes on to raise a possible objection:

> But one might separate out kindred [*sungenikē*] and companionable affection. Political and tribal and co-voyager affections, and all such types, seem more like partnership affections, for they appear to be based on a kind of agreement. One might also class affection between *xenoi* [*xenikē*] among these. (*EN* 8.12, 1161b11–6)

Political relationships are those between fellow-citizens – plural, because they may assume different forms, depending on whether they have their source in mutual usefulness, pleasure, or respect for character, the three elements that motivate love in general. Tribal friendships are those among members of the same *phulē* (the Athenians were distributed in ten such units). Affection among travelers is Aristotle's example of how even a brief collaboration produces a bond. Commonwealths or their parts arise out of a kind of accord, then, but family ties, which, though of various sorts (*polueidēs*, 1161b17), derive ultimately from paternal *philia* (*patrikē*), have another basis as well: for parents love children as being of themselves, and consequently love them as they love themselves. So too brothers are in a sense of the same substance. In addition, being raised together as children contributes to affection. In this regard, fraternal *philia* resembles the *hetairikē* or companionable sort.[23]

Aristotle goes on to explain that the bond between husband and wife is also a natural one, since human beings are by nature given to forming couples more than they are to forming civic associations (8.12, 1162a16–19; cf. *Pol.* 1.1, 1252a26–30); they do so not just for the production of children, which is a motive common to humans and other animals, but for the sake of a good life, involving a division of labor and the sharing of individual goods. The love relating to

---

[22] *Koinōnos* is the term for a business partner, e.g. Demosth. 56.10 (cf. the Latin *socius*); contrast the role of *philoi*, personal friends, at 56.50.

[23] The tendency to translate *politikē philia* as "political friendship" has given rise to an extensive, and not always relevant, literature on friendship as the ground of social solidarity; see, for example, Hutter 1978: 110: "*Philia* is thus the cement of all social and political relations"; MacIntyre 1984: 155–6; Irwin 1990: 84–95; Cooper 1990: 234–41; Pakaluk 1994.

marriage is both useful and pleasurable, and may even be based on regard for one another's virtue, if both are good, since men and women each have their specific excellence. Finally, Aristotle adds that children too bind parents together, and he notes that childless marriages dissolve more easily.

The Aristotelian commentator Aspasius seems, indeed, to attribute to Theophrastus, Aristotle's successor as head of the Lyceum, and to Eudemus the view that, although a husband naturally rules over his wife, "it is possible that a wife and her husband both [*amphoterous*] be *philoi*."[24] A brief technical excursus, however, will elucidate this surprising claim. Heylbut's critical apparatus notes that a majority of the manuscripts have *philia* rather than *philoi*; what is more, photographs provided by the Aristotle Archive in Berlin indicate that manuscript R reads *amphoterois* (i.e., "to both").[25] I suspect that Theophrastus and Eudemus said that love (*philia*) was possible for both husband and wife, and did not describe them as friends.

That love should obtain between a wedded couple is no surprise: Plutarch, for example, in his *Letter on Friendship* (fr. 167 Sandbach) writes: "For a marriage is better when it comes from blending of *philia* on both sides." This is quite different, however, from the proposition that Plutarch thought wives capable of friendship with their husbands.[26] Compare his "Precepts on Marriage," 14 (140a): "A wife should have no feelings of her own [*mēden idion pathos*]," and 19 (140c): "A wife ought not to have friends of her own [*idious . . . philous*], but use her husband's as their common stock" (trans. Russell 1993).

As a figure for loyalty, *philos* might occasionally be applied to spouses, as in the Pythagorean epistle in which Theano advises Nicostrata to put up with her husband's infidelity, for "just as hardships of the body make respites more pleasant, so too disagreements among *philoi* render reconciliations more intimate" (Thesleff 1965: 199.29–31 = Städele 1980: 172.44–6). So too, in Euripides' *Alcestis* Heracles calls Admetus a faithful friend (*pistos philos*, 1095) because of his commitment to the memory of his deceased wife (cf. *Electra* 265, cited above). Plato (*Laws* 8.839b1) praises legislation that will teach men to despise "lustful madness" (*lutta erōtikē*) and all

---

[24] Text according to Heylbut 1889: 178.13, followed by Fortenbaugh *et al.* 1992: 354; Treggiari 1991: 188 attributes the view to Aristotle; cf. Meilaender 1994: 184–5.

[25] R also reads *gunaikes*; neither is reported by Heylbut. The termination of *amphot(e)r*- in MS N is illegible.

[26] So Treu 1972: 421.

forms of excess and make them instead "proper friends," or perhaps "dear relations" (*oikeioi philoi*), to their own wives. Occasional formulas of this sort do not, I believe, constitute evidence that Greeks ordinarily thought of spouses as *philoi*.

This discussion has moved a long way from friendship in the narrow sense. But Aristotle is attending here to various kinds of *philia* or affection, from the community of purpose that exists among associations formed for reasons of collective security or other advantages, to familial love, which has, Aristotle believes, deeper sources in a shared physical identity and in the common rearing of siblings; the latter applies also, he indicates, to childhood mates. All are natural forms of love. They are not, however, the basis of affection among friends. Friends are distinct from fellow-citizens and family and their relationship has other grounds.[27]

ARISTOTLE ON THE GROUNDS OF FRIENDSHIP

Apart from nature and childhood bonding, Aristotle posits three sources of *philia*: utility, pleasure, and respect for virtue or character. We have seen that conjugal affection can involve these three principles in addition to whatever natural tendency to pairing exists among humans. Aristotle on occasion speaks as though utility or pleasure simply constituted the love that joins two people, but when he expresses himself more precisely he makes it clear that *philia* arises through or on account of (*dia*) these qualities and is thus distinct from mutual advantage, pleasure, or even respect (8.3, 1156a10–16). To make the point sharper, we may note that Aristotle never suggests that two people who are useful to one another are automatically and on that basis alone friends. But it does often happen that two people who have a mutually advantageous association *become* friends. In such a case, the origin of the *philia* is in utility, but the affection is not reducible to the mutual appreciation of one another's serviceability. Because this kind of love emerges from advantage, it may be short-lived and will tend to evanesce if there ceases to be a common benefit

---

[27] In Xenophon's *Hiero*, the Syracusan ruler for whom the dialogue is named argues that tyrants least enjoy the various kinds of love or *philia*, such as that between parents and children, siblings, wives and husbands, and *hetairoi*. In contrast to private citizens, he asserts, tyrants have often been undone by offspring, brothers, wives and comrades, "even those who most seemed to be *philoi*" (3.8). Here again, the bond between *philoi* is a subset of the broad group of relationships covered by the term *philia*, and *philos* is reserved for the category of intimate friends.

(8.3, 1156a21–2). *Philia*, however, is not a name for contracted responsibilities or for the bond constituted by reciprocal obligations. It means affection in Aristotle and in Greek generally. The varieties of loving relationships are the subject of Aristotle's treatise, and he does not exclude the sentimental attachments that evolve out of mutually advantageous association, not to mention pleasure in one another's company.[28]

Aristotle adopted from Plato the strategy of explaining *philia* by examining that on account of which (*dia*) affection arises, which he calls the lovable (*phileton*). Plato's *Lysis* is not about friendship as such, and it does not conform to the early Platonic "dialogues of definition," in which Socrates investigates questions of the sort, "What is X?" In the *Lysis*, rather, Socrates inquires about the reasons why (*dia ti, heneka tou*) a person likes someone or something, or experiences desire. Indeed, at one point in the argument (221b7–8), Socrates casually collapses the differences between *philia*, *erōs*, and *epithumia* (cf. *Laws* 8.837a1), and the discussion moves freely among cases of parental affection, erotic attraction, attachment between friends, and even the appeal of inanimate objects. Although the dialogue is aporetic, the series of critical arguments, which dismiss in turn various candidates for what is desirable (or valued) in itself, clears the ground for the possibility that the basis of desire is rooted in a metaphysical incompleteness of the human soul. In this respect, the inquiry begun in the *Lysis* is completed by the investigation of *erōs* in the *Symposium*.[29]

Aristotle, however, asserts at the beginning of his discussion that things are lovable not for one quality only but rather, as we have seen, for any of three – they may be good, pleasant, or useful (he suggests also that utility is derivative, since a thing is useful if it is a means to what is good or pleasurable: *EN* 8.2, 1155b17–21). Thereafter, he is more interested in the kinds (*eidē*) of relationship that the several likeable properties sustain than in the ultimate grounds – Plato's *prōton philon* – of human desire.

[28] Distinction between love and its grounds: cf. Nussbaum 1986: 355; contrast Hands 1968: 33: "Little or no mutual affection was essential to the relationship of either *philia* or *amicitia*"; cf. Fisher 1976: 18; Springborg 1986: 198; Heath 1987: 73–4.

[29] *Lysis* not a dialogue of definition: Sedley 1989; on the conflation of different terms for desire or affection, cf. Cummins 1981; Robinson 1986: 74–5 posits a transition from the analysis of friendship to that of desire more generally; "valued": Lesses 1986; metaphysical incompleteness: cf. Gómez Muntán 1966; Lualdi 1974: 140; Haden 1983: 351; Glidden 1981: 57; Halperin 1985: 189; relation to *Symposium*: Levi 1950: 295; Price 1989: 12–14.

Aristotle argues that people are good by virtue of what they are (*kath' heautous*), whereas they are pleasant or useful only incidentally (*kata sumbebēkos*, 8.3, 1156b6–11): one's moral character or *ēthos* is closer than wittiness or serviceability to one's essential nature, and *philia* on account of character is, accordingly, the most durable and complete. It does not follow, however, that it alone is altruistic or that the other types fail to meet Aristotle's definition of friendship. Even in the case of friendship that derives from regard for character, moreover, there is no indication that all men with sufficient virtue and consequent admiration for one another are friends; such an hypothesis is inconsistent, for example, with Aristotle's view that one can have only a few friends, among other reasons because many friends would lead to excessive and perhaps conflicting claims on one's loyalties.[30]

Respect and good will are not in themselves friendship, as Aristotle makes clear. Apart from the fact that it is possible to bear good will toward someone who is not personally known (8.2, 1155b34–56a3; 9.5, 1166b30–2), which does not count as friendship, Aristotle notes that there is no loving emotion (*philēsis*) attaching to good will, since it is not accompanied by tension or desire (1166b33–4). Such a feeling pertains to long acquaintance and does not arise suddenly, as good will may. Thus, Aristotle concludes that good will is rather to be conceived of as the beginning or source (*arkhē*) of *philia*, much the way beauty is the source of erotic attraction: someone who takes pleasure in the appearance of another is not yet in love, for this occurs only when one misses the other and is passionate for his presence.[31] Aristotle adds that those who entertain good will toward someone do indeed wish good things for the other, but are not disposed to cooperate or to go to any trouble in his behalf. It is thus a kind of lazy love, Aristotle says, but can become love over time and with personal familiarity (*sunētheia*). Aristotle (and Xenophon, loc. cit.) could not be more emphatic that *philia* is a form of affection.[32]

It should also be evident that the bond between friends based on virtue is not impersonal, as some scholars have argued. Modern views of love and friendship emphasize personal uniqueness as the

---

[30] Character closest to what a person is: cf. Price 1989: 108–9; other types also friendship: Cooper 1977; cf. Walker 1979; with some disagreement, Alpern 1983; for the *Eudemian Ethics*, see Ward 1995.

[31] Cf. Xenophon, *Hiero* 3.2, where longing for those who are absent is characteristic of *philia*.

[32] For *philia* as love, cf. Konstan 1996: 82–90.

grounds of attraction; thus Sadler (1970: 201) observes: "When interpreted from within the perspective of love, the experience of loneliness is transformed into an awareness of our singular identity. This identity is accepted and affirmed by a true friend." We speak mysteriously of the chemistry that draws two people together. "The person who is a friend must be appreciated as a unique self rather than simply a particular instance of a general class" (Suttles 1970: 100). The semanticist and psychoanalyst Julia Kristeva (1994: 3) speaks of "valorizing in our friends, students, or patients those unique aspects that escape any generalization." Finally, Martha Nussbaum (1994a: 231) remarks that the particularity of the loved one as "*that very one*" is what is "salient in the love," and renders the beloved irreplaceable.[33]

On this view, Aristotle's regard for the character or virtue of the other as the prime motive of personal attraction seems to constitute a paradox: for if affection and friendship are determined by character, or by the moral qualities of the other, then we should be equally attracted by all who possess such characteristics. Thus, Moravcsik (1988: 135) writes: "Friendships formed in the Platonic manner ultimately have character rather than the individual's possession of it as their basis. Hence if one loses a friend, it does not matter much as long as the desired character traits are still possessed by many." So too Elijah Millgram (1987: 363) says of Aristotle's view: "If the friend's virtue provides the reason for the friendship, it would seem that one has identical reason to love *all* virtuous persons, or, if this is not possible, to replace one's virtuous friends with still more virtuous persons" (Millgram suggests a way out of this dilemma).[34]

Throughout his analysis, Aristotle is concerned to clarify the conditions in which affection arises, its sources or principles. Without the enjoyment of one another's company, or some benefit that is derived, or mutual respect for character, no feeling of affection will occur, such as is necessary if there is to be friendship between two people. But the presence of these stimuli is not equivalent to *philia*. What is required in addition is the lapse of time during which two people begin to collaborate and to share difficulties (cf. *EE* 7.2, 1237b12–38a16). One does not behave in this way with respect to everyone and anyone, however fine another individual may be and deserving of esteem. The idea that one might transfer one's love to

[33] Cf. also Wiseman 1986: 198; see above, pp. 15–16.
[34] Replaceability of friends: cf. Vlastos 1973; Shoeman 1985: 278; Reiner 1991.

the next more virtuous person who comes along is not Aristotelian, though such a man will normally be the object of good will on the part of others.

Aristotle does not stress the purely personal elements that enter into love, and for good reason. For while he plainly recognizes that love is for particular persons rather than for types, he does not locate the *cause* of love in individual traits or unique aspects of personal identity, as modern theories or intuitions tend to do. Suzanne Stern-Gillet (1995: 73) observes: "Though Aristotle's insistence on the individuated character of moral virtue allows him somehow to account for the uniqueness of the friend, the equation between selfhood, reason, and goodness nevertheless pushes such uniqueness off the centre of his analysis of primary friendship." The term "somehow" has a studied vagueness about it, but Aristotle is clear enough that friendship does not exist between virtues but between people, in whom virtues are instantiated; all instantiations are particular. Stern-Gillet goes on to quote Martha Nussbaum's judgment (1986: 306): "We do not even love particular individuals in the Aristotelian way without loving, centrally, repeatable commitments and values which their lives exemplify." Here again, the emphasis is misleading. One does not feel affection for the virtue, but for virtuous persons, on account of their virtue. Whether it makes sense to speak of loving others *for* their ineffable and singular qualities may be left moot; the answer to that problem does not affect the fact that the object of love in Aristotle is the individual bearer of virtues and other qualities.[35]

In the passage we have been examining, Aristotle goes on to note that it is only just to feel good will toward a benefactor, but that this is not *philia*; as for doing favors in the hope of promoting one's own prosperity thereby, that does not even count as good will toward another, but rather toward oneself, and has nothing to do with being a *philos*. It would be difficult for Aristotle to state more clearly that friendship is altruistic, but the point needs to be emphasized because modern critics have often supposed that, according to Aristotle, love for others is derived from love for self. This is not the place to consider the more technical questions concerning the very possibility of altruism, which from an individualist perspective may seem difficult to comprehend. Aristotle himself simply takes it for granted

[35] On the unique self, cf. Laín Entralgo 1985 [orig. 1972]: 40–1, 63; love for the bearer of virtue: cf. Wadell 1989: 63.

that one can and does wish another well, as in the definition of friendship that he puts at the beginning of his discussion, immediately after his customary survey of popular opinions.[36]

When Aristotle turns to the question of self-love late in the tractate (9.4), it is not for the purpose of determining the basis of love for others but rather to inquire whether it makes sense to speak of love for oneself in the way it obviously makes sense to speak of loving another (cf. *MM* 2.11, 47.1211a16–17). To show that it does, Aristotle lists various features of friendship, such as wishing the other well, condoling with a friend, enjoying time spent together, and so forth; in dialectical fashion, Aristotle assembles these defining properties from views of friendship maintained by others rather than adducing criteria of his own, and he demonstrates that all do indeed obtain as well in respect to oneself: we wish ourselves well, like our own company, at least if we are decent sorts, etc. Aristotle concludes: "We may drop for the moment whether there is or is not *philia* toward oneself" (9.4, 1166a33–4), and he turns to the more particular topic of whether a bad man will like himself; he proves that he will not. It is best, then, to be a good person and thereby friendly to oneself and dear or likeable to others, as well (1166b25–9). The argument proceeds from interpersonal love to self-love, not the other way around.[37]

The only hint that friendship somehow comes from love of self – apart from the idea that being lovable to oneself bespeaks a character that will be appreciated by others too – is in the opening statement in the section on self-love, in which Aristotle affirms that signs of friendliness (*philika*) in regard to others and the qualities by which *philia* is defined "seem to come from those toward oneself" (9.4, 1166a1–2). Since Aristotle immediately thereafter mentions the views adopted by others, perhaps "seem" here means "seem to some" and refers to the way others have reasoned about interpersonal affection. Or else, and this is more likely, Aristotle is looking forward to the end of the paragraph and means simply that traits that are likeable to others are just the ones for which we like ourselves. This gives fair enough sense to the expression "come from," which is not a technical

---

[36] Possibility of altruism: cf. Nagel 1970; Blum 1980; Chong 1984; Gill 1996.

[37] On self-love, see Annas 1977: 539–42; Hardie 1980: 323–35; Kahn 1981: 39; Madigan 1985; Annas 1988: 12; Kraut 1989: 131–9; Calhoun 1989: 220–47; McKerlie 1991: 99; Schollmeier 1994: 53–73; Ritter 1963: 21 and 88 takes 9.4 as the beginning of the third and final part of the discussion of *philia*, in which Aristotle addresses a miscellany of controversial questions.

term in Aristotle, and removes the last support for the idea that
Aristotle somehow derives love of others from love of self, in the
individualistic manner of modern ethical philosophy.

FRIENDS AND FINANCE

In one place Aristotle seems to treat *philia* as something like a
contractual bond. After observing that quarrels and complaints arise
more often in relationships based on advantage than in those based
on pleasure or respect (8.13, 1162b5–21), Aristotle proceeds to
distinguish two sorts of utilitarian *philia*, one according to character
(*ēthikē*), the other legal or conventional (*nomikē*). Conventional *philia*
occurs on stipulated terms, whether the exchange is on the spot
(Aristotle says "hand to hand") and strictly commercial or with a
view to a future date agreed upon before a witness. Either way the
amount owed is unambiguous, though Aristotle says that the friendly
thing (*philikon*) involves a delay (1162b29). Aristotle adds that in some
places it is not permitted to go to court over such arrangements,
since people think that "those who make a compact according to
trust should be fond of [*stergein*] each other" (1162b30–1).

An affectionate relationship contracted on fixed terms sounds
strange, but this is not, I think, what Aristotle means. Rather,
partners who enter into a transaction based on good faith are
presumptive friends of the utilitarian variety; that is why they are
expected to have affection for one another. In the ethical type of
exchange, where one relies entirely on qualities of character, the
transaction takes the form of a gift to a friend. The difficulty is that
the donor expects an equal or greater return, as though he had made
a loan rather than a gift; a grievance arises because the deal is
terminated in a different spirit from that in which it was initiated.
Aristotle observes that this happens because people want to behave
honorably but end up preferring profit instead (1162b31–6).

That difficulties should arise when friends borrow from one
another is not surprising; money then as now seems to have brought
out the worst in people. The preceding passage in Aristotle is
important evidence for prestations among friends and the problems
that occur when a code of friendship based on sharing gets crossed
with expectations of return characteristic of commercial or market
transactions. Paul Millett (1991) has emphasized the considerable
importance of informal financial arrangements in the Athenian

economy, as opposed to bank loans at regular rates of interest: "There survives from Athenian sources a mass of material relating to lending and borrowing that makes overall sense only if viewed from the perspective of the gift-exchange relationship identified by Mauss." Millett goes on to specify:

Different conditions of credit were appropriate to the varying degrees of intimacy between the people who made up the *polis*. For those regarded as *philoi* (friends, relatives, neighbours and associates), the kind of borrowers with whom close reciprocal relationships might be established, loans without interest were appropriate. Where the association between lender and borrower was more distant and a reciprocal favour seemed unlikely, it was legitimate to charge interest and require security. (Millett 1990: 183)

Although the subsumption of relatives and neighbors under the rubric of *philoi* is debatable, Millett is right to note the non-mercantile character of a wide range of interpersonal transactions. But Aristotle's discussion is informed by the belief that business between friends in particular is generous rather than calculating, however often such an expectation may be frustrated in the event. Dissension arises just when affection ceases to be the operative motive in the exchange. Beyond the circle of friends, expectation of return (at whatever rate of interest) becomes legitimate.[38]

Millett illustrates the role of reciprocity in friendship through a set of Socratic conversations recorded by Xenophon in the second book of his *Memorabilia*. Like Aristotle, Xenophon is interested in various forms of *philia*, not just that between friends, and he opens the discussion with two dialogues in which Socrates attempts to reconcile a son and his mother (2.2) and a pair of feuding brothers (2.3). Xenophon then explicitly registers a change of subject: "I once heard him," he says, "discoursing also about friends [*kai peri philōn*]." With this, Xenophon offers "a considered statement by Socrates on the subject of the 'acquisition' (*ktēsis*) and 'use' (*chreia*) of *philoi*" (Millett 1991: 116).

Socrates contrasts the concern that most people lavish on possessions, such as houses, fields, slaves, cattle, and equipment, with the neglect they display toward friends, although they pretend to believe

---

[38] Generosity: cf. Democritus fr. 96 D-K: "The gracious man [*kharistikos*] is not the one who looks to a return, but the one who is committed [*prohēirēmenos*] to doing good"; also fr. 92; Cohen 1992: 207 emphasizes "the ubiquity of loans among apparently unrelated persons" in fourth-century Athens.

that a friend is the greatest good of all. He then inquires rhetorically what horse or team of oxen is so useful (*khrēsimon*) as a worthy (*khrēstos*) friend (2.4.5), and goes on to enumerate the virtues of a true friend who supplies our needs, shares our losses, acts in common, rejoices in our welfare and sets us on our feet when we have stumbled. To read this as a list of practical reasons for acquiring friends, however, reverses Socrates' emphasis. He is not encouraging his audience to seek more *philoi*, but reproaching them for failing to cherish the ones they have. Thus, he remarks that people know the exact tally of their other belongings, but are ignorant of the number of their friends, though they are few. Given the advantages of friends over property, this is indeed shortsighted, but it is also callous, and that is the main point. Xenophon's Socrates, ever the good citizen, is recommending that we appreciate the value of honest friends and act toward them accordingly: *khreia* here does not refer to the calculating exploitation of friends, as the translation "use" might suggest; rather, like the related term *khraomai* in similar contexts, it refers to the proper way to treat people as intimates: "care" might be a better equivalent. So too the pun on *khrēsimon* meaning "useful" and *khrēstos* meaning "excellent" in the moral sense (cf. *pankhrēston*) highlights the ethical dimension of friendship, as opposed to the utilitarian value of material goods.

In the next exchange (2.5), Socrates recommends that we estimate our own value as friends, just as we would the value of slaves. His aim is to embarrass a bystander who has neglected a friend oppressed by poverty. The monetary standard suggests the reciprocities of the market place, and Millett rightly points to "the double obligation imposed by *philia*: the duty to help one's friends," he adds, "is balanced by the clear expectation of help in return." And yet, this conversation, conducted, as Xenophon says, in the presence of many, is plainly staged not so much to alert the intended auditor to his failure to calculate his interests, as to humiliate him publicly for behavior unworthy of one who purports to be a friend. It is a lesson about duty, not an exercise in practical accounting.

The Greeks were generally agreed that if you mistreated your friends or failed to come to their assistance in an emergency you deserved to lose them. In this respect, friendship imposed ethical obligations, which were frequently, and understandably, illustrated in economic terms. But when Aristotle records the common view that even the rich require friends, he explains that they must have scope for liberality (*EN* 8.1, 1155a6–9); he does not suggest that they are storing up allies against some future change of fortune.[39]

A favor or service to another was commonly expressed in Greek by the word *kharis*, which also means, in appropriate contexts, "grace" or "charm." A favor places the recipient under the obligation to perform some service or *kharis* in return, and the meaning of the Greek term covers also the sense of indebtedness if one is behind in the exchange of benefits. In this latter sense, *kharis* approximates the English notion of gratitude (cf., e.g., Demosth. 49.1–2, "Against Timotheus," on Timotheus' ingratitude toward the orator's father). The rule of reciprocity in the exchange of benefactions was a vigorous one to which there was frequent appeal. Millett cites a defendant's candid explanation before the jurors of his services to the city: "It was not for the sake of the money we might get that we did you good; our purpose was that if ever we found ourselves in trouble, we might be saved by this plea, and obtain due *charis* from you" (Lys. 20.31, trans. Millett 1991: 124). Millett (1991: 119) quotes two fifth-century precepts as representative of "popular attitudes towards friendship and reciprocity." The first is attributed to the philosopher Democritus of Abdera: "When you do a favor, study the recipient first, lest he be false and repay evil instead of good" (68.93 D-K, trans. Millett, modified); the second is a fragment from the Sicilian comic poet Epicharmus: "One hand washes the other: give something and you may get something" (23.30 D-K, trans. Millett, modified; cf. also fr. 31). Epicharmus' *do ut des* advice is perhaps satirical, but the Democritean aphorism captures the wariness in matters of charity enjoined by current wisdom, though his anxiety is over a return of positive harm rather than the default of what is owed.[40]

Clearly the Athenians felt strongly about returns for favors granted and made material claims on gratitude owed. But in none of the above passages is the demand for reciprocity of services connected with the claims of friendship. This is not to say that Athenians could not be disappointed by a friend's ingratitude, but rather that the notion of *kharis* as the obligation to reciprocate kindnesses was not specifically associated with relations between *philoi*. Rather, it covered a wide range of transactions, from services to fellow-citizens

---

[39] Cf. Millett 1991: 117.

[40] On *kharis*, see Millett 1991: 123–6; on the plea of service to the city, cf. Ober 1989: 229–33; on Democritus and *philia* (including but not restricted to friendship in the narrow sense), see Spinelli 1983–4.

represented by public benefactions to the debt owed by children to their parents for bringing them into the world and rearing them; thus Xenophon's Socrates admonishes his son: "No one, then, will believe that he will get *kharis* back for having done you a good turn if he suspects that you are ungrateful [*akharistos*] toward your parents" (*Mem.* 2.2.14). If it is true that "the two concepts of obligation and reciprocity lay at the heart of the ideology of interpersonal relations" (Gallant 1991: 147), relations among friends (as opposed to neighbors, fellow demesmen, relatives, and the like) appear to be precisely the area that is exempt from such expectations of fair return. According to the adage attributed to Pythagoras (sixth century BC) and ubiquitously quoted in antiquity, "the possessions of friends are common" (e.g. *EN* 8.9, 1159b31). In friendship, it is sharing that obtains (cf. Aristoph. *Wealth* 345).[41]

So far as one may judge by the texts that survive, the ethic of friendship was not implicated in an economy of reciprocity involving interest-free loans and similar prestations. Discounting the importance of *kharis* among *philoi* may appear to contradict the commonplace complaints and warnings concerning the faithlessness of friends in time of need, but the expectation of assistance is not the same as compensation. On the contrary, the generosity of friends is imagined as uncoerced and spontaneous: instead of being motivated by a sense of debt, *philoi* are presumed to act out of an altruistic desire to be of benefit to each other. Friendship in the classical city was not embedded in relations of economic exchange (however informal in comparison to the modern market) any more than it was entangled in political alliances. It constituted in principle, like modern friendship, a space of personal intimacy and unselfish affection distinct from the norms regulating public and commercial life.

However pressing the lack of resources may have been at times of crisis, the ideal of generosity among friends was not simply a response to economic stress. Rather, it was a relationship between equals who fiercely resisted any imputation of social or financial dependency. Where long-term labor for hire on a private basis was considered tantamount to servitude, friendship was constituted as a sphere free of domination and subordination, and in this respect was a paradigm of relations in the democracy.[42]

---

[41] Friends as opposed to neighbors, etc.: Gallant 1991: 143, 155–8.

[42] Lack of resources in crisis: Gallant 1991: 143, 155–8; friendship between equals: Herman 1987: 37–8; Millett 1989: 43; the ideology of autarky may have masked inequalities: Strauss

ALLIES AND FOREIGN FRIENDS

One area in which the language of friendship is employed more widely in Greek than in English is foreign relations. While it is unremarkable today to speak of "friendly powers," and even to say that states, or their peoples, are friends, in Greek usage beginning at least in the sixth century BC, *philia*, along with *summakhia*, was the normal word for a treaty or alliance between states. Thucydides makes explicit the analogy between *philia* among individuals (*idiōtai*) and cooperation (*koinōnia*) between cities (3.10.1; cf. Xen. *Cyr.* 1.45). From the classical period onward, moreover, the concrete noun *philos* is very common in the sense of foreign ally, overlapping with *summakhos* to such an extent that it is in general difficult to draw a distinction between the two terms. When the terms are contrasted, *philos* may designate a party enjoying peaceful relations – that is, not an enemy or *polemios* – while *summakhos* indicates an active confederate, as, for example, when the Melians inquire of the Athenians: "Might you not allow us to dwell in peace as friends rather than enemies, allies of neither party?" (Thuc. 5.94; cf. 5.98). Here, then, is a context in which friendship is regulated by compact.[43]

As the term of art for relations between friendly states, *philos* frequently substitutes in the classical period for *xenos* in designating personal friends from foreign parts (cf. the expression "*philos* and *xenos*," Lys. 19.19), though friends belonging to the same community are never called *xenoi*.[44] *Xenos* and *xenia* remain in use, however, especially in connection with friendships among kings and aristocrats. A good illustration is provided by an episode recounted by Xenophon. The context is a Spartan campaign in Asia Minor in the year 395 BC, during which the Persian satrap Pharnabazus, at a conference initiated by a mutual *xenos*, "reproached King Agesilaos of Sparta for having ravaged his private estates. He complained that Agesilaos had breached the duties of friendship" (Herman 1987: 1). Agesilaus' companions were, according to Xenophon, silent with shame, but Agesilaus himself after an interval replied:

1986: 22–3; Gallant 1991: 145; cf. Oxley 1978: 53: "Most egalitarian groups do not object to some members being better off so long as they do not claim to be better"; *contra*: Arnaoutoglou 1994; friendship as a paradigm of democracy: cf. Konstan (forthcoming).
[43] For the earliest treaties, see Bauslaugh 1991: 56–64; Thucydides on *philia*: cf. Morrison 1994: 528; *philos* and *summakhos*: Gruen 1984: 54–95.
[44] See Herman 1987: 11.

I believe that you know, Pharnabazus, that among the Greek cities too men become foreign friends [*xenoi*] to one another. But these, when their cities become enemies at war [*polemioi*], wage war along with their fatherlands even against those who have become foreign friends [*exenōmenois*], and at times, if it should so turn out, have killed one another. Thus we too now, because we are waging war against your [plural] king, have been compelled to regard all of his possessions as inimical [or, at war: *polemia*]; but certainly with you [singular] we would place the highest value on being friends [*philoi*]. (*Hellen.* 4.1.34)

Gabriel Herman infers from this account a profound change in moral values between the archaic and classical periods: "Diomedes and Glaukos could exercise the rights and duties of guest-friendship freely. Agesilaos and Pharnabazos could not." Herman continues (1987: 2): "the community tamed the hero, and transformed him into a citizen. Civic obligations had come to take priority even over guest-friendship: *xenoi* who were citizens had to fight on behalf of their cities even at the risk of killing each other."

Let us examine more closely, however, the nature of Pharnabazus' complaint against Agesilaus: "O Agesilaus and all you Lacedaemonians who are present, I became a friend [*philos*] and ally to you [plural] when you were waging war against the Athenians, and by providing money I rendered your [plural] navy strong, while on land I myself fighting from horseback along with you [plural] pursued the enemies at war [*polemioi*] into the sea" (4.1.32). Pharnabazus stresses that he was never duplicitous toward the Spartans, and yet they have cut down and burned the houses and parks bequeathed to him by his father, in which he took delight; he concludes by inquiring rhetorically whether this is the way to repay favors (*kharites*).

Pharnabazus does not, in this passage, pretend to be the *xenos* or foreign friend of Agesilaus. He points rather to the services that he performed in behalf of the community of Spartans (hence the repeated use of the second person plural) as a formal ally or *summakhos*, fighting in person alongside them. If the thirty Spartans accompanying Agesilaus feel shame at Pharnabazus' accusation, it is for injury to a friendly power, not a consequence of their king's personal relationship with the satrap.

What is more, Pharnabazus bases the charge of ingratitude on narrow grounds: the Spartans have attacked his own personal estates, hardly leaving him the wherewithal to obtain dinner in his own land (4.1.33). He is not denying the necessity of carrying their campaign against the Persian king into his own satrapy, any more than Diomedes' friendship with Glaucus would have inhibited him from waging war in Lycia, had circumstances required it. Pharnabazus is requesting due consideration for his efforts in behalf of the Lacedaemonians as a whole, in the form of the exemption of his own property from pillaging.

This is the context in which Agesilaus delivers his rather patronizing homily on the occasional necessity of waging war on foreign friends. Agesilaus is seeking to excuse his previous conduct, since the purpose of the conference is to establish friendship (*philia*, 4.1.29) between the two parties, and he reaches for vague generalities about conflicting obligations as a way of putting the past behind them.

Agesilaus does not end his speech, however, with bland excuses. Rather, he invites Pharnabazus to join the Spartans and revolt against his own king.[45] Agesilaus formulates this appeal in terms of the contrast, conventional since the fifth century BC, between Greek freedom (*eleutheria*) and Persian despotism: by accepting the Spartans as allies (*summakhoi*, 4.1.36), Pharnabazus will no longer have to bow before a master, and will command his own realm. To this Pharnabazus replies:

If the king sends another general and appoints me as his subordinate, I shall elect to be your [plural] friend [*philos*] and ally. But if he assigns the office to me – such a thing, it seems, is honor – it is well to know that I shall wage war against you [plural] as best I can.

"When he heard this, Agesilaus grasped his hand and said: 'Would that such a man as you might become our friend, noblest sir. But know this one thing,' he said, 'that I shall now leave your [singular] land as quickly as I can, and for the future, even if there is war, as long as we are able to campaign against another we shall keep away from you and yours' " (4.1.37–8).

Agesilaus thus chooses, as Xenophon represents the affair, exactly the same course as Diomedes and Glaucus do in the *Iliad*: he will abstain from attacking Pharnabazus and his private lands for the sake of a friendship based this time not on past services but rather on a sense of individual admiration for the courage and honesty of the man, even though Pharnabazus has just announced his willingness to fight in behalf of his own king against the Spartans. Although their states are at war, Agesilaus is prepared to put his esteem for the

---

[45] For this type of scene in Xenophon, cf. Gray 1989: 52–8.

Persian satrap ahead of strategic considerations. I suspect that in framing this scene, in which two leaders pause in the midst of battle to affirm a personal bond, Xenophon was inspired at least in part by the Homeric dialogue between Diomedes and Glaucus.

As Pharnabazus is departing from the place of meeting, his son by his wife Parapita runs up to Agesilaus and exclaims: "I adopt you, o Agesilaus, as my *xenos.*" Agesilaus responds: "And I accept." "Remember now," the boy replies, and the two exchange gifts. Later, Xenophon notes, Agesilaus will look after the boy when his half-brother has driven him into exile (4.1.39–40).

There is a quaintness to the inauguration of *xenia* between Agesilaus and Pharnabazus' son (it may be noted that the relationship is not inherited) that suggests an institution marked by self-conscious formality and signs of privilege or distinction.[46] Such friendships were cultivated by an aristocracy that practiced and embellished a traditional code of hospitality as a way of maintaining its identity in the context of new forms promoted by the democratic cities. While *xenoi* were sometimes ostentatious in the performance of their responsibilities, symbol was as important as substance. The victory odes of Pindar, composed to celebrate the athletic achievements of aristocrats, invoke *xenia* as the emblem of social grace among the best men, and in the process translate the poet's fee into a gift bestowed upon a guest, just as his verses are a token of honor and tribute between friends. Leslie Kurke (1991: 141) remarks apropos *Pythian* 10.63–8:

> To say that he trusts to his patron's *xenia* in this context can only mean he counts on him for the future commissions to which he alludes. Yet Pindar frames this statement not as a business proposition but rather as an enduring bond of friendship between himself and Thorax.

The decorous rituals of presents and pomp convert the personal intimacy between *philoi* into courtliness.

As an "upper-class institution" (Herman 1987: 34), *xenia* was regarded with suspicion in the Athenian popular courts; thus Demosthenes (18.284; 19.295 and 314) can ridicule Aeschines' pretentiousness as self-described *xenos* of Philip of Macedon, implying both a traitorous alliance with the king and a hostility to democratic institutions. "The ideological control of the elite by the Athenian

---

[46] Cf. Bourdieu 1984.

citizen masses was not a perfect system, but on the whole it worked remarkably well" (Ober 1989: 332).

Just as friends could be called upon to offer help in a crisis, so too one might expect assistance from *xenoi*. But it ought not to be supposed that friends abroad stood ready to provide interest-free loans because of *xenia*. Apollodorus, who as trierarch had been responsible for maintaining a small fleet of ships for a year, accused Polycles of refusing to take up his responsibilities in turn at the end of Apollodorus' term of office. Having suffered desertions from the crew and finding himself severely strapped for funds, Apollodorus borrowed money from Archidemus and Nicippus at interest, "and then, having sent the pentecontarch [a naval officer] Euctemon to [the city of] Lampsacus, and giving him money and letters for the *xenoi* of my father, I ordered him to hire the best sailors he could for me" (Demosth. 50.17–8); Apollodorus himself stayed in Sestos, where he paid the crewmen who remained. Gabriel Herman (1987: 93, 96) takes it that Apollodorus requested the men in Lampsacus "to help Euktemon hire soldiers," and that Apollodorus fulfilled his trierarchy by means of "monies borrowed from his father's *xenoi*." Apollodorus, however, makes no mention of such a loan. On the contrary, he furnished Euctemon with money as well as with letters of introduction, and it is natural to suppose that the new sailors were to be recruited out of this fund, which was, presumably, a portion of the sum he had borrowed at interest. Thus, Apollodorus complains that three months later he "was still paying sailors in place of those who had deserted, having borrowed the money from bankers [*daneizomenos argurion*]" (50.23). Apollodorus did not seek to secure a loan from his father's friends in Lampsacus. The purpose of the letters was, I imagine, to provide Euctemon with a base of operations in a foreign city, and such hospitality might normally be expected of family friends abroad.[47]

PUBLIC AND PRIVATE

One of the services that *philoi* performed in Athens was to act as informal arbitrators, to whom parties to a quarrel might appeal in

[47] Ps.-Demosth. 53.12 relates how Demosthenes had offered money free of interest for one year to Nicostratus, with whom he was then intimate [*oikeiōs khrōmenos*], so that he might pay off a debt to *xenoi*; on loans in relation to friendship generally, see Cohen 1992: 34 n. 26, 207–15.

hopes of reconciling their differences before going to court (e.g. Lys. 4.2, 32.12; Demosth. 30.2, 41.1; cf. 41.14 and 29).[48] The role was occasionally performed by relatives as well (*oikeioi*, Demosth. 27.1). Mutual friends were presumably perceived as impartial and to be concerned for the welfare of their *philoi*. Loyalty would inhibit one from damaging a friend's interests even if he were in the wrong.

In his oration "Against Meidias," Demosthenes alleges that Meidias had sought to bring charges of homicide against him, but finding it impossible to make a case, he denounced Aristarchus instead in order to get at Demosthenes indirectly. When the city council or Boule was holding a meeting on the matter, Meidias

> stepped forward and said, "Don't you know the facts, Boule? When you've got the perpetrator," meaning Aristarkhos, "are you still delaying and investigating? Are you out of your minds? Won't you put him to death? Won't you go to his house and arrest him?" And he said all this, the foul brute, although he'd come out of Aristarkhos' house the day before, and until then was as intimate with him as anyone else. (22.116–17; trans. MacDowell, modified)

Douglas MacDowell (1990) comments: "Anyone who really believed a man guilty of homicide would not enter his house for fear of pollution" (cf. Antiph. 6.39). But Demosthenes, as MacDowell notes, says that Meidias left the house, not entered it.

Demosthenes' point is that Meidias has betrayed a friend for the sake of his vendetta against him; Meidias' presence in Aristarchus' house is evidence for their friendship. Demosthenes explains:

> Now, if he said this because he considered that Aristarkhos had committed any of the deeds which brought about his downfall, and because he believed the accusers' statements, even so he ought not to have acted in this way. For friends who are thought to have done something dreadful are punished moderately, by having the friendship broken off; revenge and legal proceedings are left to their victims and enemies (117–18, trans. MacDowell, modified)

One ought not to accuse a friend, whatever his crime (cf. Lys. 6.23; 12.64). At most, one may cease "to share in the affection that is left" (*tēs loipēs philias koinōnein*).

Demosthenes adds that Meidias compounded his offense by conversing with Aristarchus "under the same roof as though he had done nothing." Again, MacDowell explains that "one should avoid sharing a roof with a killer." Demosthenes, however, continues: "on

---

[48] Cf. poem 1. 37–40 Powell [1925]; Scafuro (forthcoming).

the day before he made these statements he'd gone in and conversed with Aristarkhos, and on the day after once again (now this really is the supreme example of impurity [*akatharsia*], men of Athens) he went into his house, sat down next to him, as close as this, gave him his hand" (119, trans. MacDowell), swearing on his own life, with many present, that he had said nothing in the Council against Aristarchus. MacDowell takes the word "impurity" to suggest "involvement in the pollution of homicide." But, according to Demosthenes, Aristarchus is not a murderer. The outrage is Meidias' gall in accepting the hospitality of a man he has just viciously maligned, and perjuring himself before a host of witnesses. As he sums the matter up: "isn't it a terrible thing, men of Athens, or rather impious, to call a man a murderer and then again to deny on oath having said that, to accuse a man of homicide and then to go under the same roof with him?" (120, trans. MacDowell).

Meidias' presence in Aristarchus' house is a sign that he enjoyed friendly relations with him. It is sometimes supposed that in the ethos of the classical Greek city-state the house is a wholly private space, and that apart from near relations only close friends normally had access to it. David Cohen remarks that "it is a constitutive feature of close friendship that one becomes an intimate of the family, sharing its secrets and being accepted into the house, including into the presence of its women." Cohen continues: "*Philia* embodies an idea of friendship where privacy barriers are relaxed, tempering the antagonistic social relations associated with honor and shame" (1991: 84, 85).

Cohen interprets the values of the classical city-state by analogy with modern Mediterranean villages, where public spaces are said to be arenas of struggle over masculine honor, whereas "the house is seen as sheltering the private sphere, including the sexual purity and reputation of the women on whom the honor of a family in significant part depends." Athenian texts, Cohen remarks, mostly "represent friends as belonging to the private sphere," although a "few passages treat friendship as a sort of third category, not part of public life, but not part of private life in the narrow sense either" (1991: 80, 83, 79).

The Greek compiler Aelian (second-third century AD) quotes Xenocrates, a disciple of Plato's and contemporary with Demosthenes, as saying that "it makes no difference whether you thrust your feet or cast your eyes into the house of another, for he who looks upon places he should not sins in the same way as he who enters locations he should not" (*Var. Hist.* 14.42). This might appear to support Cohen's thesis about domestic seclusion, but access to the home, at least to the men's quarters (*andrōn*), where companions were entertained, was relatively free. Demosthenes does not suggest that Meidias was considered part of Aristarchus' family. Courtesy to a friend might, on the contrary, induce a certain reserve about personal matters. In Euripides' *Alcestis*, Heracles, a *xenos* of the king Admetus, arrives during the public mourning for Alcestis, who has given up her life so that her husband's may be extended. Admetus puts Heracles up in the guest quarters of the palace but conceals his loss so as not to burden a guest with his private grief. When he learns the truth, Heracles reproaches Admetus for not having admitted a friend (*philos*: 1008, 1011; cf. 562) into his confidence. Both are behaving according to Aristotle's advice to come unbidden to the aid of friends but shrink from burdening them with one's own griefs (*EN* 9.11, 1171b15–25). While tragedy is unreliable as evidence for everyday life, it seems safe to suppose that the boundary between home life and friends was normally negotiated with a measure of tact.[49]

The division between the public and private domains did not take the form in Athens that comparison with Greek or Sicilian villages might suggest: "private" (*idion*) in the sense of individual was opposed to the political community (*dēmos*) or collective whole (*koinon*), not to outdoor social life (*dēmos*: Xen. *Mem.* 3.11.16; *koinon*: Thuc. 1.86.2; Lys. 12.83, 16.18; Demosth. 20.57, etc.). In these terms friendship is private but nothing is implied about integration into the domicile. Just as Athenian friendship was not an objective and quasi-contractual relationship, neither was it assimilated to membership in the family.[50]

WOMEN AS FRIENDS

Most of the references to friends in classical antiquity concern men, but women too have friendships. In Antiphon 1.14–15, the speaker says that his step-mother made a friend (*epoiēsato philēn*) of the

---

[49] On men's quarters in the Greek house, cf. Dunbabin 1991; Cornelius Nepos, *De vir. ill.* Prol. 6–7; also Jameson 1990: 186–91 on private space in the home; on *xenos* and *philos* in *Alcestis*, see Stanton 1990: 46–50.

[50] On *idion* and *idiōtēs*, cf. Ober 1989: 108–12; Rubinstein (forthcoming).

concubine of the man who lived upstairs. Praxagora plots with her friends (*philai*, 18; cf. 298–9) to take control of the Athenian assembly in Aristophanes' *Ecclesiazusae*; to her husband, she explains that she left the house early to tend a friend in childbirth (528–9; cf., much later, Josephus, *Jewish Antiquities* 9.65 on women as friends and neighbors). Again, these are relationships outside the home; how far and frequently women might go to visit friends is difficult to estimate, but they seem not to have suffered the severe restrictions of women in some modern Greek villages.[51]

Friendships between men and women are another matter. The term *philos* was evidently employed in everyday language for the clients or partners of a courtesan (Xen. *Mem.* 3.11; in the sense of "lover," cf. Aristoph. *Thesm.* 346; *Eccles.* 931, 952; Theocritus 14.37–8, probably of a *hetaira*; Asclepiades *Anth. Pal.* 5.7.3, *pace* Cameron 1981: 283).[52] Plutarch, in the *Life of Romulus* (4.3–5.4), explains that the Roman festival, Larentalia, was named for Larentia, the wife of Faustulus, who reared Romulus and Remus; she used to behave as a hetaera (*hetairousa*), and the Romans called such women *lupae* or she-wolves (hence the legend of the twins' nurturing). Plutarch then adds that the Romans also honor another Larentia, who was hired for a night to be the consort of the god Hercules in his temple (elsewhere, Plutarch describes her as a courtesan: *Moralia* 273a). Hercules indeed visited the woman, and told her to walk to the forum at dawn and make a friend (*poieisthai philon*) of the first man she met. This turns out to be an old, unmarried man who bequeathes her his considerable property. "Friend" here clearly signifies a courtesan's companion. This usage no doubt inhibited the application of the nouns *philos* and *philē* to relations between respectable men and women. Comparable qualms about describing men and women as friends have endured into modern times.[53]

FRIENDSHIP IN THE POLIS

Plato, Xenophon, and Aristotle all treat friendship as a subset of *philia* or affectionate attachment in general, shifting casually from one to another of its particular determinations as the emotional bond

---

[51] Restrictions in modern villages: Kennedy 1986: 129; cf. Demand 1994: 4, with bibliography, for a defense of the analogy between ancient and modern Greek practices.

[52] *Hetaira* despite the reservations of Dover 1971: 189; cf. Burton 1995: 25.

[53] See Luftig 1993: 1–16; cf. 163–9 on the encouragement, for practical motives, of friendship between the sexes in England during the First World War; for Roman usage, cf. below, p. 146.

between parents and children, friends, or members of a larger community. Friendship is one among several relationships that associate individuals in the city-state. It is respected as a particularly close connection, and the level of sociability among male friends is high. Aristotle assumes that *philoi* wish to spend the day together (*sunēmereuein*), and regards living together (*suzēn*) as the actualization (*energeia*) of friendship (*EN* 9.12, 1171b35). To be sure, the Greeks were intensely rivalrous, and contention for the same office (*telos*), for example, might damage the bond between friends; for this reason, Aristotle (*MM* 2.11, 1211a12–16) says that friendships between aliens (*xenikē*, i.e., the bond between *xenoi*) may be the most lasting kind. Ideally, however, classical friendship provided a locus of personal intimacy as powerful and fulfilling as the love between close kin. There is little mention, moreover, of conflict among the different kinds of claims on a person's feelings. As an arena of non-compulsory, altruistic sentiment and intercourse between equals, friendship nestled comfortably within the various ties and obligations to family, neighbors, demesmen and fellow-citizens that defined the social world of the polis.[54]

[54]   On competition between friends, cf. Black 1980: 55; absence of conflict: cf. Klein 1957: 72.

CHAPTER 3

The Hellenistic world

UNEQUAL FRIENDS

Among the epistles ascribed to the orator Isocrates is a letter of recommendation on behalf of a disciple of his named Diodotus (*Ep.* 4); the letter is addressed to Antipater, regent in Macedonia during Philip's absence. Assuming that the text is genuine and not a later composition passed off as classical – such exercises were fashionable in subsequent centuries – it may be dated to the year 340 or 339 BC. In the letter, Isocrates praises Diodotus for his moderation, thrift, and sense of justice, as well as for his pleasant nature and fluency (*ligurōtatos*), qualities that make him an excellent companion with whom to share the day or spend one's entire life. In addition to this, Isocrates says, Diodotus possesses *parrhēsia* or frankness in the highest degree – not an inappropriate outspokenness, but rather the kind of candor that manifests itself as the truest sign of good will toward his *philoi*. Isocrates continues:

Those princes who have a laudable gravity of soul honor this [frankness] as useful, whereas those whose nature is more feeble than the powers they possess take it ill, as though it compelled them to do what they do not choose; they do not realize that those who most dare to disagree concerning what is advantageous are the very ones who afford them the maximum capacity to do what they wish. For it stands to reason that monarchies, which involve many inevitable dangers, cannot endure in power by relying on those who elect always to speak with a view to pleasing; not even civic polities can do so, and they have more security. If they rely, however, on those who speak frankly for the best then much is salvaged even in situations that seem headed for ruin.

Isocrates observes that Diodotus has had bad experiences, on account of his *parrhēsia*, with some Asian princes with whom "the flatteries [*kolakeiai*] of men of no sort had weighed more heavily than the good services of this man." Isocrates expresses his confidence, however, in Antipater's awareness that "the most pleasant and profitable thing of all is to acquire and treat well friends [*philoi*] who are trustworthy and useful by virtue of their good services," and he concludes by affirming his commitment to his friends who have become very dear (*prosphilestatos*) to him (4–7, 9, 13).[1]

Isocrates' letter presents an aspect of friendship entirely different from those discussed in the previous chapter. Isocrates is writing to the regent of a king and recommending that he take into his confidence a man who is seasoned as an adviser in royal courts. Though the position for which Diodotus is being promoted is evidently semi-official, Isocrates urges that he be accepted by Antipater as a friend or *philos*. The qualities that Isocrates endorses have nothing to do with providing material assistance in adversity; the regent of Macedon does not depend on someone like Diodotus for loyalty or help of this kind. Rather, Isocrates speaks of forth-rightness or *parrhēsia*, which he represents as a mean between rude presumptuousness and dishonest flattery. Plainly, such frankness is a virtue in a counsellor, who must risk the ire of princes foolish enough to be offended when contradicted, even if the advice is in their own interest. To dare to speak the truth in such a context represents the genuine fidelity of a friend and is to be prized. In addition to this, Diodotus, according to Isocrates, is good company and pleasant to spend the day with; in this, at least, he conforms to the image of the *philos* sketched by Aristotle.

When Aristotle turns from the topic of love (*philia*) characterized by equality (*en isotēti*) to that involving surplus (*kath' huperokhēn*), such as exists between fathers and sons or husbands and wives, he remarks that in all relations of the latter type the affectionate feeling (*philēsis*) must be proportional (*analogos*), which entails that the superior partner is loved more than he loves (*EN* 8.5–6, 1158b1, 12, 23–5). Aristotle notes further that with *philia*, unlike justice, quantitative equality takes priority over the equality that is produced by adjusting for merit (*kat' axian*), and he adds:

it is clear when there arises [between people] a great differential in virtue or vice or affluence or anything else: for they are no longer friends, nor do they think they deserve to be. This is most obvious in the case of the gods,

---

[1] Isocrates' letter genuine: Lesky 1976: 618; cf. [Plato] *Ep.* 6, 323a–c, recommending Erastus and Coriscus, evidently disciples of his, as friends to Hermeias, the tyrant of Atarneus; on friendship in the Platonic epistles, see Holzberg 1994: 12.

for in all good qualities they excel most. But it is also clear in the case of kings: for those who are far inferior do not think that they deserve to be friends [or dear: *philoi*] to these, nor those who are worthless to the best or wisest. (8.7, 1158b33–59a3)

The relationship of a king to his subjects is comparable, Aristotle says, to that of a father to his children (8.10, 1160b24–5), and the latter, as he notes elsewhere, are not called friends (cf. *EE* 7.4, 1–2.1239a1–7, quoted in ch. 2).

Aristotle comments in passing that people in power tend to split their friends between those who are entertaining and those who are good at carrying out orders. True, an upright individual is both pleasing and useful, but prominent people do not have that sort of friend (8.6, 1158a27–34). Because they seek honors (*dia philotimian*), most people prefer to be loved rather than to love, and this is why they are attracted to flatterers: "for a flatterer is an outclassed friend, or one who pretends to be such [i.e., a friend] and to love more than he is loved" (8.8, 1159a15–17).

FRIENDS AT COURT

Although Aristotle was from Stagira in Chalcidice, on the fringe of Macedonia, and a tutor to Alexander the Great, his analysis of friendship with kings is far different from the image of the expert counsellor and companion that Isocrates advances in his letter to Antipater. To appreciate the context of Isocrates' conception, one may look to the structure of royal courts in the Greek world during and after the reigns of Philip and Alexander. D. Musti (1984: 179) points out, for example, that alongside the king, inscriptions from Hellenistic Syria mention "friends (*philoi*) and the military forces of land and sea (*dynameis*)." He adds that the "term (*philoi*) stresses the personal structure of the kingdom: it indicates a characteristic aspect of the monarchical institution as such." Frank Walbank (1984: 69–70) observes more generally:

Friends are to be found in all Hellenistic courts, where they form a council of state in daily session, advising the king on matters of policy – though it remains his prerogative to take the decision ... During the fourth and third centuries the king's Friends are distinguished by social and geographical mobility and personal initiative; but in the second century there was a gradual hardening into a bureaucracy.

The active career of Isocrates' pupil Diodotus illustrates the move-
ment and opportunism characteristic of this cohort.[2]

The surprising feature in Isocrates' epistle – and one that has cast
some doubt on its authenticity – is its early date in relation to the
Hellenistic practice. Walbank (1984: 69) dates to around 285 BC the
earliest contemporary reference to friends as officials of the king: a
letter from Lysimachus to the city of Priene (Welles 1934: no. 6). The
absence of explicit mentions of the titles of royal friends in earlier
documents may be due to a deference on the part of rulers to the
sensibilities of newly subject cities. There is evidence that the
Macedonian kings traditionally resorted to a cabinet of companions
or, in Greek, *hetairoi*, who may also have been identified as *philoi*
(*hetairoi* always in Arrian; Plutarch regularly employs *hetairoi* but
occasionally varies it with *philoi*; Diodorus favors *philoi*). Apart from
Macedon, the term *philos* may have antecedents in Near Eastern
courts. It is perhaps relevant that in Aeschylus' *Persians* (472 BC), the
queen mother Atossa regularly refers to the chorus of trusted advisers
as *philoi*. Xenophon (*Cyr.* 8.7.13) gives as Cyrus' final instructions to
his eldest son, Cambyses: "Know that it is not this golden scepter
that preserves your sovereignty, but rather that faithful friends (*pistoi
philoi*) are the truest and safest scepter kings have." Cyrus observes
that fidelity is not in-born; rather, "each man must create those who
are faithful to him, and their acquisition is never by force, but rather
by benefaction [*euergesia*]." Cyrus proceeds to rank the protectors of
kingship from subjects (*politai*) to mess-mates (*sussitoi*) and, most
reliable of all, brothers (8.7.14: the reference is to Cambyses' brother
Tanaoxares). However, whether such friends and comrades are
represented as having an official status is quite unclear (conceivably,
Xenophon is adapting Spartan usage).[3]

There is perhaps an allusion to the bureaucratic function of
friends in a pamphlet that Isocrates addresses to Nicocles, son of the
ruler of Cyprus, in which he advises the youth to "honor the closest

---

[2] On royal Friends, cf. Herman 1980–81: 115–16; for a detailed discussion of the Friends of
Antigonus the One-Eyed, see Billows 1990: 246–50, with prosopography 361–452.

[3] Absence of Friends in early documents: Herman 1980–81: 111–13, 117; cf. Price 1984: 34;
and note the hymn to Demetrius Poliorcetes (Athenaeus 6.253d–f) vv. 9–12; companions of
Macedonian kings: Hammond 1989: 53–8; whether the Macedonian language was Greek is
still debated: see Borza 1990: 90–4 for discussion; *hetairoi* vs. *philoi* in Macedonian court:
Hamilton 1969: 39 *ad* 15.3; cf. Herman 1980: 111 n. 24; Heckel 1992: 68 notes a distinction
between Alexander's comrades and the friends (*suntrophoi*) he grew up with; Eastern courts:
Musti 1984: 179; Cyrus' friends as officials: Herman 1980–81: 112 n. 28; Spartan usage: cf.
Cartledge 1987: 139–59.

[*oikeiotatoi*] of your friends with appointments to office [*arkhai*], and those who are most well-disposed with the most significant ones" (2.20). He continues: "Do not acquire as friends all those who wish to be, but rather those who are worthy of your nature, nor again those with whom you will spend your time most pleasantly, but rather those with whom you will manage the city in the best way" (2.27).[4]

The institution of royal friends – in whatever degree of official formality – is a striking instance of the application of the language of friendship to distinctly hierarchical relations between people of different social station, such as noblemen and individuals in their entourages, that is widely encountered in contexts outside the Athenian democracy and its sphere of cultural influence. Within the democracy, there was a tendency to avoid mentioning unequal rank and indications of superiority and dependency among the citizen body. Paul Millett (1989: 17) comments: "It seems a plausible hypothesis that the democratic ideology, with its emphasis on political equality, was hostile to the idea of personal patronage." In particular, as Aristotle makes clear, friendship was interpreted as a relationship between equals, which could be subverted by a substantial disparity between the partners (cf. the saying, "amity is parity," cited at *EN* 8.5, 1157b36, 8.8, 1159b2–3; *EE* 7.4, 1239a1–6, 7.10, 1242a9–11).[5] So too, the emphasis on helping friends in a crisis reflects an ethos in which equally vulnerable parties voluntarily cooperate in a spirit of reciprocal generosity: the ideal is more an affirmation of political equality than of economic interdependency.

There had been monarchies and aristocracies among the city-states of classical Greece, but the social world of great courts and powerful lords that arose after the conquests of Alexander the Great succeeded in eclipsing Athens as the cultural center of the Greek-speaking world. Vast cities like Alexandria were the administrative seats of kingdoms in which Greeks gathered in a few urban concentrations dominated a native hinterland. Walbank (1984: 69) remarks that "The Friends were almost invariably Greeks or Macedonians; Egyptians, Syrians, Jews and Iranians were alike excluded." In this context, relations with potentates became a literary theme – one that

---

[4] Cf. the advice of Plato (if he is indeed the author) to Dionysius of Syracuse "to acquire loyal *philoi* and *hetairoi*," *Ep.* 7.331e; also 332c, 333e on friends of Dion who become his *hetairoi*; see further Ribbeck 1883: 7.

[5] Sophocles' image in the *Ajax* of the heroic champion as friend to his vassals is antiquated; cf. Blundell 1989: 73; Konstan (forthcoming).

was readily adapted as well to the new conditions of Roman domination of the Greek east, culminating in the integration of Egypt into the Empire in 30 BC (conventionally the terminus of the Hellenistic period). In view of the cultural continuities, Greek evidence for this topic dating to the first century AD and somewhat later is freely cited in this chapter.[6]

To take an example: Vettius Valens, an astrologer active at Rome in the second century AD, records in his handbook, written in Greek, signs that promise advantageous friendships with powerful figures. People born when Zeus and Ares are in conjunction will be "famous, ostentatious, friends of greater men or of kings, generals" (1.19.12 = 38.8–12). Other signs indicate "friends of potentates [*megistanes*], closeness to kings" (2.11.6 = 64.27–8). One man, in conformity with his horoscope, "became ambitious and political and liberal with gifts and obsequious to the masses and a friend of kings and rulers" (2.21.35 = 82.4–5). At the same time, various signs point to crises in which the assistance (*boētheia* or *ōpheleia*) of friends will be required, in accord with the traditional image of friendship as a symmetrical relationship between peers.[7]

FRIENDS AND FLATTERERS

The topics broached in Isocrates' brief letter are developed at length five centuries later by Plutarch in his treatise entitled "How to Discriminate a Flatterer from a Friend," written in approximately 100 AD and dedicated to C. Julius Antiochus Philopappus, a patron of the arts who was titular king of Commagene and suffect consul in 109 under the emperor Trajan. Plutarch too explores the triad of friendship, flattery, and frankness of speech: once again, candor is the mark of the friend, as opposed to toadyism or *kolakeia*.

Plutarch's leisurely didactic essay exhibits a certain anxiety over the flatterer's ability to mimic the behavior of a true friend. He observes that "just as false gold and counterfeit coin imitate only the brilliance and sheen of gold, so the flatterer, who imitates the

---

6　Hellenistic kingdoms: Lewis 1986: 14–36 (Egypt); Grainger 1990: 148–69 (Syria); on the difference between Hellenistic and earlier monarchical institutions, cf. Price 1984: 25–7; Friends chiefly Greeks: cf. Herman 1980: 115; McKechnie 1989: 207; Plato *Ep.* 7.337b advises rulers to select Greeks as their associates.

7　Friends of kings: cf. also 4.8.17 = 159.21; 2.32.7 = 98.33; assistance in times of crisis: e.g. 4.8.20 = 159.33–4; 4.21.1 = 184.22; 5.6.114 = 219.12; 5.6.117 = 219.17; 5.6.121 = 219.26 (alternate numbers = page and line in Pingree 1986).

pleasantness and graciousness of the friend, seems always to present himself as cheerful and radiant and never opposes or objects to anything" (50a–b). But a genuine friend too will have occasion to offer praise, and constant complaint is the sign of a misanthropic and unfriendly nature. Thus, Plutarch affirms: "one might say that it is difficult to discriminate the flatterer and the friend" (50c).

Plutarch makes it clear that he is not talking about the shameless spongers or parasites, as they were called, who hung about the tables of the rich and were a stock type in New Comedy (fourth–third centuries BC) caricatured for their limitless appetites. These free-loaders, who are interested in their bellies and nothing else, are easy to recognize, Plutarch says. A fragment attributed to Archilochus (seventh century BC) already describes the type: "You drink a lot of wine straight, you don't contribute your share …, and you come uninvited as though you were a *philos*, but your stomach has turned your mind and wits to shamelessness" (fr. 124b West). Parasites are never mistaken on the comic stage for upright citizens, and they wore special masks that immediately announced their role; as a literary convention they were a caricature of subservience generally rather than representatives of a social type.[8]

A parasite in one of Libanius' declamations complains of having fallen off his horse and missed dinner in his haste to respond to an invitation of an acquaintance (*gnōrimos*, 28.6 = 576.13), not a friend; in another, the parasite laments that he has a philosopher as his master (*trophimos*, 29.2 = 593.9, etc.).[9] A parasite in a comedy by Antiphanes (fourth century BC) boasts that his kind is "both the noblest and securest friend," and that "no parasite wishes that his friends do badly, but on the contrary that they all always prosper" (fr. 80.7, 3–4 K–A), but the absence of envy is in this case merely a sign of servility: his well-being depends entirely on the wealth of his patron.

The name of flatterer might be applied to these stylized free-loaders, as Plutarch's remark indicates, but such starvelings were a far cry from men of real influence (whether flatterers and parasites were distinct types in comedy is questionable). Comic poets perhaps occasionally called attention to the wider social consequences of flattery, as in a fragment of Diphilus' *Marriage* (Athenaeus 6.254e =

---

[8] For the stereotype of the parasite, see Nesselrath 1990: 309–17; the parasite as a literary convention: Damon 1996.

[9] Alternate numbers = page and line in Foerster 1911; Libanius is a late source (fourth century AD), but he draws on New Comedy for his stereotype.

fr. 23 K–A): "For the flatterer ruins with a mischievous word general and prince and friends and cities, though pleasing a short while"; Gabriel Herman (1980–81: 119) suggests that friends of kings were "the real-life counterparts" of a high-class variety of parasites in comedy. However that may be, the literature concerning the effects of adulation in great houses and councils of state is not preoccupied in earnest with brazen gluttons. In his oration "On Friendship" (22.276c = 66.18–23), the fourth-century AD rhetorician Themistius contents himself with a passing allusion to the type:

For a friend is nowhere near a flatterer, and is furthest removed in this, that the one praises everything, while the other would not go along with you when you are erring; for the former is set on making a profit or stuffing his belly by his efforts, and is not impressed with you, but with your money or your power [*dunasteia*].[10]

As opposed to the wheedling gourmandizer, the kind of person seriously to be on guard against is "the one who seems not to flatter and says he does not – him one cannot catch in the kitchen" (50e). The insidious kind of fawning, however, "often coincides with friendship" (50f); "mingling itself into every feeling and every gesture, into the practices and communion of friendship, flattery is difficult to separate out" (51a). Worst of all, the accomplished sycophant knows that frankness is "the voice of friendship," and does not neglect to imitate that characteristic as well (51c).

There are, nevertheless, ways to catch the charlatan out. Because the flatterer has no stable center to his character, but forever adapts himself to the manners of others, he may be identified by his fickleness: pretend to change your own views, and see whether he accommodates, Plutarch recommends (52f), thereby approving a temporary adoption of the truckler's style. Flatterers, moreover, are betrayed by their innate tendency to approve base behavior, which

---

[10] Flatterers distinct from parasites in comedy: Gil: 1981–3: 46–57, Nesselrath 1985: 99–121; see however Brown 1992: 98–106, and cf. Pollux *Onomasticon* 6.123. Alternate numbers for Themistius = page and line in Schenkl, Downey, Norman 1971.

In Plautus' *Captives* (141–2), Hegio acknowledges that the parasite Ergasilus has been *amicus* (perhaps = "friendly") to his son and his son to him. Terence's Phormio, however, is ambiguous – part parasite, part sycophant in the technical Greek sense of litigious busybody (Dziazko-Hauler 1898: 70 n. 1; cf. Arnott 1970), and part altruist – and he earns the appellation "friend" (324, 562, 598, 1049) for his services. Donatus (2.463 Wessner) reports that 562 translates "he alone knows how to love his friends [*philein tous philous*]" in Terence's model, Apollodorus of Carystus' *Epidikazomenos* (fr. 23 K–A; as cited by Donatus, the line does not scan); the Latin rendering *amicus amico* is proverbial for intimate friends (Dziazko-Hauler 1898 ad loc.; cf. Plautus *Bacchides* 386, *Mercator* 887, etc.).

one may recognize by the usual signs of dissipation: one is reminded of Isocrates' warning to Nicocles about friends who cater only to pleasure (compare Cicero's vivid description of the depravity of Quintus Apronius, who attended on Gaius Verres: *Against Verres* 3.22–4, 157–8). Plutarch explains that the soul contains one part that loves what is noble (*philokalon*) and another that loves what is false (*philopseudes*); the genuine *philos* takes the side of the former, which is rational and true, while the flatterer lines up with the emotional and irrational component (61d). Within the soul there is thus reproduced the tension between the honest friend and the dissimulator: each has its ally inside.

Discernment, accordingly, is not enough; the rational element must be able to prevail over the irrational. Plutarch's essay is thus in large measure an exhortation to virtue – he himself is the good friend and counsellor who with his admonitions strengthens the better self of his reader and tips the balance in favor of probity. There is no guarantee, however, that good judgment will win out, especially if the addressee is surrounded by flatterers who have the advantage of accommodating themselves to the tastes of their patron and thus appearing all the more to be genuine friends, since friends are, in Aristotle's phrase (e.g. *EN* 9.4, 1166a31–2), another self. In such circumstances, real friends manifest themselves by their independence (53b). Separating forthrightness from feigning is exacting work; one writer (Little 1993: 19) drily concludes: "there's nothing in Plutarch to flush out the flatterer or mere echo of ourselves."

Isocrates remarked in his letter to Antipater on the flattery in Asian courts that had thwarted Diodotus' good influence as an honest friend. While adulation was not unknown in democratic Athens (it was a topos in connection with childless men cozened into adopting an heir, e.g. Isaeus 8.37; Demosth. 44.63), it was not normally articulated as an imitation of friendship. Flattery implicitly acknowledges the superior station of another, and, as we have observed, the egalitarian ideology of the democracy discouraged the representation of relations of dependency among free citizens. As Aristotle says, "all flatterers are hirelings and humble people flatterers" (*EN* 4.3, 1125a1–2). Having friends in high places, such as the Macedonian court, laid one open to suspicion of greed and servility. In the democratic ethos, friendship presupposed equality.[11]

---

[11] Adulation in democratic Athens: cf. also Demosth. 45.65 on Stephanus as a flatterer of the well-to-do who betrays them in adversity; Demosth. 19.21; Plato, *Rep.* 7.538 A; Arist. *Pol.* 2,

Aristotle defines the flatterer as one who is ingratiating (*areskos*) with a view to his own advantage (*EN* 4.6, 1127a7–10); on the spectrum along which virtues are a mean and vices the extremes, he characterizes obsequiousness as excessive sociability; at the other extreme is the *duskolos* or grouch (*EN* 1126b11–27a12; Theophrastus treats the *kolax* and *areskos* separately in *Characters* 2, 5). Sociability, Aristotle notes, has no name of its own (1126b19, 27a7: the commentator Aspasius ventures the label *homilētikē* [121.8 Heylbut]); it resembles *philia* but differs from it in that the sociable person lacks feeling and affection (*pathos, to stergein*) for those with whom he mingles (1126b20–3).[12] In the *Eudemian Ethics* (3.7, 1233b30–34a32), the mean between enmity or hostility (*ekhthra*) and flattery (*kolakeia*) is called *philia*, which is here presumably equivalent to "friendliness." Discriminating the dissimulator from an actual friend is not a problem that attracts Aristotle's attention.[13]

In the democracy, only the sovereign populace (*dēmos*) could claim deference, and politicians who catered to its desires might be accused of flattery. Isocrates reprimands the Athenians (8.4) "because you know that many and great houses have been ruined by those who flatter [*tōn kolakeuontōn*], and although you hate those who possess this art in private situations, you are not disposed in the same way toward them in public situations." He adds (8.14): "although there is a democracy, there is no freedom of speech [*parrhēsia*] ... but toward those who rebuke and advise you you are as grudgingly disposed as toward those who are doing the city harm." Centuries later, Maximus of Tyre ("By What Means One May Separate a Flatterer from a Friend," *Or.* 14.7) asserts that democracies rather than aristocracies are breeding grounds of flattery, and gives as examples Cleon and Hyperbolus, *kolakes* of the *dēmos*. The opposition between *parrhēsia* and *kolakeia* or obsequiousness is reminiscent of the contrast between frank and flattering counsellors in Isocrates' letter to

---

1263b21–3; flatterers as servile: cf. Arist. *Pol.* 5.11, 1314a1–4; Ussher 1993: 43–4 on Theophrastus' depiction of the flatterer in the *Characters* as "an utterly base and servile occupation"; Maximus of Tyre 14.6–7 on the *isēgoria* or free speech of the friend vs. the abject attendance [*therapeia*] of the flatterer; suspicion of friends in high places: Herman 1980–81: 121–2.

12 A modern writer (Raphael 1993: 16) comments: "gregariousness is a parody of friendship, just as promiscuity is a travesty of passion"; the idea goes back to Plutarch, *On Having Many Friends* 93c and Lucian, *Toxaris* 37, who however compare men's desire for many friends with women's licentiousness.

13 On *philia* as "friendliness," cf. Arist. *MM* 1.28, 1192b30–2, 1.30–2, 1193a12–39; so too *philos* at *EN* 2.7, 1108a26–30 is adjectival and means "friendly"; cf. also *EN* 8.8, 1159a14–15, cited above; Nesselrath 1985: 112–13 contrasts *EN* and *EE* too sharply on this point; identifying dissimulators in Aristotle: *pace* Gallo and Pettine 1988: 14.

Antipater. Unlike relations with kings, however, one does not talk of being friends with the Athenian assembly. The issue of *philoi* vs. flatterers falls outside the discourse of the democracy.[14]

FRANKNESS AND FREE SPEECH

The last third of Plutarch's tractate on distinguishing the flatterer from the friend (chs. 25–37) is devoted to frankness, complementing the analysis of flattery.[15] Like flattery, *parrhēsia* too is subject to abuse in the form of overly harsh criticism or the boorish directness that Isocrates censured in praising the discreet candor of Diodotus. Just as one must learn to discern friends from dissimulators, there is need also for instruction on how to give counsel in the gracious manner befitting a friend. Few people speak openly to friends as opposed to indulging (*kharizesthai*) them, and those few do not know how to do so, since they mistake blame and abuse for candor (66a; cf. 66e). Timing (*kairos*) is of the essence: neglect of the right moment "ruins the utility of frankness" (68c); the phrase is reminiscent of an aphorism attributed to Democritus (86B 226 D–K) to the effect that "*parrhēsia* is intrinsic [*oikēion*] to freedom: the difficulty lies in diagnosing the *kairos*." Thus, one must recognize the season when a friend is open to correction (70d). Further, frankness is not to be employed with friends in the presence of others (70e); criticism must be tempered with praise (72b), nor must *parrhēsia* be answered with *parrhēsia* (72e). Tact is of the essence: Plutarch fondly recalls (70e) the way his teacher Ammonius, rather than directly chastise some of his students who lunched too luxuriously, had his slave beaten for a like offense but cast a knowing look at the guilty parties.

Contrary to the usage witnessed in Plutarch, in the classical democracy frankness was not regarded as the specific virtue of *philoi*, any more than flattery had been perceived as the antithesis to friendship. A friend might offer helpful criticism, but such forthrightness was assumed rather than enjoined. In democratic Athens, indeed, the word *parrhēsia* normally did not refer to personal candor

---

14 Flattery of *dēmos*: cf. Aristophanes, *Knights* 48; Isocrates 8.3; Arist. *Pol.* 4.4.1292a15–7; Ribbeck 1883: 9–14; Romilly 1975: 43–7; Gil 1981–3: 47–8; Konstan 1996a; Aristophanes, *Peace* 756, however, alludes to flatterers of Cleon; cf. Demosth. 19.162, of Aeschines; friends vs. flatterers: cf. Procopé 1991: 962–5. Outside the democratic context, Pindar *Pyth.* 2.81–8 (to the tyrant Hiero of Syracuse) contrasts the "fawning" and "straight-speaking" man in connection with the behavior of friends.

15 Gallo and Pettine 1988: 19, following Brokate 1913: 2–11, overstate the separateness of the two parts of Plutarch's treatise.

but rather to freedom of speech as a liberty pertaining to all citizens. As Arnaldo Momigliano (1973: 258) remarks, "In the second part of the fifth century and during the greater part of the fourth century every Athenian citizen had the right to speak [in the assembly] unless he disqualified himself by certain specified crimes." This freedom is, Momigliano supposes, "an Athenian fifth-century idea," and the term of art that expressed it was *parrhēsia*: "*Parrhēsia* represented democracy from the point of view of equality of rights" (Momigliano 1973: 259).[16]

Thus Phaedra, in Euripides' *Hippolytus*, intones (421–2): "May free men, flourishing in freedom of speech [*parrhēsia*], dwell in the city of renowned Athens." In the *Phoenissae*, Jocasta asks her son: "What is the wretched thing for exiles?" Polyneices replies: "One thing above all, that he does not have *parrhēsia*." To which Jocasta responds: "What you have said – not to utter what one thinks – pertains to a slave"; the city is Thebes but the ideology is thoroughly Athenian (390–2; cf. Plato, *Rep.* 557b4–6).

The change from the political to the moral sense of *parrhēsia* was not abrupt. Free speech remained a value in the Hellenistic period: for example, the cynic Teles (third century) notes that exiles lack *parrhēsia* ("On Exile," in Stobaeus, *Eclogae* 3.40.8 = 23.5); on the other hand, the letter of Isocrates would indicate that the personal dimension of the term was available in the mid-fourth century. With the rise of palace monarchies as centers of power, however, courtesy and individual honesty among friends assumed particular importance. In illustrating *parrhēsia*, Plutarch draws almost all of his examples from the sphere of kings and courtiers, and it is usually the inferior party whose frankness is at issue. As Momigliano (1973: 260) puts it, "Menander replaced Aristophanes, and *parrhesia* as a private virtue replaced *parrhesia* as a political right."[17]

Outside the sphere of democratic discourse, friendship is reconfigured in such a way as to include hierarchical relationships, and a judicious candor is perceived as the touchstone that distinguishes the true friend from the flatterer, who assumes, in turn, a new importance on the political scene. Philo of Alexandria expresses it crisply: "*Parrhēsia* is kin to *philia*" (*Her.* 21), whereas "*kolakeia* is *philia*'s

---

[16] *Parrhēsia* as a civic liberty: cf. Scarpat 1964: 29–37, 46–69; Hunter 1985: 487–9.

[17] No sharp change in sense of *parrhēsia*: Gallo and Pettine 1988: 21–2; Spina 1986; Teles: alternate numbers = page and line in Hense 1909, cit. Herman 1980–81: 125; Plutarch's examples: cf. Engberg-Pedersen 1996; *parrhēsia* as private virtue: cf. Peterson 1929.

disease" (*Leg.* 2.10). There is an interrelated shift in the semantics of all three terms.[18]

FRIENDS AND RULERS

The difference of status between the partners, the deference expected of underlings, and the semi-official role of the courtier who performs services all contribute to the suspicion that friendship of the sort Plutarch describes is less personal and affectionate, more formal and calculating than the classical ideal. Horst Hutter (1978: 10) expresses a modern qualm: "Friendship tends toward equality. One of the strongest barriers against the formation of a friendship bond is structurally-conditioned inequality". In his petition to the Duchess Mazarin entitled "Sur l'amitié," composed in 1689, Charles de Saint-Evremond states flatly: "It is certain that one cannot regard one's prince as one's friend. The distance that exists between rulers and subjects does not permit the formation of that union of wills that is necessary to true love" (1966: 307–8; my trans.). Saint-Evremond accordingly concludes (1966: 308–9; trans. Silver 1996):

> The usual relationship of kings and their courtiers is a relationship of interest ... [But] the flatteries of adulators make [kings] wish for the sincerity of a friend ... With these, they wish to taste all the pleasures that familiarity of association and freedom of conversation may endow on private friends. But how dangerous are these friendships to a favorite who dreams more of love than of watching his own conduct! Wishing to find his friend, this confidant meets his master; [his] familiarity is punished as the indiscreet freedom of a servant who forgets his place.

Such knowing commentaries acknowledge the force of sentiment only to make it appear naive and irrelevant to the realities of absolute power.

Plutarch's essay is about friendship, not statecraft or the courtier's art. He assumes that a disinterested relationship may obtain between king and subordinate just as it may between social equals, and nowhere does he draw a distinction between equal and unequal associations. Candor is necessary to intimacy at any level. As Maximus of Tyre puts it (*Or.* 14.7), "friendship is equality of character [*tropos*]." Plutarch cites Alexander the Great's refusal to be

---

[18] New importance of flatterer: cf. Brown 1992: 102; *parrhēsia*: cf. also Philo *Her.* 19–21, *Ios.* 74; *kolakeia*: cf. Philo *Leg.* 3.182; *Plant.* 104–5; *Conf.* 48; *Agr.* 164; *Migr.* 111–12; the index to Philo (Leisegang 1926–30) is particularly useful; for a further semantic shift, see below, pp. 155–6.

compared to a god to illustrate the need we all have for honest criticism from friends in our private affairs (66a).

A section (13) of Plutarch's *Political Precepts*, addressed to aspiring politicians in Greek city-states under Roman rule, is devoted to the choice of friends (806f–809b). It is peppered with anecdotes concerning Solon, Themistocles, Cleon, and other old-time statesmen, but Plutarch is manifestly reading contemporary conditions back into the political life of democratic Athens. Plutarch relates (807a-b), for example, how Themistocles once replied to a question about ruling fairly: "May I never sit on such a throne in which friends will not weigh more with me [retaining *par' emoi*] than non-friends" (the "throne" seems more a royal seat than an Athenian magistrate's chair). Plutarch comments huffily: "But he was not right in pledging the state to friendship and subordinating what is in common and public to private favors and concerns" – though curiously enough, he at once attributes the contrary view to Themistocles himself, to the effect that "a ruler [or archon] is not equitable who grants favors [*kharizesthai*] contrary to the law" (807b).[19]

Plutarch goes on to compare the relationship between a political leader and his friends to that between a master architect and his subordinates and craftsmen, or between a carpenter and his tools: "for friends are the living and thinking instruments of men of politics, and one must not slide along with them [i.e., the politicians] when they err, but be alert so as not to transgress even when they may be ignorant of it" (807d).[20] Plutarch then indicates the kinds of benefits that are not begrudged when awarded to friends, for example prestigious missions as envoys (808b-c). A little later (813b), Plutarch cunningly recommends letting two or three friends take the other side in public debate, only to declare themselves persuaded in the end. It is always wise to be gracious to colleagues in office even if they are not *philoi* (816c); truly powerful friends – i.e., Romans – are indispensable (814c-d; cf. 819b). Friends in politics are not treated as part of the regular administrative apparatus: their influence and their utility, as well as the threat they pose to just government, derive from the fact that the relationship is first and foremost personal.

Undoubtedly, rulers selected intimates to serve in official capa-

---

[19] For the tendency, see Andrewes 1978: 3–4; Connor 1971: 44–5 treats the episodes cautiously as evidence for classical practices; *par' emoi*: cf. Caiazza 1993: 227 n. 152.

[20] Contrary to the translations of Fowler 1927, Carrière 1984, Caiazza 1993: 101, and Russell 1993: 154–5, it is the friends, I think, and not the statesmen who must remain upright.

cities; this is in part a function of the personal nature of Hellenistic monarchies. Kings were commonly advised to look to the virtue of their associates, not their administrative talents. In his third oration "On Kingship," probably recited as a panegyric before the Roman emperor Trajan, Dio Chrysostom, having begun with due cautions about flattery (3.2–3, 12–25) which among other things has the vicious consequence of undermining the value of true praise (18), concludes (86–132) with a eulogy of friendship as the finest and most secure possession of a king – better than walls and armies (86). Whereas the safety of subjects is sustained by laws, a king has no protection other than to be loved, and for this reason must be sure of his friends before granting them power (89). Dio slips easily into general commonplaces on the benefits of *philoi*: they alone are both pleasant and useful (91–5); good things are better if shared with friends (96–8, 101–3, 108–9). More pertinent to rulership is the idea that friends are superior to eyes, ears, tongue, and hands because they function at a distance and render one omnipresent (104–7; cf. the so-called Eyes and Ears of the Persian king, 118; Xen. *Cyr.* 8.2.10– 12). Since the king should outshine all others in *philia* as in other virtues, his people love him (*agapan*) more than their own parents and children, and he in turn is exemplary in his fondness for his relatives and his wife (111–13, 119–22), desiring that they earn their offices through merit, not kinship (120). The idea of *philia* has here widened into affection generally, and Dio enters the qualification that one can break with friends but not with relatives (121). Friendships are made, and the king is best equipped to acquire them since he can bestow whatever others want, whether fame, authority, military or bureaucratic posts: if *philia* can be bought, an emperor can do it better than the rest (130–2).[21]

Dio's theme is that a good king inspires love and loyalty. He can be served by *philoi* and have confidence in his ministers in part because his choice is limitless (130); tyrants, by contrast, are friendless (116–18). Dio is not recommending granting appointments to intimates so much as the cultivation of affection and allegiance within the administration (including the imperial family). By representing fidelity in terms of love and friendship inspired by the virtue of the ruler, Dio is simultaneously fostering the king's rectitude (one of the

---

[21] Kings advised to look for virtue: Saller 1982: 96–102; Eyes and Ears of the king: cf. Hirsch 1985: 101–30; also Libanius, *Or.* 8.6–7.

purposes of panegyrics as a genre) and affirming the force of personal attachments, which are treated both as genuine and reciprocal.

Alexander the Great had provided an example of extreme devotion in his love for Hephaestion, his age-mate and "dearest of all his friends" (Quintus Curtius 3.12.16), upon whose death he displayed inordinate grief – "reminiscent, as he was doubtless aware, of Achilles' sorrow at the fate of Patroklos" (Heckel 1992: 65). Modern critics have intuited an erotic motive that is absent in the sources and effectively excluded by the label *philos*. More to the point is the tension occasionally noted between Hephaestion's special status and the collective fellowship of the *hetairoi*. Friendship is strong enough a tie, and this is the bond that concerns the political moralists, both for the danger of confidence in undeserving associates and the blessing of trust based on honest and mutual affection.[22]

PHILOSOPHICAL FRIENDSHIP: EPICUREANISM

When Galen, writing in the second century AD, instructs his readers on how to cure themselves of vehement passions (*On the Passions Specific to Each* 1.3), he advises them to take as a friend (*philos*) a man not given to flattery (*kolakeia*). The test is whether he frequents the houses of the rich and powerful: only one who avoids such connections can be trusted to speak the truth and correct one's faults (*elenkhein, epanorthousthai*). Correspondingly, one who is wealthy or holds high office cannot expect honest counsel. Galen directs his lesson, accordingly, to those of humbler station.[23]

Galen's treatise thus presents the triad of admonishment, sycophancy, and friendship in a context involving social peers outside the domain of political or courtly life. In doing so, he reflects a tradition of philosophical pedagogy to which he was heir and which, in the Hellenistic period, gave rise to intense discussion concerning the proper mean between strictness and indulgence among teachers and disciples engaged in the pursuit of moral improvement. Out of this milieu, for example, come two treatises by the Epicurean thinker Philodemus, one entitled "On Flattery" (*Peri kolakeias*), the other "On

---

[22] Alexander's grief: cf. Plut. *Alex.* 72.3 with Hamilton 1969: 223; Arrian 7.14.2–4; Diod. Sic. 17.114.4; erotic motive: Hamilton 1969: 130 ad 47.9; Heckel 1992: 65–6; cf. also above, pp. 37–9; tensions between friends and *hetairoi*: Heckel 1992: 72–5; on the problems that beset a courtly fellowship based on personal ties, cf. Archibald 1992 on Thomas Malory's *Morte Darthur*.

[23] Text of Galen: Marquardt 1884; for translation, see Harkins 1963.

Frankness" (*Peri parrhēsias*), preserved in damaged condition among the scorched papyri recovered from a house in Herculaneum, near Naples and the slopes of Mt. Vesuvius, that was buried when the volcano erupted in AD 79. The villa, which contained Philodemus' library, belonged to his friend and patron, the Roman aristocrat Lucius Calpurnius Piso.

The Epicureans cultivated ties of friendship within their communities, and the Hellenistic practice of referring to adherents as friends seems to go back to Epicurus' own time (later fourth and early third centuries BC; cf. Cicero, *De finibus* 1.20.65 on Epicurus' houseful of friends).[24] References to *philoi* in Epicurus' own writings are relatively few. One aphorism (*Vatican Saying* 34) reads: "we have use not so much for usefulness [*khreia*] from our friends as for trust in their usefulness." In another (*VS* 39), Epicurus says that "neither is he who continually seeks usefulness a friend, nor is he who never connects them." Utility or benefit is again associated with friends, but constant recourse to their help is like "trading exchange in favors" (*kapēleuei tēi khariti tēn amoibēn*); on the other hand, never to rely on them "cuts off confidence concerning the future." One more saying in the Vatican collection (66) advises that we should "condole with our friends not by wailing but by taking thought," presumably for practical ways to be of use (cf. "Sayings of Clitarchus" 91 Chadwick). That friends may be relied on for help or *boētheia* in times of crisis was, of course, a commonplace in the classical Athenian democracy, but Epicurus' concern with confidence or trust seems intended to allay a sense of individual vulnerability in the face of chance rather than to affirm the values of loyalty and generosity between equals.

Also attributed to Epicurus is the view that the wise man will never betray a friend and will on occasion die for one (Diog. Laert. 10.120–1), and that "the memory of a friend who has died is a sweet thing" (fr. 213). Perhaps these pronouncements too reflect Epicurus' preoccupation with the pragmatics of security (*asphaleia*). Preserved in the collection at Herculaneum is a fragment of an essay by one Carneiscus, a contemporary of Epicurus, that discusses the proper attitude toward the death of a friend. The work derives its title from Carneiscus' fellow-Epicurean Philistas (appropriately named), who manifests the right outlook and demeanor. In the portion of book 2 that is legible, Carneiscus attacks a treatise dealing with friendship

---

[24] Harnack's well-known aphorism (1905: 25), "The history of the Greek schools of philosophy is at the same time the history of friendship," is, however, something of an exaggeration.

by Praxiphanes, a pupil of Theophrastus; the polemic reflects the energetic controversy over the issue that has now all but vanished from sight. Only Epicureanism, Carneiscus suggests, with its understanding of the psychology of limitless desire and fear, is helpful with respect to needs or utility (*khreiai*, col. XIX.7). Another of the Herculaneum papyri (1089) says that "a friend is promptly at hand in need."[25]

Philia in its broadest sense is "the attractive principle in human nature generally" (Stock 1913: 136), and where Epicurus speaks of *philia* rather than *philoi*, he is prone to extravagant claims, such as the assertion that within the limited span of human affairs we may acknowledge "the complete security of *philia*" (*Kuriai Doxai* or "Principal Tenets" 28). Again: "of the things with which wisdom furnishes itself for bliss in an entire life, much the greatest is the possession of *philia*" (*KD* 27). In *VS* 78 the noble person is said to "exist above all in the ambit of wisdom and *philia*"; Epicurus adds that the one is a mortal good, while the other – apparently *philia* – is immortal.[26]

In these sentences, *philia*, which is more lasting than wisdom and connected with blessedness, seems to exceed the practical advantages of friendship and perhaps has a more ample significance. In *VS* 23 Epicurus says: "All *philia* is an excellence [*aretē*] in itself, but it has taken its origin from service [*ōpheleia*]." The word "all" suggests a wide range of affectionate ties or fellow-feeling, but the proposition that such sentiments have arisen out of service or *ōpheleia* seems analogous to the utility (*khreia*) Epicurus ascribes to friendship in the narrow sense. A distinction may be in order, however: friends (*philoi*) are recommended for their usefulness (*khreia*) to us here and now, insofar as trust in them is conducive to tranquillity; *philia*, on the other hand, arose originally because of mutual need and support (*ōpheleia*) among human beings, and comes to be valued for its own sake.[27]

The context for the latter idea is likely to have been Epicurean anthropology. Epicurus believed that primitive human beings did not have need of one another, but led isolated and self-sufficient

---

[25] Carneiscus: see Capasso 1988; on pap. Herc. 1089, see the edition in Acosta 1983, esp. pp. 130–2.

[26] *Philia* immortal: cf. Gemelli 1978: 62–3.

[27] For a distinction between "friends" and "friendship" in Epicurus, cf. O'Connor 1989: 185; *philia* as an *aretē* so MSS., Bollack 1975, Long and Sedley 1987; other editors (cf. Gemelli 1978: 60) adopt Usener's emendation *hairetē*, "choiceworthy."

lives. Affection, accordingly, arose historically out of the need for mutual benefit only after humans had developed to the point of being sociable. Thus Lucretius reports that in the beginning the human race was hardier than now, and "not easily capable of being harmed by heat or cold or unusual food or any damage to the body ... Nor could they have the common good in view ..." Lat'er, however, "the human race first began to soften ... Sex sapped their strength, and children by their charm easily broke their parents' stern demeanour. Then too neighbours began to form friendships [*amicities*], eager not to harm one another and not to be harmed; and they gained protection for children and for the female sex" (5.929–30; 958; 1014–21, trans. Long and Sedley 1987: 127).

Amicities translates *philia*; Lucretius is talking not about the acquisition of friends in the restricted sense, but rather about the origin of sympathy in general, the sensibility or disposition to care for spouses, children, and neighbors. Parental love is an early form of such affection, though it is not natural in the sense of innate to the race (cf. Demetrius Lacon, quoted in ch. 2 n. 21). Rather, *philia* is a product of evolution (cf. Hermarchus in Porphyry, *De abstinentia* 1.9.4 = Long and Sedley 1987: 130). Once human beings have become social creatures, they can make compacts (*foedera*, 1025) and acquire a sense of fairness (*aequum*, 1023).

In *VS* 52, *philia* is described as "dancing round the world bidding us all to wake up and felicitate each other." The striking image seems to refer to affection as a capacity of the species rather than to the assurance to be derived from individual friendships. When Epicurus mentions *philoi*, he appears to be referring to particular intimate relationships that inspire confidence and peace of mind; "friends" in this limited sense corresponds to ordinary Greek usage. By reinterpreting the security friends afford as an interior conviction, Epicurus may have been responding to a narrowly utilitarian view of *philia* in the post-Socratic tradition that construed affection as such as a consequence of *khreia* ("need" or "usefulness"), as in Aristippus' dictum: "*philia* is born in *khreia*." Epicurus had a more complex, historical conception of the origins of *philia*, and his celebration of this faculty goes beyond the composure to which a small circle of personal friends may contribute.[28]

---

[28] Aristippus is quoted in Diogenes Laertius 2.91 = Giannantoni 1983–5 4 A 172; for further examples, see Capasso 1988: 258–61; on utility and friendship in Epicureanism, see Brescia 1955: 317–19; Mitsis 1987; Mitsis 1988: 98–128.

Later Epicureans entertained a variety of views on love and friendship. Cicero (*De finibus* 1.66–70) reports three opinions: that feelings for friends derive from and become bound up with the pleasure they afford; that with familiarity love flourishes so that friends are cherished for their own sakes independently of advantage; and that friendship involves a contract or pledge (*foedus*) among the wise to love each other as themselves. But the role of friendship also acquired a new pedagogical dimension that, to judge from surviving sources, goes beyond the methods elaborated by the founder of the school.

In his essay on candor, Philodemus (first century BC) is concerned with the proper use of *parrhēsia* or frank criticism as a means of improving or "saving" (*sōzein*, fr. 36.1) fellow-disciples.[29] Philodemus says that only the sage will know how to be forthright in a way that is attuned to the individual nature of the student and is therefore neither too harsh nor too indulgent (cols. IV–VII); initiates, however, are encouraged to report on the failings of their peers, provided they do so for the sake of correction (*diorthōsis*) and not slander (fr. 49.7–50.12), and they may also be treated (*therapeuthēnai*) by one another (fr. 79.1–4). Like Plutarch (70e), Philodemus (fr. 84) recommends discretion in the use of *parrhēsia* when others are present, and suggests that one leaven blame with praise (fr. 68; cf. frs. 7, 10, 58 and Plutarch "How to Distinguish" 72b, 73c–74a). He allows too that the teacher himself may stand in need of criticism on occasion (col. VIII), and recognizes that differences in social status complicate the task of the teacher: a humble Greek instructing a powerful Roman aristocrat must be discreet, and Philodemus offers some practical advice on how to treat students of high station (cols. IVb, xa, and especially XIVa; contrast Cicero's uncomplimentary portrait of Philodemus' relation to Piso, *Against Piso* 68–71).

The other side of the coin of honest criticism is openness on the part of the aspirant, who must willingly reveal his or her faults (frs. 40–1, 49; the term for such confession is *mēnuein*, "to reveal").[30] A deficiency of frankness, in turn, is flattery – "the adversary of *philia*" (P.Herc. 1082 col. 2.3–4) – to which Philodemus devotes more than one book of his treatise, *On Vices*.[31] As in Plutarch, moreover, the

---

[29] Olivieri 1914: vii–x (references to Philodemus, *On Frankness* are to this edition); Glad 1992: 229–320; *parrhēsia* occurs in Epicurus only in *VS* 29, of his intention to speak openly about his physical theories.

[30] On disclosure in Philodemus, cf. Glad 1995: 124–32.

[31] See Gargiulo 1981; Longo Auricchio 1986.

exercise of *parrhēsia* is specifically associated with relations among *philoi* (*On Frankness* frs. 8, 41, 50, 55, 70, 81, 84; *philia*, fr. 28; *philotēs*, fr. 86). Members of local Epicurean societies were evidently encouraged to conceive of themselves as friends or to develop ties of friendship with one another; Diogenes of Oenoanda, who in the second century AD had a summary of Epicurean philosophy inscribed upon a wall, speaks of friends in Athens, Chalcis, Thebes, and elsewhere (fr. 62 II 5 Smith 1993; cf. frs. 21 III 14, 117.2, 126 III 2). Friendship remains a bond between individuals, but it is communally fostered and exploited in the service of philosophical instruction and development. By contrast, the *hetairoi* (including Piso) invited by Philodemus (*Epigram* 27 Sider) to celebrate Epicurus' birthday perhaps represent a wider circle of Epicurean companions, gathered after the fashion of the traditional symposium.

FRIENDSHIP AND STOIC PERFECTION

The Stoics had small interest in friendship as opposed to human attachments generally (Epictetus, *Disc.* 4.5.10 notes that mankind is "a mutually affectionate [*philallēlon*] animal"; cf. the role of *oikeiōsis* or "affinity"). On a strict account, sages and no one else are capable of being friends (Diog. Laert. 7.124; cf. Cic. *De amicitia* 5.18), and they, secure in their autarky and impassiveness (*apatheia*), are impersonal in their affections: "the sage acts from moral virtue, not because of strong feeling for another" (Lesses 1993: 71). Seneca (*Ep. mor.* 9.5–6) affirms that the wise man, as a craftsman in the art of making friends, can always replace a deceased friend with a new one. Epictetus, who examines various sorts of love in his conversation concerning *philia*, affirms that friends, country, kin, and justice itself are commonly outweighed by interest when they conflict (*Disc.* 2.22.18). To be a true friend or son or father depends on the identification of self with moral commitment (*prohairesis*, 2.22.20). For those who believe that commitment and the good coincide, there is no need to wonder whether they are "father and son or brothers or went to school together for a long time and are comrades, but knowing this alone you may confidently declare that they are *philoi*, and likewise faithful, and just" (2.22.29). True friendship is a function of wisdom: in all other relationships, loyalty is contingent. Epictetus indeed discourages his disciples from socializing with outsiders or laymen (*idiōtai*, 3.16.3, 16) and from consorting with former acquaintances and friends (4.2.1).

Epictetus may reflect a severe strain of Stoic thought in respect to friendship, virtually evacuating the concept of its ordinary content; if Panaetius (second century BC) was indeed a source of Cicero's treatise *De amicitia* (see above, pp. 131–2), he perhaps promoted less rigorous criteria. The definition of *erōs*, attributed to the Stoic founders Zeno and Chrysippus, as "an impulse to make friends [*philopoiia*] on account of the conspicuous beauty of youths in their prime" looks to eliminating the sexual component of pederasty in favor of a disinterested and educative affection identified as *philia*. Perhaps the effect of such virtuous passion is to convert the beloved into a Stoic friend.[32]

PYTHAGOREANISM AND THE CULT OF FRIENDSHIP

Among the pairs of friends celebrated for their fidelity in antiquity are the Pythagoreans Phintias and Damon (e.g. Plut. *On Having Many Friends* 93e). In the version recorded by Iamblichus (fourth century AD) in *On the Pythagorean Way of Life* (234–6), Phintias, having been condemned to death by the tyrant Dionysius (early fourth century BC), asks Damon to serve as hostage until he can arrange his personal affairs; to universal amazement, not only does Damon consent, but Phintias honors his pledge and returns to custody.[33] Dionysius then requests to be admitted into their friendship, but they refuse.

Whether or not the lore attributed to Pythagoras (sixth century BC) goes back to the founder's own time, it certainly had a vogue in the Hellenistic world, when various Pythagorean pseudepigrapha were in circulation. A number of adages laud friendship, such as the dictum recorded by Diodorus Siculus (10.8.1 = 232.15–17) that "the good will of friends is the worthiest good," or the aphorism contained in an alphabetically arranged collection of Pythagorean sentences: "consider that they above all are friends who help you toward

---

32 Stoic definition: Arius Didymus, quoted in Stobaeus, *Ecl.* 2.115.1–2; cf. Diog. Laert. 7.130 = *SVF* 3.180.17–19; disinterested affection: so Diog. Laert.; cf. Dio Chrysostom, *Disc.* 3.98–9; Plut. *De comm. notit.* 1073b–c; schol. ad Diogenes Thrax = *SVF* 3.181.22–4; beloved as friend: so Schofield 1991: 34; cf. Arist. *EN* 8.4, 1157a10–12 on the conversion of *erōs* into friendship.

33 Text in Dillon and Hershbell 1991; cf. Cicero, *De off.* 3.45; Diod. Sic. 10.4.3–6, followed by Valerius Maximus 4.7: foreigners 1; Hyginus, *Fables* 257.3–8 (probably second century AD) reports a similar story about the friends Moerus and Selinuntius, also at the court of Dionysius, without reference to Pythagoreanism.

wisdom" (33; cf. 34; Clitarchus, "Sentences" 88–92; "Golden Verses" 5–8 = 160.3–6). The tale of Phintias and Damon, however, departs from such commonplaces in its emphasis on the complete and exclusive loyalty between adherents of the group.[34]

Iamblichus also relates how Dionysius, having unsuccessfully sought the friendship (*philia*, 189) of the Pythagorean circle, takes Myllias and his wife Timycha prisoner. He offers to share his rule with the couple, but they refuse; when he demands to know why the sect avoids treading on beans, Timycha, determined not to betray the reason, bites her tongue off so as not to succumb to torture (192–4). Iamblichus comments: "so slow were they to make friendships [*philiai*] outside the school" (194, trans. Dillon and Hershbell 1991: 201). This anecdote, which is similar in form to that of Phintias and Damon, again celebrates strict allegiance within the cult, this time symbolized by silence concerning its secret doctrines. *Philia* here seems less a matter of personal sentiment than of sectarian solidarity. Perhaps the maxim, "*philia* of all toward all," that Iamblichus ascribes to Pythagoras (69) is to be understood as restricted to initiates.

PARABLES OF FRIENDSHIP

Philosophical theories and anecdotes are not the place in which to discover the day to day realities of friendships and betrayals. A more promising source might have been documents preserved on papyrus, but they yield surprisingly little evidence on this subject. The terms *hetairos* and *epitēdeios* occur only in literary texts. According to Katherine Evans (1996), *philos* and *philia* are also rare: of 18,000 documents that she examined, only 203 exhibit either term. In Christian texts of the sixth and seventh centuries AD, well beyond the period surveyed in this chapter, "friend" and "your friendliness" start to be used in greetings and titles.[35]

It is necessary, then, to rely on narrative texts to fill out the picture adumbrated by didactic literature. Episodes related by historians and biographers provide sketches of friendships, invented or embellished, that exhibit the strategic deployment of the values attaching to loyal

---

[34] Pythagoras' own time: de Vogel 1966; cf. Zhmud 1996: 101–5; Hellenistic vogue: Thesleff 1961: 71; alternate numbers = page and line in Thesleff 1965; Pythagorean "Sentences" and Clitarchus cited according to Chadwick 1959.

[35] Papyri: see Preisigke 1925–71: s.vv.

affection. To take but one example, a moment in the imaginative reconstruction of early Roman history by Dionysius of Halicarnassus, a Greek residing in Rome at the end of the first century BC, indicates how the language of friendship employed in formal pacts and alliances permits the appeal to personal values in relations between states. When the Roman king Tullus and Mettius Fufetius, the commander of Rome's parent city Alba, decide to compose their differences, Fufetius observes: "I hold that mutual reconciliation is the best and the most becoming to kinsmen and friends [*philian kai sungeneian*], in which there is no remembrance of past injuries, but a general and sincere remission of everything that has been done or suffered on both sides" (*Roman Antiquities* 3.7.3, trans. Cary 1939). "Kinsmen and friends" alludes simultaneously to a common formula in treaties, and to the bond between colony and metropolis as Dionysius conceives it. Tullus takes up the offer, on condition that the Albans move to Rome and thus eliminate the competition between the cities: "for no one can be a firm friend to one who distrusts him" (3.9.4). Fufetius predictably rejects the proposal, and the quarrel is left to be decided by a duel between three brothers on each side, the Horatii and Curiatii. But the mention of trust conjures up the confidence that obtains between personal friends as a way of justifying the assimilation or synoecism of two polities.[36]

It is noteworthy that the playwrights of New Comedy prefer not to portray disloyalty between friends: apparent rivalry in love, as in Plautus' *Bacchides* or Terence's *Andria*, is invariably revealed to be based on a misunderstanding; the same cannot be said about competition between kin, especially across generations (e.g. Menander's *Shield*; Plautus' *Asinaria*). Friends commonly offer counsel and comfort to young men distracted by desire (Menander's *Shorn Girl*) or to fathers who are either too harsh or too lenient with their wayward sons (esp. Terence's *Self-Tormentor*).[37]

The Greek novels exhibit the bond between male friends as complementing the erotic attraction between the hero and heroine, which in this genre alone is regularly represented as symmetrical. In *The Ephesian Tale* by Xenophon of Ephesus (probably first century AD), for instance, Hippothous of Perinthus, although he has adopted

---

[36] Remission of what has been done: an allusion to the classical idea of amnesty, like that enacted in Athens in 403 BC; on friendship in Dion. Hal., cf. Balch 1996.

[37] On friendship in New Comedy, cf. Zucker 1950; Menander's *Shorn Girl* and Terence's *Self-Tormentor* (based on a Menandrean original) are discussed in Konstan 1995a.

the life of a bandit, is fiercely loyal to his Ephesian friend Habrocomes, and checks his passion for Anthia, Habrocomes' wife, the moment he learns her identity (4.9). The two erotic attachments that Hippothous forms within the novel are with male youths, but, characteristically, there is no suggestion that he has an amorous interest in Habrocomes himself. Because pederastic relations are asymmetrical, involving a division of roles between lover and beloved, they operate over a different domain from that of friendship. In Chariton's *Chaereas and Callirhoe* (roughly contemporary with Xenophon's novel), the ever-faithful Polycharmus abandons home and family in Sicily to accompany his friend in the search for his kidnapped wife, and when he can no longer curb Chaereas' suicidal despair, proposes that they sacrifice their lives jointly in a reckless gesture of retaliation against the king of Persia (7.1).[38]

Alexandrian poetry offers some illuminating, and less romantic, vignettes of friendship in the cosmopolitan world of big cities and international travel. Callimachus (*Aetia* fr. 178), for example, describes a symposium at the home of one Pollis, an Athenian (Athenaeus 11.477c) who lives in Egypt but continues to celebrate the Athenian festivals, on this occasion the Aiora. To this banquet (*daitē*, 178.5) Pollis has invited various *homētheis* (loosely, "friends"), among them a *xeinos* from Icos named Theogenes, recently arrived in Egypt on private business. Callimachus is happy to share a couch with him because he is of a similar temperament (*homoios*) and dislikes drinking to excess. In Theocritus, *Idylls* 14, Aeschinas describes to Thyonichus, an old friend (not necessarily a countryman) whom he has not seen for a while, a party he hosted at which an Argive, a Thessalian horse-trainer from Larissa called Agis, and a soldier named Cleonicus were present (12–13, 31–2), as well as a girl-friend of Aeschinas' with whom he had a fight. Thyonichus approves Aeschinas' plan (55–6) to go abroad as a mercenary, and encourages him to sign up with Ptolemy in Egypt (58–9). In *Idylls* 15, two women originally from Syracuse (they speak with a Doric accent) have maintained a friendship in Alexandria, in part, no doubt, because of their ethnic connection, even though they live at a considerable distance from one another.[39]

Friends can be petty, too. In a witty comment on coteries within the art world, Callimachus (*Epigrams* 59 = 59 Gow-Page) claims that

---

[38] On the Greek novels, see Konstan 1994.
[39] On friendship and mobility in the Hellenistic world, cf. Burton 1995: 34–40.

Orestes' madness did not constitute a true test of Pylades as a friend (*philos*); by writing one play he himself has lost many Pylades.

Many of the themes concerning Greek friendship that have been discussed so far are woven into a series of clever stories recounted in a dialogue entitled *Toxaris or On Philia*, by the second-century AD satirist Lucian. The essay takes the form of a debate between a Scythian, for whom the work is named, and a Greek called Mnesippus, over which of the two peoples holds friendship in higher regard – Mnesippus began by teasing Toxaris about the Scythians' reverence for Orestes and Pylades, although the pair had plundered their homeland. The terms of the match are that each presents five tales of avowed authenticity in support of his claim.

Mnesippus' first contribution tells of two men who were childhood friends, the one, Agathocles, of a poor family from Samos, the other a rich Ephesian named Deinias. Deinias is courted by flatterers who encourage him in luxurious pleasures, and he soon grows weary of the sober admonitions of Agathocles (12). The clash between a true friend and counsellor and a horde of sycophants in attendance on a profligate young man conforms to the situation addressed by Plutarch in his treatise on friends and flatterers.

Deinias' unscrupulous companions cozen him into falling in love with a dissolute woman, the wife of the leading politician in Ephesus, who pretends to be pregnant by Deinias. When he has squandered his patrimony on her, she abandons him for another youth, and the band of flatterers deserts him as well (16). In this extremity he turns to Agathocles, who recognizes that this is the wrong moment (*akairon*) for reproaches; instead, he sells his ancestral home and gives Deinias the money. The sharing of wealth among friends has good Greek credentials, but failure to correct a friend in error is a mistake, and Deinias, flush once more, takes up again with his mistress. This time her husband catches him in the act, however, and Deinias brutally murders the couple. The authorities in Rome banish Deinias to a tiny island, whither Agathocles accompanies him and tends him (*therapeuein*; cf. Arist. *EN* 8.4, 1157a6–8), remaining there after Deinias has died so as not to abandon his *philos* even in death.

This is an edifying fable of devotion, but the loyalty is all in one direction: Agathocles (*agathos* = "good") sticks by Deinias (*deinos* = "terrible") through thick and thin. For his maturity he seems more the custodian of his comrade than his coeval, as though he were the faithful minister of a rash prince. The asymmetry in their roles suggests the pattern of lover and beloved as much as that of mutual friends, and Deinias' affair with a married woman may be seen as a negative example of erotic exploitation in contrast with the affirmative ideal, such as that preached by Plato and perhaps the Stoics, of nurturing a youth into virtue (cf. Demosthenes, *Erōtikos* 57). The image of the wise counsellor lends itself to this model of unequal partners, which Lucian's wit has folded into a story of mutual friendship between age-mates.[40]

Mnesippus' fifth and final entry in the competition has a similar plot. Two Athenian friends and schoolmates – Demetrius, who took courses in the Cynic regimen, and Antiphilus, who studied medicine – move to Egypt, and while Demetrius is touring monuments in the south, Antiphilus is falsely accused of temple robbery and imprisoned. On his return, Demetrius, ever faithful, takes a menial job, as Agathocles had done, and tends (*therapeuein*, 31) his ailing friend. Denied admission to the jail, he denounces himself before the authorities so as to be incarcerated along with Antiphilus. When at last the innocence of the two friends comes to light and they are compensated for their suffering, Demetrius bestows his portion upon Antiphilus and departs to join the Brahmins in India, confident that this time it is pardonable to desert his friend when he is prosperous and "no longer has need of a *philos*" (34).

Demetrius' self-sacrificing fidelity is again one-sided, like that of Agathocles. His autonomy is that of the Cynic or Stoic sage, and having done his duty by his friend he abandons him to pursue his own spiritual perfection. Lucian pushes the ideals of independence and selfless generosity to the point at which reciprocity becomes impossible, and he thereby illustrates one of the paradoxes of philosophical friendship even as he acknowledges its ethical vigor. Perhaps, by projecting the extreme of self-sufficiency onto distant India with its tradition of contemplative self-realization, Lucian also renders it foreign: in leaving personal intimacy behind, Demetrius leaves the Greek world too.

Toxaris in turn describes the Scythian custom of courting friends as the Greeks do wives, securing the bond with pacts and oaths and drinking of blood (37). Most of his stories tell of extreme sacrifice in combat or hunting. The centerpiece recounts how a young Scythian

---

[40] For fuller analysis, see Konstan 1994: 8–12.

falls in love with the daughter of a neighboring king and asks for her hand. As evidence of his resources, he announces that he has two noble friends, but the king prefers a suitor with more material wealth. Back home, the Scythian tells his friends of his disgrace: they decide to kidnap the bride and kill her father, and gather a large force for the purpose. In the war that follows, the Scythians emerge victorious.

In contrasting the nomadic society of the Scythians with that of the Greek states, Lucian ascribes to the Scythians a structured form of friendship based on ritual vows of fealty. National institutions are correspondingly deficient: informal ties of personal allegiance draw the entire tribe into war. The patterned opposition between Greek and Scythian conventions highlights the private nature of friendship among the Greeks, who assist one another individually under conditions imposed – justly or not – by magistrates and courts. This is not to say that Lucian's picture of Scythian practices is necessarily inaccurate; *The Herald* of Zimbabwe reported recently that "The wounded honour of a spurned suitor touched off a clan battle in which 108 people were killed in western Sudan" (31 July 1993: 2). The point is rather that the Scythians function as an ideological other against which Lucian, himself a Hellenized Syrian, is able to articulate Greek friendship as a domain of unconstrained altruism within the official carapace of the state.[41]

FRIENDSHIP IN THE "GREAT WORLD"

In the Hellenistic world, Greeks traveled great distances, occupied cities that were at the same time garrisons in the midst of foreign populations, paid court to kings who were revered as gods, participated in wars between imperial powers as nationals and hired troops (the term *xenos* in this period had as its primary meaning "mercenary soldier"), committed their lives to philosophical doctrines and communities, built libraries and museums, consulted astrologers, farmed as ever, traded, paid taxes, and maintained the traditions of the classical city-state both in cult and political institutions to a remarkable degree. In these conditions, friendship served new needs and was subjected to new strains. Intimacy with powerful figures or royalty brought influence and with it the need for honesty (*parrhēsia*)

---

[41] Patterned opposition: cf. Hartog 1988; Cartledge 1993: 36–62.

and a sense of responsibility: flattery, as Plutarch notes ("How to Distinguish" 49c), does not attend the poor and insignificant. The collective solidarity of the philosophical schools demanded an equal candor in the service of moral development. In an expansively ecumenical mood, Dio Chrysostom declares (*Or.* 1.40; cf. 12.76) that "Zeus is surnamed *Philios* and *Hetaireios* because he draws all human beings together and wishes that they be friends [or friendly: *philoi*] to one another." Plutarch, stressing rather the exclusiveness of friendship, asserts (*On Having Many Friends* 93e) that "*philia* is a companionable animal, not herdlike or flocking, and to consider a friend another self and a comrade [*hetairos*] as one's other [*heteros*] is just what they do who use the number two as the gauge of friendship." Commonly the Greeks thought of a person's friends as constituting a small group of intimates: in the special case of the king's *philoi*, the term served as a title without losing the sense of private devotion. Friendship thus continued to be conceived of as a personal relation between people bound to one another not by kinship or ethnicity, or by palace duties and offices, but by mutual loyalty, trust, and love.

CHAPTER 4

Rome

ROMAN FRIENDSHIP

The earliest Latin texts that can count as literature date to the latter half of the third century BC, when Rome was already master of most of Italy, and the ruling aristocracy could look back to three hundred years or more of continuous supremacy within the state. What is more, Roman culture was already deeply indebted to Greek: the first literary work in Latin is a translation of Homer's *Odyssey*, and the earliest surviving compositions are the plays that Plautus and Terence adapted from Greek New Comedy. No original Latin text of any size written before the first century BC survives complete (a few brief epigrams and the prologues to Terence's six dramas are the exceptions). When Roman ideas on friendship become available for study, they are already the product of a complex interaction between cultures.

Unlike Greek, Latin has a word for friendship. Though *amicitia* has a certain breadth of meaning, as does the English "friendship," and may assume, especially in philosophical contexts, some of the wider connotations of *philia*, it does not normally designate love in general but rather the specific relation between friends (*amici*). The term corresponding to *philia* in the more sweeping sense is *amor*, just as *amare* is the Latin equivalent to the Greek verb *philein*, though both words may be employed also for erotic passion which in Greek is distinguished by *erōs* and its cognates.

There is thus no need to demonstrate for Latin as for Greek that the vocabulary of friendship marks off a field of relations different from kinship, ethnicity, and utilitarian associations such as business partnerships. To take a single illustration, Cicero, in his defense of Publius Quinctius, violently attacks Sextus Naevius, an in-law and associate of Quinctius', for abusing several bonds at once (*Pro*

Quinctio 26): "If friendship is fostered by veracity, partnership by good faith, and family ties by piety, then a man who has tried to strip his friend, partner, and in-law of name and fortune must confess that he is vain, faithless, and impious." The view was long prevalent, however, that *amicitia* was "the good old word for party relationships" (Taylor 1949: 8) and entailed no necessary sentiment of personal intimacy. The idea developed in reaction to the notion that factions in Roman politics, as the *populares* and *optimates* were assumed to be, worked like modern political parties that are based on allegiance to platforms and social principles. In contrast to this anachronistic image, Roman partisanship was presumed to be a function of contingent convergences of interests among the nobility in the course of their continual campaigns for office as prescribed by the traditional *cursus honorum*. The parties to these shifting alliances grounded in private favor were said to be *amici*, which captured the individual nature of such ties and at the same time reduced them to a matter of practical affiliation having nothing to do with real and lasting affection. This, moreover, was taken to be the entire content of Roman *amicitia*.[1]

The evacuation of emotional content from the concept of friendship was facilitated by the Roman concern with reciprocity. Like the Greek *kharis*, the Latin term *gratia* refers both to the return that is due for a service (*officium* or *beneficium*) one has received, and to the sense of debt or gratitude that is morally incumbent on the beneficiary; thus Cicero (*De officiis* 2.20.69) observes: "even if one cannot return *gratia*, one can certainly have it" (cf. Seneca *De beneficiis* 7.14.4–6). This ethic of obligation was assumed to be associated particularly with relations between friends, which accorded with the picture of pragmatic give and take as the foundation of personal alliances among political leaders.[2]

In an elegant and richly documented study, Peter Brunt (1988 [orig. version 1965]) challenged the assumption that "if a Roman called a man *amicus*, it meant that he was a political ally" (1988: 352). In fact, he argues (367), "complex personal relationships could cut across political discords": men remained close despite political differences, and those with no private ties are frequently aligned on the same side in political conflicts. Furthermore, Brunt adduces the many passages in the writings of Cicero in which "*amicitia* is not

---

[1] No sentiment of intimacy: cf. Syme 1939: 157.

[2] On the Latin vocabulary of reciprocity, see Pöschl 1940: 97–103; Saller 1982: 15–22.

restricted to a connection founded solely on mutual services and common interests, still less to membership of the same faction" (356). The Roman word for friendship, he observes (354), derives from the verb *amare*, "to love" (Cicero, *De amic.* 26; cf. *Partitiones oratoriae* 88 on *caritas* and *amor* as the constitutive elements of *amicitia*); even the superficial connections that gentility denominated as *amicitia* "took their name by external analogy from the true affection which is the primitive significance of the word" (360). Brunt concludes (381): "The range of *amicitia* is vast. From the constant intimacy and goodwill of virtuous or at least like-minded men to the courtesy that etiquette normally enjoined on gentlemen, it covers every degree of genuinely or overtly amicable relation."

CICERO AND HIS FRIENDS

The correspondence and political speeches of Cicero illustrate the way friendships were negotiated among the elite classes at Rome, about which information is most abundant. Cicero is naturally at his most reflective when a relationship is under stress. Thus, in a letter of 5 December 61 BC (1.17 = 17) addressed to Atticus, Cicero is moved to an explicitness that tact usually inhibited (17.7) by a quarrel that had erupted between Atticus and Cicero's brother Quintus, who was married to Atticus' sister.[3] "Your liberality and great-heartedness are entirely clear to me," Cicero writes, in response to Atticus' mention of the profitable opportunities he had let pass in Cicero's behalf, "nor have I ever believed that anything separated you and me except for our choice of way of life" (17.5), his own being the path of political office while Atticus preferred a private status.

In the true accomplishments of uprightness, integrity, conscientiousness, and scrupulousness, I put neither myself nor anyone else before you, while as for your love toward me, if I leave aside my brother's love and that at home, I award you first prize. For I have seen – seen and observed profoundly – your worries and your joys during my various vicissitudes. Your congratulations on my accomplishments have often been pleasurable to me and your solace of my anxiety welcome. Now, indeed, when you are absent I most miss not only the advice which is your forte but also our exchange of conversation, which is sweetest of all to me with you ... In

---

[3] Alternate numbers refer to the editions of Cicero's letters to Atticus (*Ad Att.*) and to his friends (*Ad fam.*) by Shackleton Bailey, who departed from the traditional order in favor of as strict a chronological arrangement as possible; subsequent references are to these editions.

short, neither my work nor rest, business or leisure, affairs at the forum or at home, public or private, can long do without your sweet and loving advice and conversation. (17.5–6)

Cicero acknowledges the benefit he derives from Atticus' support and thus implicitly the sacrifices he has made, but he specifies also elements that are shared rather than given: their common qualities of character, Atticus' love, which is manifested in his identification with Cicero's ups and downs, and their mutual talk, on which Cicero placed high value: "What leisure activity can be more delightful or more suitable to mankind than witty and broadly cultivated conversation?," Cicero asks in his treatise *On the Orator* (1.32; cf. *Ad fam.* 9.24.3).

Atticus is a special case: toward the end of his life (46 BC), Cicero is still writing that the Isles of the Blest are not worth whole days apart from him (*Ad Att.* 12.3 = 239.1). To turn to a less close relationship, in mid-January of 62 BC, just after Cicero's consulship, Quintus Metellus Celer, who as proconsul was waging war in cis-Alpine Gaul, complained to Cicero about his attacks on Metellus' brother back in Rome (*Ad fam.* 5.1 = 1): their mutual spirit (*animus*) and restored favor (*gratia*), as well as the stature (*dignitas*) of his family and his eager services (*studium*) both toward Cicero himself and toward the republic, had led him to expect better treatment. Cicero replies (5.2 = 2): "As to the 'mutual spirit between us,' I don't know what you consider to be mutual in a friendship; I for my part believe that it is when like sentiments (*voluntas*) are received and returned" (2.3). He affirms that he had consistently supported Metellus abroad, and deserved the same treatment in his post within the city. Cicero further denies that favor has been restored, since it had never, he claims, been curtailed (2.5).

He then comes to the quarrel with Metellus' brother: he understands fraternal loyalty very well, but begs pardon for preferring the interest of the republic, "for I am as much a friend of the republic as anyone can be." If at the personal level he defended himself, Metellus should be content that Cicero did not go further and complain to him directly of his brother's affront (*iniuria*, 2.6). Cicero alleges that he tried privately to get Metellus' wife and their sister to discourage the brother from the offense, which consisted among other things in vetoing his right to give an oration upon laying down his magistracy, and also sent common friends to reason with him (2.7–8). Given that Metellus' brother had behaved as an enemy,

Cicero had been the soul of generosity (*humanitas*, 2.9). Fraternal affection is a noble thing, but since Cicero had been attacked without provocation, Metellus should have come to his assistance, army and all. He concludes:

I have always wished you to be friendly [or a friend: *amicus*] toward me, and I have worked hard to have you know that I am most friendly [*amicissimus*] toward you. I continue in that sentiment, and shall continue as long as you desire it, and I shall sooner cease to hate your brother out of love for you than subtract anything from our good will [*benevolentia*] out of hatred for him. (2.10)

The episode illustrates the sense of protocol that obtains between statesmen who can exploit some link of cordiality. One shows one has not been behindhand in reciprocating kindnesses; if a quarrel has arisen, one claims not to have precipitated it and to have sought arbitration to allay it. Under attack, one responds with moderation, and invokes the public interest whenever possible. Fairness should be respected, but one is willing to bury the hatchet with a declared enemy for the sake of preserving friendship with his kinsman. There is no suggestion of great intimacy between Metellus and Cicero; indeed, Cicero protests at the threatening tone of Metellus' note (2.10). But he perceives it as worth his while to maintain the forms of a personal attachment because it has value for maneuvering in the tricky terrain of republican politics (and with the Catilinarian troubles still fresh in mind).[4]

When, near the end of his life, Cicero attacked Caesar's ostensible successor Mark Antony in a series of orations known as the *Philippics* (44/3 BC), he was obliged to answer Antony's charge that he had violated their friendship. None of his former foes, he alleges at the beginning of the second *Philippic*, fell out with him deliberately; all were assailed in the interest of the republic (2.1). But Antony doubted his associates would accept him as public enemy (*hostis*) of his country unless he were a personal enemy (*inimicus*) of Cicero's (2.2). With this flourish, Cicero proceeds to the topic of *amicitia*, the betrayal of which he regards as a most serious accusation.

Antony had complained (according to Cicero) that Cicero had begun hostilities by opposing him in some legal business (the details are obscure). Cicero replies that he was defending an intimate

---

[4] Public interest: cf. Brunt 1988: 368–9, 380.

against an outsider. But his opponent – evidently a tribune who had interposed a veto – had acted out of a sense of obligation (*gratia*) toward Antony that Antony had earned by means of sexual favors. Thus Cicero was in fact responding to an attack (*iniuria*) on the part of Antony which he had initiated through the services (*beneficium*) of that foul tribune (2.3). Hence it was Antony who breached the *amicitia*, and what is more did so by trading in *beneficia* and *gratia* – the coin of personal relations – of a dirty and improper sort. Cicero's skill at deploying the Roman ethical lexicon is stunning.

Cicero denies further that Antony had frequented his house and that he had yielded to him his candidacy as augur nine years earlier (2.4). He then comes to the *beneficium* for which he is supposed to be grateful (*gratus*), that Antony saved or spared his life at Brindisi – the kind of benefit bestowed by bandits, Cicero asserts (2.5). But suppose it a service, in what was he ungrateful? Ought he not to have complained about the destruction of the republic so as to appear grateful to Antony? Here again is the argument from patriotic commitment, followed by the personal justification that his first *Philippic* had in fact been temperate and indeed friendly (*amice*) in tone (2.6). Now that, says Cicero, was indeed a *beneficium*. Antony had also read aloud from some letters Cicero had sent him, which, Cicero avers, no one with the least cultivation would do, for it abolishes the communion between distant friends (2.7). What Antony sought to prove is unknown, but the trick rebounded, according to Cicero, because the letters were full of good will (*benevolentia*, 2.9). Yet Antony's letters – were Cicero to read them! – would prove that he had received a favor from Cicero himself.

The claim of a personal connection or of friendly offices evidently carried weight in public discourse, and when declared enmity was unavoidable a speaker sought to cast himself as the injured party. Cicero is thus at pains to be seen neither as defaulting on a moral debt (*ingratia*) nor as terminating an amicable association, however superficial, by a gratuitously hostile gesture that might count as *iniuria*. Reciprocity of benefits is in principle distinct from the relationship between friends, who ideally act from motives of generosity and do not require that every kindness be repaid in full. In his treatise *De beneficiis*, Seneca the younger, who had been tutor to Nero, exhaustively analyzes expectations of return on loans and favors, but rarely raises the subject of friendship; the only time he discusses *amicitia* specifically is to respond to the paradox that friends cannot grant *beneficia* because they possess all things in common (7.12). But helpfulness is traditionally the mark of a friend and services may be interpreted as a sign of good will or amicableness. Mutual support is the point at which the vocabularies of friendship and exchange of benefits intersect, and Cicero moves naturally between the two issues, defending his integrity on both the counts of refraining from offending a supposed friend and of being conscientious in respect to any genuine debts of gratitude he may owe.[5]

FRIENDSHIP IN POLITICS

Cicero's relationship with Atticus is a world apart from those with Metellus or Antony, and Romans of his class were conscious of the difference between intimate friendships and polite or useful connections in public life. To Atticus, Cicero writes (18.1):

those politicking and powdered-up friendships of mine have a certain brilliance in the forum but are profitless at home. Though my house is quite full [of greeters] in the morning, though I go down to the forum hemmed in by droves of "friends," I can find no one out of that great crowd with whom I can freely make a joke or sigh familiarly. That's why I am waiting for you, longing for you, even beckoning you now.

An electioneering manual attributed to Cicero's brother Quintus, and at all events written by someone "well versed in the manners of the age" (Brunt 1988: 360), coolly lays out the vote-getting meaning of friends:

The support of friends should be acquired by benefits and services and long acquaintance and agreeableness and a pleasant personality. But this word, "friends," extends more widely in campaigning than in life generally, for whoever displays any sign of favor toward you or attends to you or visits you at home is to be considered among the circle of your friends. (16; cf. Seneca, *Ep. mor.* 3.1)

Friendship here is not wholly stripped of a personal dimension. The

---

[5]   Friends and *beneficia*: cf. Sen. *De ben.* 6.35 on the unseemly wish for the occasion to repay a friend's help; on *officia* and *gratia*, cf. Cicero's *Ad fam.* 5.5 = 5 to Gaius Antonius (23 December 62); on *beneficentia*, *De off.* 1.42–60 (discussed in Atkins 1990); Valerius Maximus 5.2–3 illustrates gratitude and ingratitude with scarcely a reference to friendship; for the widespread assumption that Sen. *De ben.* and Cic. *De off.* discuss gifts and gratitude in the context of friendship, cf. (e.g.) Dixon 1993: 452, 454; services as an expression of good will: Brunt 1988: 356; for Greek ideas of friendship and gratitude, see above, pp. 81–2.

author assures Cicero that he can win the support of anyone not already committed to his competitors if he creates the impression that he is earnest and sincere and that "his friendship will be solid and enduring, not transient and electoral [*suffragatoria*]" (26). In reference to Cicero's rival for the consulship of 63, C. Antonius, he adds: "nothing seems more stupid to me than to imagine that a person you do not know is your supporter" (28). One must know one's people by name. With this energetic method of canvassing votes through direct acquaintance with a very large constituency, Quintus (if he is the author) conveys a picture not of established networks of personal affiliation so much as of active competition among a changeable electorate at every level of the social hierarchy.

The broad participation of different classes in the campaign process has a democratic ring, and Fergus Millar has indeed argued that politics in republican Rome resembled that of classical Athens more than scholars commonly suppose; Polybius, he notes (1986: 3), assumed that "the categories of political analysis relevant to Greek cities could be applied to Rome" (Polybius, writing for a Greek audience, may not be an entirely reliable reporter). On the one hand, the popular vote mattered; otherwise, it would not have been courted so systematically through oratory, not to mention bribery. Traditional patronage was a lesser factor. On the other hand, personal obligations among the nobility did not determine the distribution of power. Friendships and enmities might have an effect on senatorial decision-making, but this does not demonstrate the existence of "larger groupings" or factions. Where relatives and friends did count was precisely in the solicitation of mass support through the ballot; thus Cicero writes to Atticus (2.1.9): "Favonius carried my tribe with even more credit than his own, but lost that of Lucceius" (trans. Yakobson 1992: 46). In the contentious arena of "open, mass politics" (Millar 1995: 103), moreover, issues were as important as personalities.[6]

---

[6] Rome resembles Athens: Millar 1984: 2; cf. 14; popular vote matters: Millar 1984: 2; courted through oratory: Millar 1995: 103; through bribery: Yakobson 1992: 32–5; vs. patronage: Yakobson 1992: 34; vs. personal obligation: Millar 1986: 2, criticizing Gelzer 1969; friendship in senatorial decisions: Millar 1984: 15, citing Livy 39.4.1–6, 40.45.6–46.15, on the enmity between M. Aemilius Lepidus and M. Fulvius Nobilior and their formal reconciliation; support of relatives: Millar 1984: 13; campaigns for the ballot: Yakobson 1992: 36, citing Cicero, *Pro Murena* 72 for role of friends in providing spectacles, etc.; cf. *Comm. pet.* 44; also Cicero, *Planc.* 45 on *amici* helping to secure their tribes in an election; issues in elections: Millar 1995: 99–100.

CICERO ON FRIENDSHIP

In a youthful rhetorical treatise (*c.* 84 BC), Cicero had defined friendship in Aristotelian terms (*EN* 8.2, 1155b31–1156a5) as "the willing good things to another person for the own sake of him whom one loves, together with the same will on his part towards you" (*De inventione* 2.166, trans. Stock 1913: 137, modified).[7] Shortly afterwards (80 BC), in a speech which established his reputation as an orator, Cicero describes good faith in friendship as crucial to human affairs (*Pro Roscio Amerino* 111):

in matters to which we cannot ourselves attend, the delegated trust [*fides*] of friends is substituted for our own labors; whoever damages this trust attacks the common safeguard of all and, to the extent he can, disrupts the sociability of life.

Cicero goes on to say that friendships are formed for the sake of dependable partnerships: "For we are not able to do all things by ourselves: one is more useful in one business, another in another. Hence friendships are acquired, so that a common advantage [*commodum*] may be driven by mutual services." These rather abstract reflections are designed to magnify the perfidy of his opponent; *amici* were undoubtedly relied upon for the faithful execution of a commission (112), but Cicero is here explaining the social function of friendship in general, not reducing particular attachments to utilitarian motives.

When in the last year of his life (44–43 BC), marked by the assassination of Julius Caesar and the outbreak of civil war, Cicero meditated in earnest on friendship, he defined it (*De amic.* 6.20) as "nothing other than the agreement over all things divine and human along with good will and affection [*caritas*]." To a certain extent, the view was a commonplace. Sallust (*Catiline* 20.4) had remarked: "to want and not want the same things – that is firm friendship."[8] But the coincidence of tastes or desires is less than the rigorous intellectual accord that Cicero prescribes. Cicero himself, as a thoroughly political man, had long regarded a community of views and values as a basis for friendship; in his letter to Appius Pulcher (*Ad fam.* 3.13 = 76.2), written in 50 BC, he affirms that their friendship is its own

[7] Cf. also 2.167–8 for the role of advantage versus friendship for its own sake; Brunt 1988: 353–4.

[8] Cit. Powell 1990 ad loc.; cf. Plautus *Persa* 489 with Woytek 1982; Plautus *Rudens* 1045; Aristotle *NE* 9.4, 1166a7.

reward, above all for the common pursuits by which they are bound: "for I pronounce you my ally [*socius*] in the republic, concerning which we think alike, and my colleague in daily life, which we nourish with these studies and interests" (cf. *Against Verres* 2.3.6, delivered in 70 BC; *Pro Plancio* 5 on friendship as "consensus and partnership of counsel and will").[9] But in the crisis leading up to and following Caesar's assassination, Cicero seems to have been especially preoccupied with the relationship between friendship and political allegiance.[10]

FRIENDS VS. COUNTRY

In his discussion of the grounds on which a friendship may be dissolved, Cicero follows Aristotle (*EN* 9.3, 1165b13–22) in identifying "a change in character or interests"; he adds to these motives, however, a "disagreement over sides [*partes*] in respect to the republic" (21.77). The most telling indication, however, of Cicero's concern with patriotism is the vigor with which he denies that loyalty to friends can ever justify rebelling against the state: "Coriolanus had friends; should they have borne arms along with him against their country?" (11.36). Laelius, Cicero's spokesman in the dialogue, professes horror at Gaius Blossius Cumanus' confession that at the command of his friend Tiberius Gracchus he would have set fire to the Capitol (11.37): "it does not excuse a crime that you committed it for the sake of a friend."[11]

Critics differ over whether Cicero followed a specific Greek model in composing *De amicitia*; Fritz-Arthur Steinmetz, who has argued that Cicero's immediate source was the Stoic Panaetius, nevertheless considers that the section devoted to violence against the state (36–44) is Cicero's own, inspired by contemporary events and, more particularly (70–6), by his correspondence with Gaius Matius, a partisan of Caesar's, who remarks, apropos his grief at the death of Caesar (11.28 = 349.2; *c.* October 44 BC), that people "say that one's country [*patriam*] should be put ahead of friendship, as though they

---

9 In rather an extreme vein, Ludwig Wittgenstein wrote to Bertrand Russell early in 1914: "I can see perfectly well that your value-judgments are just as good and just as deep-seated in you as mine in me, and that I have no right to catechize you. But . . . for that very reason there cannot be any real relation of friendship between us" (trans. Wright 1974: 50).

10 Cf. *De off.* 3.43–6; Brunt 1988: 381.

11 Fuller discussion of the Blossius episode in Konstan 1994/5: 1–2; cf. Klein 1957: 1–23; contrast Appian *Mithr. Wars* 101, where Mithridates slays his treacherous friends but spares his son's because they were obliged personally to the latter.

had already proved that his death was good for the republic." This commonplace in itself, however, is unlikely to have made much of an impression on Cicero.[12]

That Cicero was worrying about the issue at this time is evident from the second *Philippic* (15.38, delivered in December 44), where he explains that he and Pompey succeeded in remaining friends even though they "disagreed concerning the highest matters in the republic (*de summa re publica dissentientis*)." Cicero adds that each knew the view of the other, and suggests that they differed over priorities more than aims, thus rendering their dissension more endurable (two decades earlier, in April 62, Cicero had aspired to play Laelius to Pompey's Scipio: *Ad fam.* 5.7 = 3.3).

If the ambience of civil war and tyrannicide helps account for Cicero's politicized definition of friendship, he found philosophical precedent for an analysis of the tension between loyalty to friends and duty in Theophrastus' treatise *On Philia*. According to Aulus Gellius (*Attic Nights* 1.3.9), "whether one ought to assist a friend contrary to what is just, and to what extent and in what ways" was a popular subject in the philosophical schools, and Theophrastus dealt minutely with it in book 1 of his tractate. Gellius adds that Cicero abbreviated Theophrastus' technical discussion, simply allowing that one may, in matters of life and death, support a friend's unjust aspirations provided that serious disgrace will not ensue (Cic. *De amic.* 17.61, cit. Gell. 1.3.13). Gellius complains that this advice is too vague. That one must not bear arms against one's country (*contra patriam*: Cic. *De amic.* 11.36, cit. Gell. 1.3.19) for a friend is obvious. Pericles, Gellius continues, put the limit at swearing falsely.[13] Theophrastus, for his part, calculated that moderate dishonor might be balanced by an important service to a friend (1.3.21–6).

There is nothing in Aristotle's analysis of *philia* comparable to Theophrastus' punctilious examination of the conflict between morality and obligation to friends. The suggestion that one ought not to require anything bad of friends (*EN* 8.8, 1159b5) finds an echo in

---

[12] Sources of *De amic.*: cf. Powell 1990: 20–1; influence of Panaetius: Steinmetz 1967: 191, 199; cf. Fortenbaugh 1984: 111–13, 288–9; of contemporary events: Steinmetz 1967: 66–76 (Clark and Reubel 1985 argue that after events in the early 50's altered Cicero's views on political violence he sought support in Stoic theories); of Matius: cf. Kytzler 1960: 109–10, who suggests that Matius is appealing to Cicero's own principles; also Heuss 1956; Klein 1957: 126–52.

[13] Cf. Plut. *Reg. et imperat. apophthegm.* 186c; *De vitioso pudore* 531c; Stobaeus 27.10 Meineke (under *Peri horkou*), where the thought is attributed to Lycurgus.

Cicero's essay (13.44), but the Greek thinkers of the fourth century BC did not usually fear that a virtuous disposition such as *philia* might demand the transgression of what is just or honorable. Theophrastus did, however, and if he was not just filling in a gap in his teacher's exposition he may have been responding to changed political conditions in Athens following the conquests of Alexander the Great. In particular, Theophrastus was intimate with the philosophically minded regent of Athens, Demetrius of Phalerum (in power 317–07 BC): perhaps the imposition of a regime backed by Macedonian military power set the climate for concern about the ethical limits of personal allegiances, whether in the circle of the ruler or among a possibly restive citizen body. Although it is only conjecture, I am inclined to see in Theophrastus' anxiety óver friendship versus right a symptom of a new extrinsic sense of public responsibility, represented and enforced by state institutions, that dissolved the unquestioned compatibility between personal and civic life projected by the democratic ideology.[14]

There is a reflection of Theophrastus' theme in Cicero's dictum, cited above, concerning a crime committed for a friend (11.37), but Cicero gives the argument a further twist when he specifies the offense of waging war against one's country (*contra patriam*). Whether this issue too is Hellenistic in provenience is difficult to determine. The Greek historian and critic Dionysius of Halicarnassus, writing at Rome some years after the death of Cicero, expatiates rhetorically on the example of Gnaeus Marcius Coriolanus mentioned in *De amicitia* (11.36). In defense of his support of the Volscians in their war with Rome, Coriolanus lectures his friend Marcus Minucius, who had pleaded with him to assist his own people:

When you still call those my friends, Minucius, who banished me, and that my country [*patris*] which has renounced me, when you appeal to the laws of nature and discourse about sacred matters, you seem to me to be alone ignorant of the most common things, of which no one else is ignorant: that neither the nature of one's appearance nor the imposition of a name defines what is friendly [*to philion*] or inimical [*polemion*], but both are revealed by services [*khreiai*] and deeds, and that we all love [*philoumen*] what does us good and hate what does us harm ... For this reason we renounce friends when they wrong us and make friends of our enemies when some favor [*kharis*] is done for us by them; and we cherish [*stergomen*] the city that gave

---

[14] *Philia* does not entail transgression: cf. Klein 1957: 72; Kraut 1989: 125; Bodéüs 1993: 42–6; but note Lysias 12.51; Lycurgus 1.6; democratic ideology: cf. Osborne 1985: 7–8.

us birth when it helps us, but abandon it when it harms us, liking [*agapōntes*] it not for the place, but for advantage's sake. (*Roman Antiquities* 8.34.1–3; trans. Cary 1945, modified)

Coriolanus is made to articulate a view of friendship based on reciprocity and apply it both to personal associates and loyalty to homeland. Having denied that ethnic characteristics ("appearance") and the appellation "Roman" ("name") constitute a basis for civic allegiance, Coriolanus concludes that Romans generally may be treated as inimical if the city has wronged him, and those who have given him shelter are by the same token friends. In reducing patriotism to the status of an individual bond Coriolanus exploits the convention by which states and peoples are described as friends and enemies (cf. Alcibiades' speech defending his desertion to the Spartans in Thucydides 6.92.3–4, which is likely to have been one of Dionysius' models; Dionysius wrote a treatise on the Athenian historian). But by having Coriolanus prefer friends at war with Rome to Rome itself, Dionysius has articulated the reverse of the principle that the republic takes precedence over all claims of friendship. He is clearly alert to the issue. Whether he is elaborating on a Roman problem, or has drawn upon Hellenistic sources (in which case, perhaps Cicero's own), is uncertain.

Patriotism was construed by Cicero and his contemporaries as loyalty to the republic, and with the coming of the empire, the theme lost its immediacy. Valerius Maximus, who composed a collection of edifying anecdotes during the reign of Tiberius (early first century AD), adduces the case of Blossius' fidelity to Tiberius Gracchus to illustrate the virtue of *amicitia*, despite the fact that he was an enemy of his nation (*inimicus patriae*, 4.7 Romans 1). The next vignette tells of the dedication of two friends to Tiberius' brother Gaius, after his revolutionary plans had been foiled and his confederates were being hunted down; one of them, Laetorius, gave his life so that Gaius might escape, standing guard for friendship's sake over the very bridge Horatius Cocles had defended out of love of country. Another story tells of Rheginus, who released his friend Caepio from prison and fled with him into exile. Finally, Valerius recounts an example of friendship "without any harm to the republic": Titus Volumnius stayed by the body of Lucullus, who had been a partisan of Brutus and Cassius, rather than flee the sword of Mark Antony. Volumnius' gesture might be read as republican in the sense of anti-Caesarian, a risky posture under Tiberius, but Valerius seems oblivious to the subversive innuendo. Friendship proves itself in adversity, as he says, and fidelity in defeat entails defiance of the victors. The Ciceronian anxiety over seditious constancy to friends has evanesced.

STATUS AND THE QUESTION OF PATRONAGE

Rome was a profoundly stratified society, and Cicero's Laelius (*De amic.* 19.69) is at pains to insist that "in a friendship it is crucial to be a peer to one's inferior. For there are often certain outstanding cases, like Scipio in our pack, if I may put it so: never did he put himself above Philus, or Rupilius, or Mummius, or friends of lower rank [*ordo*]." Cicero further cautions (20.71) that "just as those who are superior in a relationship of friendship and association should equalize themselves to their inferiors, so too inferiors ought not to take it ill that they are surpassed in ability or fortune or station." Though Cicero alludes to stories of princely foundlings who retain, when their identity becomes known, an affection (*caritas*) for the shepherds who raised them (19.70), he is not contemplating friendships over such social distances. Later, Laelius mentions the comic playwright Terence, said to have been brought to Rome from Carthage as a slave (Suetonius, *Life* 1), as his *familiaris* (24.89), a vague word that refers to anyone who is deemed part of the household, and hence may signify "intimate" (e.g. *Ad fam.* 13.50 = 266.1); by itself, however, it does not convey the model of equality implied by the word *amicus*.

Cicero extols honest criticism (*monitio*), which is proper to true friendship, in the measure that he detests flattery (*adsentatio, De amic.* 24.89), and, like Plutarch, he advises (25.91) that it be applied candidly (*libere*), not harshly. Again, the adulator is condemned for having no character of his own but adapting himself to another's every whim (25.93; cf. Juvenal *Sat.* 3.100–8). Comic parasites like Terence's Gnatho are dismissed as having no bearing on the issue of friendship, but upper-class and clever flatterers are a genuine menace, and it takes diligence to distinguish the ingratiating friend from the true (25.95; cf. 26.99).[15] One give-away is comportment when addressing the populace (25.95–6), and here Cicero, drawing

---

[15] Cicero in *Pro Quinctio* caricatures Sextus Naevius as a toady or *scurra* who depends upon influence (*gratia*, 1, 93) with powerful friends (96, 98; cf. Damon 1996: part 3, ch. 1), while his client Quinctius has only "a slender supply of friends" (2). It serves Cicero's rhetorical purposes to suggest that Naevius has won allies through depravity, but his friendships are evidently reciprocal and reliable.

on Roman examples, develops the Greek democratic topos of the toady to the *dēmos* or people. For friends to rejoice in vain praise, however, exposes them to deception and mockery (26.98–9). Although Cicero shares some themes with Plutarch's essay on discerning friends from flatterers, his treatment is not adapted to a world of courtiers but to friendships between equals or else those who woo the favor of the masses.

Relations between superiors and inferiors at Rome were governed by an etiquette that is commonly described in the language of patronage, according to which a powerful benefactor (*patronus*) lent protection and support to his dependents or *clientes*, who are supposed to have owed him the more humble services of obeisance and allegiance in return. Clientship in the strict and archaic sense of obligatory fealty has little or no bearing on historical friendships of which we have knowledge in the last century of the Roman republic or the first two centuries of the empire; the 500 "clients [*pelatai*] and friends" that the young Scipio collected as part of his private militia in 134 BC (Appian, *Roman History* 6.14.84) were presumably distinct groups, though Scipio is said to have applied the label "troop of friends" to the entire company of 4000. Interpreted more broadly, however, as an asymmetrical personal relationship involving expectations of reciprocal exchange with a potential for exploitation, patronage certainly played a role in Roman social life, as it did in Greek hierarchies as well. Friendships between people of different social stations were embedded in a culture of authority and deference entirely different from that of classical Athens. Moreover, the role of personal status assumed a new and more intense form with the emergence of the principate, under which enormous power was concentrated in the hands of the emperor and his associates.[16]

Historians have sometimes concluded, accordingly, that friendships between superiors and inferiors under the empire are euphemisms for relations of dependency that in truth are better called patronage, whether or not they were sustained by a formal code of

---

[16] Decline of clientship: see Rouland 1979; Brunt 1988: 382–442; *patronus* remains the term for a legal advocate, who might also be a friend: e.g. Tacitus, *Dialogus* 9.4; Statius, *Silv.* 4.5.50–2; patronage as asymmetrical relationship: Saller 1989: 49; cf. Saller 1982: 8–11; Eisenstadt and Roniger 1984: 2; exploitation: Millett 1989: 16; patronage in Greece: cf. Cartledge 1987: 140–2 on Sparta, though the connection with friendship is more doubtful; patronage in general: Wolf 1966: 16; cf. Pitt-Rivers 1954: 140 for the definition of patron-client relations as "lop-sided friendship"; contrast with Athens: Strauss 1986: 22–3; Millett 1989: 16; Gallant 1991: 145; status under the principate: Brunt 1988: 440.

clientela. Thus, Barbara Gold (1987: 134) writes: "The word *amicus* ...
is a nicely ambiguous word which applies equally well to political
allies or personal intimates, to the patron or the client."[17] Richard
Saller (1989: 57) states in turn:

> To discuss bonds between senior aristocrats and their aspiring juniors in
> terms of "friendship" seems to me misleading, because of the egalitarian
> overtones that the word has in modern English. Though willing to extend
> the courtesy of the label *amicus* to some of their inferiors, the status-
> conscious Romans did not allow the courtesy to obscure the relative social
> standings of the two parties. On the contrary, *amici* were subdivided into
> categories *superiores, pares* and *inferiores* (and then lower down the hierarchy,
> humble *clientes*). Each category called for an appropriate mode of behaviour,
> of which the Romans were acutely aware (Pliny, *Ep.* 7.3.2, 2.6.2; Seneca,
> *Ep.* 94.14). Resemblances between the behaviour of aristocratic *amici*
> *inferiores* and *clientes* suggest that *amici inferiores* can appropriately be analysed
> under the heading of patronage.

Saller's description collapses unequal *amicitia* into clientship.
However, even though the snobbery of the prosperous and social
climbing among their lessers may compromise the quality of an
association, friendship as a bond of generous affection, loyalty and
intimacy can coexist with the recognition that degree must receive its
due. Once the reduction of *amicitia* to a purely practical quid-pro-
quo exchange of services is abandoned, there is no prima-facie
reason to doubt that Roman writers who speak of friendship intend a
relationship of mutual fondness and commitment, whatever the rank
of the partners. To put it differently, not *every* connection between
patrons and protégés is described as *amicitia*; when it is, it may be
supposed that the pair also are, or wish to be thought of as, friends.

THE DINNER-PARTY SCENE

One context in which expectations of equality characteristic of
friendship might clash with protocols of rank was the Roman dinner
party. John D'Arms (1990: 318) observes: "Unlike the practice at the
early Greek sympotic gatherings ... Roman convivial equality can
never have been other than a very fragile kind." D'Arms vividly
evokes the upper-class fixation on prestige, to which munificence was
handmaiden. Individuals of lower station might further their ambi-
tions at such parties: "*clientela* and *amicitia* linked together and

---

[17] Cf. Gold 1987: 40, 71, 104; Strauss 1986: 22.

integrated persons of varied rank, origins, and status, inside as well as outside the dining-room," and "the brisk exchange of *officia* and *beneficia* can be assumed to have flowed continuously, along with the wine and the conversation" (319). However, in "a world where a host might appoint a slave to keep watch on the behaviour of guests of different ranks" (318), the comfortable and egalitarian social ambience of the symposium was out of the question.

That a great man's table might be the scene of humiliating condescension is true, but the Romans do not normally represent such relations as friendship. It is Seneca (*Ep. mor.* 47.8) who provides the detail about a slave assigned to report on guests whose "flattery and exorbitance of gullet or tongue will get them invited on the morrow." This is revealing, but Seneca's concern here is with the abuse of the slave. The letter compliments Lucilius for dining together with his slaves, who are, Seneca insists (47.1), "human beings – tent-mates – humble friends – fellow slaves!" It is his character (*mores*) that makes a slave or free man worthy of one's table (47.15): "There is no reason, my dear Lucilius, to seek a friend only in the forum and senate house; if you look closely, you will find one at home as well" (47.16). Supping with such friends is just the opposite of the hierarchical banquets at which adulators are scrutinized for their comportment. Even allowing for Stoic didacticism, Seneca is contrasting, not assimilating, the treatment of friends and sycophants (cf. Epictetus, *Disc.* 4.1.48).

Juvenal's fifth satire wittily portrays the mortification of lesser guests at the kind of dinner party Seneca decries. Because Juvenal ridicules the pretensions of Trebius, a middling aristocrat, to friendship with the wealthy Virro, the poem is sometimes cited as testimony for the equation of friendship and clientship. Juvenal warns:

Consider in the first place that when you've been summoned to take your seat you've received the full value for your former services. The reward for your great friendship [or friendship with the great: *magna amicitia*] is a meal ... If after two months it pleases him to beckon his forgotten client so that the third cushion won't go vacant on an empty couch, he says: "Let's get together." (5.12–18)

Having demeaned Trebius with the appellation *cliens*, Juvenal goes on to imagine him among the common greeters at Virro's door each morning.

At the meal itself, Virro, as Juvenal depicts him, openly displays his contempt for guests like Trebius by serving them inferior wine and food, and subjecting them to the abuse of slaves who are "indignant at serving an old client" (64). Juvenal attacks his stinginess: "No one's asking for what Seneca used to send to his modest friends ... We just request that you dine in a civil manner" (108–9, 112). The sole question is money, according to Juvenal; if Trebius were suddenly made rich, "what a great friend of Virro's you would become!" (134) – if there are no heirs: "A sterile wife makes for a charming and dear friend" (140). With roles reversed, Virro becomes the fawning legacy-hunter.

Trebius imagines himself to be free and equal as a guest, but Virro, says Juvenal, "thinks you've been caught by the aroma of his kitchen." "Not a bad guess, either" (162–3), Juvenal comments, assimilating Trebius to the comic parasite. The diatribe concludes: "One of these days you're going to let him shave your head and pound it, you'll lose all fear of submitting to the stinging whip – you'll be worthy of these feasts and such a friend" (171–3).

The point of Juvenal's irony is that, whatever Trebius imagines, he is not Virro's friend. Trebius' own motives are exposed as no less calculating than Virro's show of power and disdain. That his abjection gains him no reward in wealth or influence only proves that Trebius is foolish as well as servile. The meaning of the satire depends precisely on the difference between friend and toady (the latter rudely equated with client, parasite, and even slave), which Juvenal does everything to expose. Juvenal's sarcasm would be otiose if the humbler nobility never masked the status-coded formalities of the *convivium* as friendship, but it would be futile if the two relationships were not understood to be distinct.[18]

Martial exposes the reverse side of purchased friendship in his epigrammatic quip (9.14) addressed to a naive patron: "The man your table, your dinners have made your friend, do you suppose he is the soul of faithful friendship? He loves boar and mullet and udder and oysters, not you. If I should give such nice dinners, he'll be my friend." In the game of cadging a meal, however – at least as it is represented in Martial's lampoons – hosts are not normally identified as friends. Indeed, the two categories may implicitly be contrasted:

---

[18] Contrast LaFleur 1979: 171, who takes *amicus* as "equivalent to either *cliens* or *patronus*"; Cloud 1989: 208 remarks that "Juvenal...uses *amicus* in a consistently derogatory or ironic manner" in *Satires* 1 – but always in reference to pretenders masquerading as friends; for fuller discussion, see Konstan 1995: 336–8.

thus, if Selius is depressed, it is not, says Martial (2.11), on account of
a friend or brother, wife or slaves, but rather because he finds himself
obliged to dine at home.[19]

Seneca reports (*De ben.* 6.34) that the regal practice of ranking
masses of friends by allowing them differential access to one's house
was introduced to Rome by Gaius Gracchus and Livius Drusus, and
indignantly denies that the crowds of greeters who attend notables in
the streets deserve the name *amicus*. No one who must wait his turn at
the morning salutation, he says, can attain frankness (*libertas*). Among
the retinues of the rich, the vocabulary of friendship evidently was
debased, and Trebius' pretensions were no doubt encouraged by this
semi-formal usage. Moralists and satirists assumed the responsibility
of reanimating the true meaning of the word, but it is unwise always
to take literally the sketches that lend bite to their irony.

GREAT FRIENDS

In the following century, Lucian composed a caustic exposé of
Greeks who took hired positions as resident professors or philosophers in the houses of rich Romans. They are seduced not only by
the attractions of wealth and distinction, but also by the prospect of
counting the best of the Romans as their friends (*philoi*, 3). In fact,
the conditions of their employment amount to voluntary servitude
rather than *philia* (1, 5): they gain neither fortune nor favor (5–9), but
are subject to the whim of the doorman and nomenclator (10).
Lucian conjures up the anxiety of the first dinner party, where
everything is unfamiliar (on the unequal treatment of guests, cf. 26);
what is more, the grandee's old *philoi* (15, 17) will be resentful of the
newcomer. Since he too is a "friend," the saw that all is common
between friends is exploited to shame him into accepting meager
wages (19–20).

Lucian is playing on the classical Greek analogy between labor for
wages (*misthos*) and slavery (23–4), as well as on the contrast between
the free man and the flatterer, who lives his life for another (30; cf.
28, 38). The friendship to which his addressee aspires is incompatible
with both these demeaning roles: as a paid purveyor of culture in
Roman mansions, the title "friend" only renders him vulnerable to
further manipulation and abuse. Crossing the familiarity and affec-

---

[19] Cf. Martial 2.55, 10.58 on the difference between affection [*amare*] and paying court [*colere*];
also Damon 1966: part 2, ch. 4.

tion appropriate to friendship with the regard for status increasingly characteristic of the Roman nobility was a tricky business, and the satirist took advantage of this tension (contrast Plutarch's endorsement of friendly association between philosophers and men in power, in an essay devoted to the topic: *Mor.* 778a-b).

Horace was particularly sensitive to the pressures that result from relations with figures in power, and he prescribes a simple life as a way of escaping dependency (cf. *Ep.* 1.7 to Maecenas; 1.17 to Scaeva). In his epistle to Lollius (1.18), Horace takes up the particular problem of unequal friendships. Lollius is a man of an exceptionally free or independent temper (*liberrime*, 1), and Horace reminds him that friendship is a mean between flattery and boorishness, which poses as freedom (*libertas*, 8). The doctrine derives from Aristotle, who defines friendship – or rather, a sociable disposition that resembles friendship but has no name of its own (4.6, 1126b20, 1127a11; cf. 2.13, 1108a27–30) – as midway between flattery and surliness or quarrelsomeness. But mention of *libertas* evokes the contrast between frank speech (*parrhēsia*) and flattery elaborated outside the democratic discourse of classical Athens. Rude or excessive candor in this tradition is also a flaw in relations between friends, as Plutarch makes clear ("How to Distinguish" 66a, 66e). As one who is *liber* in the extreme, Lollius must guard against coarse forthrightness (for the meaning of *liber*, cf. *Sat.* 1.3.51–2: "rather crusty [*truculentior*] and immoderately *liber*").[20]

Horace accordingly recommends a more accommodating manner: a rich friend (*dives amicus*, 24), whatever his own vices, rightly reproves one who has ruined himself by love affairs or gambling, for he can afford what the other cannot (Plutarch had cautioned against answering frankness with frankness: 72e). "Yield to the gentle commands of your powerful friend [*potens amicus*]" (44–5), Horace counsels: if he wants to hunt, do not stay home writing poetry; do not fall in love with his household slaves, and be cautious about introducing others into his company. "Cultivating a powerful friend seems nice to those who have not experienced it; one who has fears it" (86–7), and Horace reminds Lollius once again that he will have to be compliant: "Sad types hate a cheerful fellow, jocular types hate a sad sack; fast people hate a sedentary fellow, relaxed types hate one

---

[20] Aristotle: cf. Hunter 1985: 483–4; above, p. 102; excessive candor: cf. Philodemus, *On Frankness* cols. IV–VII; De Witt 1935; Michels 1944; *liber*: not quite "irrational behavior" (Kilpatrick 1986: 29); cf. Bowditch 1994: 411; Gold 1987: 130; Cicero, *Pro Plancio* 33; *Pro Quinctio* 11.

quick and clever" (89–90). In curbing Lollius' tendency to gruffness, Horace comes near to endorsing the assumed expressions and attitudes characteristic of the flatterer.[21]

The threatened collapse of the distinction between polite but honest speech and sly adaptability generates a discursive crisis in the poem, which abruptly takes a different tack: Horace urges Lollius to study philosophy and learn to live in peace, free from desire, fear, and the hope of vain things, to discover what eradicates anxiety (*curas*), "what will restore you as a friend to yourself" (*te tibi reddet amicum*, 101), and whether it is fame and money or rather quietude that confers tranquility. The latter, Horace assures his friend (*amice*, 106), is his own way: he prays to retain what little he possesses and to live "for myself" (*mihi uiuam*, 107). It is for Jupiter to bestow wealth and years, but it lies within ourselves to achieve a calm mind.[22]

This Epicurean turn is in accord with Philodemus' doctrine that only a wise or realized (*teleios*) person is in a position to employ frankness properly (*On Frankness* cols. IV, VIII). When Lollius is at peace with himself, he will be able to be candid with others without giving needless offense. The wise man can thus enjoy a relation of true friendship with a social superior, as Philodemus himself presumably did with Piso. Otherwise, *libertas* or *parrhēsia* is bound to be misapplied, erring in the direction of unseemly and perhaps risky brusqueness or else giving the appearance of an ingratiating complaisance.[23]

Given the pitfalls involved in friendship with the rich and powerful, Lollius is best off eschewing it: the necessary delicacy and courteous dissimulation, which in themselves are honorable and necessary among friends (cf. *Sat.* 1.3.41–4, 54–6), run counter to his spirited nature, and Horace's account is designed to discourage him and to lead him to philosophy instead, which will also purge him of any element of ambition in the formation of such ties. Then he will be prepared to befriend great men.[24]

---

[21] Accommodating manner: Hunter 1985: 481; attitude of the flatterer: cf. Plutarch "How to Distinguish" 51a; Hunter 1985: 484; cf. *Latin Anthology* 403 Shackleton Bailey.

[22] Friend to yourself: cf. Gantar 1976, and contrast *Sat.* 1.2.20; "live for myself": cf. *Ep.* 1.7; Ovid, *Trist.* 3.4.5–6: "live for yourself and steer clear of great names"; also vv. 43–4 on acquiring "equal friendships."

[23] For Horace's possible debt to Philodemus in the *Art of Poetry*, see Armstrong 1994.

[24] Cf. Konstan 1995: 338–41 for a somewhat different analysis.

PATRONS AND POETS

The question of patronage and friendship has attracted special attention in connection with relations between poets and sponsors such as Maecenas and Messalla, in part because of who the characters are, in part also because the term patronage is still alive in this sphere and evokes modern controversies over the freedom of the artist. In the last century, Theodor Mommsen complained in a lecture transcribed by his students:

That this age is justly called "The Age of Maecenas" is a damning criticism. It is Maecenas, Asinius Pollio, Valerius Messalla, etc., who produce literature – more accurately, who cause it to be produced. The industrious composition and recitation of verse are everywhere dependent on orders from above (trans. Armstrong and Calder 1994: 88; orig. Mommsen 1992 [1882/6]).

Nicholas Horsfall (1981: 5) comments in a similar vein on Horace's introduction to the circle of Maecenas (*Sat.* 1.6): "The line between *amicus*-'friend' and *amicus*-'client' should not be drawn, now or at any point later in the relationship."[25]

As an Epicurean and composer of convivial love lyrics, verse epistles, and chatty "conversations" (*sermones*), Horace was disposed to prefer private friendships to public life, and his poetry is rich in tender expressions of affection, of which the description of Virgil as "half my soul" (*Odes* 1.3.8) is the most memorable (cf. Ovid, *Ep. Pont.* 1.8.2: "great part of my soul"; Statius, *Silvae* 3.2.6–7). His version of a dinner party that includes Maecenas (*Sat.* 2.8) is correspondingly genial, and though there are touches of comedy, as the genre requires, it exhibits the "freedom for frank exchange that obtains between friends" (Baker 1988: 229). Horace was secure enough in his intimacy with Maecenas to publish what are ostensibly personal letters and small talk between them, thus exposing their confidential exchanges to the gaze of the greater world.[26]

Was he also in any sense Maecenas' client? The commentator Porphyrio (third century AD), in a note on Horace's use of *amicus* in the first *Epode* (189.12–13 Holder), remarks: "It does not seem to suit Horace's modesty that he calls himself the friend of Maecenas when he ought to call himself his client." Peter White (1993: 32) comments: "Porphyrio clearly conceives of the word 'client' not as an eccentric

---

[25] Cf. White 1978: 81–2; Konstan 1995: 328–9.
[26] For the paradox, cf. Oliensis 1995.

or invidious substitute for 'friend,' but as the proper name for the relationship." Perhaps the more rigid social stratification of the later empire made Horace's claim to friendship with Maecenas seem presumptuous; alternatively, Porphyrio is conscious that at the writing of this early poem Horace has not yet achieved the familiarity implied by the word *amicus*.

Though Horace calls himself Maecenas' friend, it does not follow that he would refuse the label "client." In a late ode (4.12), Horace invites to a symposium a certain Virgil, whom he identifies as "a client of noble young men" (15). A majority of the manuscripts identify the man as a banker, which sits well with the description of him as having an "interest in profit" (25); on the other hand, this seems rude in reference to the poet, now dead. Timothy Johnson (1994: 62) suggests, however, that the formula is typical of Horace's invitations; as for *cliens*, Virgil "is a poet with patrons, and his patrons are the leading men of Rome." The gift that Horace demands is, indeed, as Johnson notes (63), a poem. If Virgil is Virgil, then it was no insult to be called a client of such sponsors.[27]

Peter White (1993: 14) captures the nuanced quality of such asymmetrical friendships in Augustan Rome:

It is in terms of social and cultural affinities that poets can count as the equals of great men like Maecenas and Messalla and can practice the kind of reciprocity which we associate with friendship. Thus a genuine ground of rapport does exist between them, and the affect-laden language which pervades their discourse is probably to be interpreted as an effort by both parties to neutralize those status differences which do still stand between them.

Statius enjoyed celebrating the beneficence of wealthy hosts – he seems to have been the first poet to eulogize gorgeous villas. He was also accommodating toward the difficult Domitian: his poems provide an early example of the use of the term *dominus*, "master," in addressing the emperor (e.g. *Silv.* 4 praef. 27; 4.2.6; Suetonius records in his *Life of Domitian* 13.2 that the emperor expected to be addressed as *dominus et deus*). This combination has cast suspicion on the nature of his friendships; one commentator (Van Dam 1984: 2) sums up his situation:

In Rome he earned his living as a poet ... St[atius] never employs the word *patronus*, for to him his rich protectors are *amici*: the old interpretation of one kind of *amicitia* as the devoted attachment of a poorer man to a rich one also

[27] Putnam 1986: 206 allows that "Virgil" may be the poet.

applied to the poet and his Maecenas. *Amicitia* in this sense is a career or a vocation.[28]

Another (Coleman 1988: 177) treats an expression of gratitude (*Silv.* 4.6.1–4) as subtly disingenuous, for Statius' "phrasing disguises the fact that, by the operation of *amicitia* fundamental to his livelihood, he was obliged to accept an invitation to dinner." However, this same poem concludes (4.6.89–93, as transposed):

Now too, if the gods are concerned to know the character and hearts of mankind, it is not your mansion, Tirynthian, nor its royal splendor that favors you, but the pure and guiltless mind of their master, with his austere fidelity and everlasting covenant of friendship, once begun.

Loyalty to friends is not inflected here according to rank.

Silvae 4.9 is a droll complaint addressed to Plotius Grypus for having sent Statius an inferior collection of writings as a gift on the Saturnalia – just as slim as Statius' present to him but penned on poorer paper. Statius concludes (46–55) with a series of contrasts between the favors appropriate to friends of different social station (49–52): if he saluted Grypus in the morning, would Grypus return the greeting at Statius' door? Having dined Statius magnificently, would Grypus expect like entertainment in return? The premise is that "*amicitia* between social unequals precludes strictly reciprocal behaviour" (Coleman 1988: 238), but Statius gives the argument a twist by extending it to poetry, on the one hand flattering Grypus by suggesting that he ought to have given better than he got, on the other hand tempering the compliment by restricting the comparison to the packaging, where Grypus' wealth might indeed have shown itself. Statius in fact does not mention *amicitia* in this poem, perhaps just because the representation of exchange is too economic: Cicero (*De amic.* 9.31) had observed that

we are not beneficent and generous in order to demand recompense [*gratia*], for we do not make a loan of our benefits, but are disposed by nature to generosity; so too in the case of friendship we are not drawn by the hope of profit but believe that it is to be sought because its entire reward resides in the love itself.

But the ease with which Statius acknowledges the gap in social position between himself and Grypus while playfully intimating their equality in the realm of art suggests that common tastes were the basis of a frank and jocular amity as genuine and intimate as any.

---

[28] Cf. Coleman 1988: xxiv–xxv.

FRIENDSHIP BETWEEN MEN AND WOMEN

The phrase "everlasting covenant of friendship" (*perenne foedus amicitiae*) with which *Silvae* 4.6 concludes clearly echoes Catullus' prayer (109.6) for an "eternal covenant of sacred friendship" (*aeternum sanctae foedus amicitiae*) with his mistress, Lesbia, instead of the pleasant love-affair (*iucundus amor*) that she promises him. Catullus' appropriation of friendship as an image for an enduring relationship between a man and woman is striking. The term *amica* or "girlfriend" had pejorative connotations, and husband and wife were no more likely to be described as friends in Latin than in Greek. Cicero (*Pro Caecina* 14) suggests that there is something suspicious about a man who makes himself the friend (*voluntarius amicus*) of a widow, without having been the friend of her father or husband.[29]

The abstract noun may indeed be used to describe a non-sexual relationship between the sexes: Ovid recommends feigning *amicitia* as a means of seduction (*Art of Love* 1.720–2; cf. 579–80, where Ovid suggests making friends with the husband). Statius, however, returns to the model of Catullus in order to represent as friendship the bond between a married couple, Pollius Felix and Polla (*Silv.* 2.2.154–45, as transposed):

No other hearts adhere under a better divinity, no other minds has Concord instructed. Learn from her in security: your marriage torches, intertwined in your hearts, have coalesced forever, and a sacred love [*sanctus amor*] preserves the laws of chaste friendship [*pudicae amicitiae*].

Concord and partnership (*societas*) are central themes in the Roman conception of marriage, but the reference to friendship is unusual. Statius has reverence enough for the quality of *amicitia* to invoke it as the name of an equal and loving alliance between spouses.[30]

---

[29] *Amica* pejorative: cf., for example, Plautus, *Bacchides* 193, *Curculio* 593, *Epidicus* 702; Terence, *Andria* 216, *Self-Tormentor* 328, also 911–12 for the contrast between *amica* and *amicus*; Catullus 110.1–2; Martial 11.49(50).10; Greek usage: cf. above, p. 91; note too the story (Val. Max. 4.4 Romans 4) that when Marcus Plautius slew himself at the funeral of his wife, his friends raised a tomb for the couple with the inscription *tōn philountōn*, "of the lovers"; they would not have written *philoi*; in Lucian, *Toxaris* 61 a Scythian prefers a friend to a wife; cf. Konstan 1994: 4–5, and King Arthur in Thomas Malory's *Morte Darthur*: "And much more I am soryar for my good knyghtes losse than for the losse of my fayre quene; for quenys I myght have inow, but such a felyship of good knyghtes shall never be togydirs in no company" (Vinaver, 1990: 1184 = 20.9 in the Caxton numeration).

[30] Roman conception of marriage: Treggiari 1991: 249–53; Van Dam 1984: 279 suggests that Statius may be alluding to Pollius' Epicureanism.

FRIENDSHIP IN IMPERIAL SOCIETY

Friendship among the Romans was a voluntary bond of mutual devotion. A fragment of a declamation attributed to Quintilian (308.21–3 Winterbottom) explicitly mentions the role of choice (a friend is contesting an inheritance claimed by kinsmen of the deceased): "The name of friend in itself seems to me even holier [than that of relative]. For the one comes from the intellect, comes from a decision; the other chance bestows, a circumstance of birth and things that are not elected by our will." The stratification of Roman society threatened at times to render hollow the intimacy and affection associated with friendship as the term was used for relations marked by hierarchical display and dependency, but the strong sense of *amicitia* remained available as a means of unmasking such appropriations.

In the palace milieu, the problem of friendship was complicated by the absolute authority of the emperor and the proud tradition of the senatorial class. With distrustful rulers such as Nero or Domitian, deference amounting to sycophancy was perceived to be imperative, and insincerity touched the sense of friendship as it did other ideals such as liberty. Tacitus (*Hist.* 1.15) has Galba, who was to be emperor for half a year in AD 69, say to Gaius Calpurnius Piso, the leader of the failed conspiracy against Nero in 65, whom he plans to adopt:

You to be sure will preserve with the same constancy good faith, freedom of speech [*libertas*], and friendship, the outstanding values of the human soul, but others will erode them through obsequiousness; adulation will break through, and flattery, and the worst poison to true affection, each man's own interest.

The term of art for the pretense of friendship in Tacitus is *species*, and it is part of a systematic staging of experience, as Tacitus represents it, that puts in jeopardy the line between reality and playacting.[31]

Even when the compulsion to counterfeit admiration abated under regimes more hospitable to the senate, the heritage of hyperbole abided in expressions of good will and gratitude addressed to the emperor. In his panegyric to Trajan in 100 AD – close to the time of Dio Chrysostom's third discourse on kingship (see above, pp. 107–8) – Pliny the Younger declaims (85.8): "So great a capacity

---

[31] On liberty under the empire: cf. Roller 1994; on hypocrisy: Bartsch 1994: 24–5; *species*: Seager 1977; staging of experience: Bartsch 1994: 1–35; cf. Rudich 1993: xxii-xxxii on *dissimulatio*.

do you have for putting your friends under obligation that no one but an ingrate could fail to love you more." Hannah Cotton (1984: 266) comments: "the over-embellished argument is its own undoing; it destroys the very relationship it set out to establish."[32] But Pliny also implies (44.7) that friendship with Trajan depends on the moral equality between the emperor and those who are, by reason of their virtue, similar (*similes*) to him.

Personal ties within the aristocracy and between political candidates and their followers in the Roman republic furnished new contexts for friendship; under the empire, conditions again altered, as vertical relations among the nobility became more openly hierarchical. Ideas of friendship were adapted to different practices, but the core sense of a private bond based on mutual affection, esteem, and liberality – within the capabilities of the respective partners – abided. Extreme differences in wealth and power inspired a tendency to classify friends by social station, but also provoked a more radical sense of moral egalitarianism, exemplified in Seneca's injunction to take meals together with the virtuous among one's slaves, that transcends Aristotle's vision. The distance between inner worth and outer position was perhaps one of the factors contributing to a new interest in sincerity as opposed to services between friends, exhibited also in the concern with candor and flattery both among political commentators and in the pedagogical therapies of the philosophical schools.

---

[32] Cf. Bartsch 1994: 148–87; Wallace-Hadrill 1982: 40 is more positive; on imperial *amici*, see also Crook 1955: 23–7 and Rudich 1993: xxvii.

CHAPTER 5

Christian and pagan

SELF-DISCLOSURE AND CHRISTIAN FRIENDSHIP

During the third and fourth centuries AD, the Roman state endured as a central political authority controlling a vast empire that included Western and South-Eastern Europe, North Africa, and the Near East up to the borders of Persia. The periphery of this territory and Italy itself were subject to invasions by warlike peoples that had been partly assimilated to Roman social life; destruction was at times massive, and regions periodically achieved varying degrees of local autonomy. Internally, class divisions hardened into statuses: laws prescribed different treatment for citizens according to rank, and the lowest stratum was reduced to a serf-like state of dependency (the "colonate") that was often little different from slavery. At the same time, traditional civic institutions, or at least forms, exhibited a remarkable tenacity, and many cities preserved ancient offices and titles under radically changed conditions. Finally, Constantine's decision to grant religious freedom to all Christians in 313 confirmed the pre-eminence of the church, and created the conditions for vigorous campaigns of conversion as well as confrontations between rival Christian sects.[1]

Within the church, attitudes toward friendship were conditioned both by theological or ethical principles and by organizational considerations. Monastic life, which took various forms in different parts of the empire, had a profound influence on Christian social thought. When the church fathers wrote about friendship, they were as often concerned with relations among monks, priests, or other devotees who lived together in religious communities as with forms of familiarity among lay people.[2]

---

[1] Cities: cf. Millar 1993: 254.
[2] On the influence of Pachomius, see McGuire 1988: 17–20; Rousseau 1985: 94–5; on the transfer of Greek monastic ideals to the Latin west, McGuire 1988: 38–40.

We may take as an example the treatise *On the Duties of Ministers* by
Saint Ambrose, bishop of Milan in the late fourth century. The tract,
in three books, is clearly modeled on Cicero's *On Duties*; in the final
portion (3.21.123–22.137), which deals with *amicitia*, Ambrose draws
also on Cicero's essay *On Friendship*, which Cicero himself saw as
supplementing the larger work (*De off.* 2.9). There is controversy
among scholars over the degree of Ambrose's independence in
respect to classical authorities, and to Cicero in particular, in his
treatment of friendship. One way in which Ambrose appears to
depart significantly from the tradition represented by Cicero,
however, is in the emphasis he places on self-disclosure between
friends.[3]

Ambrose advises the novice priests (3.22.128): "Open your bosom
to your friend, so that he may be faithful to you and that you may
derive from him pleasure in your life. 'For a faithful friend is the
medicine of life, and the blessing of immortality' [Eccl. 6:16]."
Again, he recommends (3.22.131):

Preserve, then, my sons, the friendship that has been entered upon with
your brothers, than which nothing in human affairs is more lovely. For it is
the solace of this life that you have one to whom you may open your bosom,
with whom you may share hidden things, to whom you may commit the
secret of your bosom.

Yet a third time he exhorts (3.22.135):

[God] gave the form of friendship we follow, that we may perform the
wishes of a friend, that we may open our secrets, whichever we have in our
bosom, to a friend, and that we may not be ignorant of his hidden things.
Let us reveal our bosom to him, and let him reveal his to us. "Therefore,"
he said, "I have called you friends, because all that I have heard from my
Father, I have made known to you" [John 15:14]. Therefore a friend hides
nothing, if he is true: he pours forth his mind, just as Lord Jesus poured
forth the mysteries of his Father.

The idea of openness between friends advanced by Ambrose (cf. also
3.22.136) is not without classical antecedents. Cicero, for example,
exclaims (*De amic.* 22): "What sweeter than to have one with whom
you are bold to speak as with yourself?" Pliny, in turn, remarks in a
letter (5.1.12): "I speak no differently with you than with myself."

---

[3] Ambrose's independence: White 1992: 121 regards Ambrose's innovations as minimal;
Pizzolato 1974 argues for Ambrose's subtle transformation of his sources; cf. Boularand
1972: 113; Pizzolato 1993: 269–75; more generally, Coyle 1955; further bibliography in
Pizzolato 1974: 54 n. 5.

Nevertheless, a recognition of the advantages or delights of speaking openly with a friend is a different matter from Ambrose's injunction to disclose one's inmost concerns.[4]

Closer to Ambrose's concern with self-disclosure is Seneca's counsel on how to behave with a friend (*Ep. mor.* 3.2–3): "Speak as boldly with him as with yourself ... share with your friend all your worries, all your thoughts ... Why should I hold back any words in the presence of my friend?" Seneca's *Moral Epistles* are addressed to one Lucilius, and are designed to instruct an apprentice in Stoic philosophy. Seneca is writing within a tradition in which the candid revelation of one's fears and desires was an element in a program of philosophical therapy that would enable the disciple to overcome resistances to the claims of reason. We have already had occasion to note (see above, pp. 112–13) how the social ideal of frank criticism or *parrhēsia* was embraced by the Hellenistic philosophical schools as a pedagogical practice. The Cynics went in for stinging reproaches, as illustrated by the phrase attributed to Diogenes by John Stobaeus in the section of his chrestomathy devoted to *parrhēsia* (3.13.44): "Diogenes said: Other dogs bite their enemies, I [bite] my friends – so that I may save them."[5]

Philodemus, in his treatise on frankness, sought to refine the exercise of correction and to define a mean between excessive harshness, which may discourage the moral improvement of the learner, and too accommodating a leniency. For the treatment to work, however, openness and the revelation of personal faults are also required on the part of the disciples or friends, as adherents of the school were called; Philodemus indicates this kind of forthright-ness by the verb *mēnuein*, meaning "disclose" or "declare" (or, in legal contexts, "inform"), rather than by *parrhēsia* and related forms (frs. 40–1, 49). The distinction in terminology deserves attention. While Philodemus encouraged both the practice of balanced criticism undertaken by the sage and the divulging of private sentiments for the purpose of improvement on the part of disciples, he considered them to be two parallel activities, rather than one and the same. Similarly, Augustine, in a letter to Jerome written in 405 (*Ep.* 82.36), explains that he takes pleasure not only in the affection but also the frankness of their friendship (*libertas amicitiae*; cf. *Ep.* 155.11);

---

[4] Classical antecedents: Pizzolato 1974: 63; with a friend as with oneself: cf. Powell 1990: 90; also Augustine, *De diversis quaestionibus* 83 q. 71.6, cit. McNamara 1958: 204.

[5] Seneca's epistles: see Graver 1995; philosophical therapy: cf. Nussbaum 1994b.

the other side of the coin is to be open about one's own faults.[6] The
English words "frankness" or "candor," which cover both operations, may obscure the difference.

The role of self-disclosure in Ambrose's treatise may seem to have
affinities with the twentieth-century interest in intimacy and personal
communication among friends as a means of bridging the existential
gap between unique selves (cf. above, pp. 15–17). Certainly, Christian
thought recognized in a special way the idea of the inner man as the
locus of faith. An illustration of this orientation is the gloss that John
Cassian (early fifth century) provides on Jesus' injunction (Matthew
5:39), "if someone has struck you on the right cheek, offer him the
other as well"; Cassian comments (*Conferences* 16.22): "understood,
undoubtedly, is [the other] right [cheek], and this other right [cheek]
cannot be taken except as that on the face, so to speak, of the inner
man [*interior homo*]"; similarly Basil, varying a trope of epistolary
theory, remarks to Ambrose (*Ep.* 197) that through Ambrose's letters
he has become acquainted with "the beauty of the inner man [*ho esō
anthrōpos*]."

There is, however, a deep gulf between ancient, including Christian, conceptions of the self and modern notions of authenticity, and
Ambrose's purpose in recommending openness between friends is
not that of encouraging personal intimacy as an end in itself.
Ambrose is concerned rather with friendship among a company of
"brothers" whom he addresses as his sons, and whose relationship
depends on their common faith and participation in the offices of the
church. In insisting on the importance of self-revelation, Ambrose is
seeking to promote a harmony of sentiment and collective loyalty
within a community organized around a shared vision of life. In this
regard, the object as well as the techniques of spiritual improvement
in Christian communities were analogous to those of the Hellenistic
philosophical schools.[7]

Self-disclosure, indeed, may work to advance the cohesion of small
societies precisely by inhibiting private relations among individuals.
Where Seneca advises candor with a friend, Ambrose encourages it
among all the brethren (contrast Epictetus' warning against the rash
disclosure of secrets to casual acquaintances, *Disc.* 4.13.11, 15). Injunc-
tions against secrecy are a feature of rules for monastic life. Here

---

6   Cf. McNamara 1958: 209.
7   Inner man: cf. Augustine, *Ep.* 2; on interiority in Augustine versus Plato's vision of external
    forms, see Taylor 1989: 131; modern authenticity: cf. Gill 1994.

again, the connection with the philosophical schools may be relevant, though Markus (1990: 80) overstates the case when he concludes that "the Stoic ideal of friendship found its fulfilment in monasticism" (Pythagoreans had perhaps a larger influence). Under conditions of collective living, where group cohesion and spiritual progress were central concerns, the emphasis fell more on generalized charity and the need for honesty than on ties between pairs of individuals, which might be disruptive to the community, quite apart from the dangers of erotic attachments, to which the Greek fathers were particularly alert. In this way, the classical ideal of friendship is subtly altered, as particular bonds between individuals are displaced by a concern for a broader concord among communicants as such. The effects of this shift are discernible as well outside the restricted sphere of the cloister and seminary.[8]

HYPOCRISY AND FRIENDSHIP

The 22nd oration by the fourth-century AD rhetorician Themistius, a pagan who opened a school in Constantinople and was tutor, under Theodosius I, to the future emperor Arcadius, is entitled "On Friendship" (*Peri philias*). Early in the speech, Themistius observes:

For a friend [*philos*] is nowhere near a flatterer [*kolax*], and is furthest removed in this, that the one praises everything, while the other would not go along with you when you are erring; for the former is set on making a profit or stuffing his belly by his efforts, and is not impressed with you, but with your money or your power [*dunasteia*]. (276c; cf. Maximus of Tyre, *Or.* 14.6)

Here Themistius reproduces the conventional Hellenistic contrast between friendship and adulation (cf. above, pp. 98–103), cheerfully tossing in an allusion to the comic figure of the parasite in the process. But Themistius also remarks that the pursuit of friendship is endangered above all by "that which is called hypocrisy [*hupokrisis*] by people in our time" (267b). Themistius ends his discourse with a version of the tale of Heracles' choice, related first by Prodicus in Xenophon's *Memorabilia* (2.1.21–34). In Xenophon's version, the two allegorical female figures between whom Heracles is invited to choose are identified as Virtue (*Aretē*) and Vice (*Kakia*); the latter describes

---

[8] On self-disclosure in a monastic context, see Gould 1993: 30–3, 63–6; Pythagoreans: see Wilson 1975: 59 on Athanasius', and perhaps Basil's, acquaintance with Iamblichus' writings; erotic attachments: McGuire 1988: xli–xlii; broader concord: Treu 1972: 431.

herself as Happiness (*Eudaimonia*, 26). Themistius has drawn also upon Maximus of Tyre, who opens his oration on friendship with a brief adaptation of Prodicus' fable, in which the two alternatives are labeled Virtue and Pleasure (*Hēdonē*, 22.1). Themistius retains Xenophon's personae, but gives each a companion: Friendship (*Philia*) for Virtue, Hypocrisy (*Hupokrisis*) for Vice (280b). In contrasting friendship with hypocrisy, Themistius is varying the traditional opposition between the friend and the flatterer; indeed, Themistius locates Flattery (*Kolakeia*) on the approach to the mountain where Hypocrisy dwells, and casts Flattery as Hypocrisy's forerunner.

Flattery is a form of self-interested deception: the flatterer, as Aristotle observes, differs from the ingratiating person (*areskos*) in that his obsequiousness is in the service of his own gain (*EN* 4.6, 1127a7–10). Hypocrisy in Themistius appears to be a less calculating kind of pretense, a kind of inauthenticity that displays itself as friendship but does not have friendship's unfeigned simplicity.

Hypocrisy had a painted face, not a genuine beauty; instead of a peaceful smile she had a deceitful grin. In order to appear desirable, she pretended to feel desire for those who came to her. Since no one would come any distance to her on his own, she would run out and submit herself to people, go meet them herself and take them back with her. (282a)

This Hypocrisy seems a forlorn and desperate sort rather than an artful cheat, such as flattery is conceived to be. No motive is offered for her self-prostitution, save for the wish to be liked. She is less concerned to extort benefactions than to represent herself as better than she is.

In Themistius' discourse, then, the opposite to friendship is not so much betrayal or the exploitation of an intimate relationship, as the earlier tradition had represented it, but rather a failure of sincerity that presents a false image to the admirer. Hypocrisy in this sense is almost devoid of practical content: it is revealed not in one's actions or motives so much as in a fundamental bad faith with oneself.

There are some signs in Themistius' discourse that the classical priority of virtue as the basis of friendship has begun to give way, albeit partially, to a conception of friendship founded on a more or less arbitrary attraction. Themistius follows Xenophon's lead (*Mem.* 2.6) in identifying the qualities of a potential friend as a sense of gratitude, ability to endure physical hardships, generosity, and an absence of spite and arrogance (268c-9b), but he then introduces a new point that is perhaps of his own invention: given that it is difficult to achieve moral perfection, one ought at least to seek as a friend someone whose vices are the opposite of one's own (270c-1b); similarly, Themistius later advises that one may avoid invidious competition by selecting friends whose occupations are different from one's own (275d). After first recommending that one make oneself as virtuous as possible in order to attract the other (271d; cf. Xenophon *Mem.* 2.6.14, 35), Themistius goes on to suggest that one cast winning glances, trace out the haunts of one's prey, offer praise, ingratiate oneself with the other's relatives (272a-3b) – such wiles have more in common with Ovid's *Art of Love* than with Plato's or Xenophon's prescriptions on securing worthy friends. In this part of the discourse, the question of the character of the friend recedes to the point of indifference. What one is tracking is simply the object of desire. The very image of hunting down a friend, inspired by Plato's *Lysis* (218c) and by Xenophon (*Mem.* 2.6.8) but blown up into a conceit by Themistius, involves just the skills that are emblematic of Friendship's antitype, Hypocrisy, and her entourage of Deception (*Apatē*), Plotting (*Epiboulē*), and Trickery (*Dolos*, 282b).

The opposite of the flatterer is the plain speaker, who is prepared to discourage, however tactfully, the errors or vices of his companion, irrespective of his social position. It is tacitly assumed that such frankness is the expression of a virtuous disposition; the *kolax* or adulator, subtle as he may be, betrays himself by a systematic compliance with his patron's base desires, from which he hopes materially to benefit. The hypocrite, however, is intent upon concealing his own nature with a view to being desired, rather than seeking selfishly to exploit the faults of another. The antithesis to the hypocrite, accordingly, is not one who honestly confronts the deficiencies of his associates, but one who shuns masquerades as such and prefers to be seen for what he is. This kind of candor is not the outspokenness associated with the Greek term *parrhēsia* or the Latin *libertas*; rather, it has more to do with the personal honesty or openness to which Ambrose exhorts his neophytes (his word is *aperire*, "reveal"), and which Philodemus, in his treatise on frank speech, identifies by the term *mēnuein*.[9]

The complex of ideas involving hypocrisy, self-disclosure, and friendship based on spontaneous attraction rather than on qualities of character has the appearance of a new mutation of the Hellenistic

---

[9] The discussion of Themistius is adapted from Konstan 1996a.

triad of friendship, frankness, and flattery. The three elements cohere as an expression of a concern with integrity for its own sake, rather than as the basis of social relations in public life. There is a temptation to regard this structure as an intimation of the modern conception of an inward and asocial self (see above, pp. 16–18), and the juxtaposition of Ambrose and the pagan Themistius may suggest a greater consistency in the *mentalité* of the age than is in fact justified. And yet, the Greek word *hupokrisis* in the sense of inner bad faith is characteristic of biblical usage (e.g. Matt. 23:28: "outwardly you seem just to men, but inwardly you are full of hypocrisy and lawlessness"), although there are parallels elsewhere (the more common meaning of the term in classical Greek is "role"). The question of Themistius' relation to Christian vocabulary requires further investigation.

FRIENDSHIP VS. BROTHERLY LOVE

It is commonly recognized that many Christian writers eschewed the classical vocabulary of friendship, particularly in the fourth century and later. Earlier, the Greek Clement of Alexandria (late second-early third century) had cordially adopted a modified version of Aristotle's threefold classification of types of friendship, with the best type based on virtue or *aretē* (*Stromateis* 2.19), though Clement goes on at once to describe affection based on *aretē* as *agapē*; the Latin Christian writer Minucius Felix (first half of the third century), in turn, harks back to Cicero and Sallust when he remarks that friends share a single soul and wish the same things (*Octavius* 1.3). It is true that neither *philos* nor *philia* has great currency in the New Testament, but in John 15:13–14 Jesus speaks of those who obey him as his friends (cf. Luke 12:4–5), and in Acts (2:44–7, 4:32–7) Luke appeals to the classical commonplaces of shared hearts and holding possessions in common, though he ascribes these ideals to the entire community of believers.[10]

In general, however, the preferred metaphors for Christian solidarity were derived from kinship, for example brothers or father and

[10] Eschew vocabulary of friendship: Vischer 1953: 175–6; Clement's classification: cf. Vischer 1953: 175; Treu 1972: 427; single soul and wish the same things: cf. Gregory of Nazianzus, *Or.* 43.20; *Ep.* 15.2, 31.1; Augustine, *Ep.* 28, etc.; *philia* in New Testament: full discussion in Stählin 1974: 159–69; cf. also Pizzolato 1993: 228–38; in the Old Testament, Proverbs and Ecclesiastes in particular provide examples; Luke: see Mitchell 1992.

son, rather than from the domain of *amicitia* or *philia*. Thus, Tertullian, writing at the end of the second century (*c.* 197), observes: "we are designated by the name of brothers.... How much more worthily are they called and deemed brothers who have recognized a common father in God" (*Apologeticum* 39.8–9). Similarly, the 451 sayings of Sextus, which seem to represent a late second-century Christian redaction of Pythagorean or suchlike aphorisms, contain virtually nothing on friendship (as opposed, for example, to comparable collections like the Pythagorean Sentences or the sayings of Clitarchus). Only one aphorism comes close (86b), and it illustrates the distance between Sextus and the classical tradition: "the goal of piety is *philia* toward God" (443, quoted from Aristotle, on the attraction of like to like [neuter] hardly counts). Contrast the tenor of 213: "pray that you may be a benefactor to your enemies" (cf. 105, 210a–b; note also *agapan* in 106a–b). Sayings subsequently added to the original collection (perhaps fifth century) mention brotherly love (496–7).[11]

In the fourth century, some Christians, it has been argued, came to regard friendship as a pagan ideal distinct from Christian love. Thus, Paulinus of Nola (late fourth century), for example, mainly uses the term *caritas* for love among Christians, though he also employs *affectus* and *affectio*, *amor*, and *dilectio*.[12] "On the other hand," writes Pierre Fabre (1949: 148), "there is one word that, by contrast, Paulinus never uses to express friendship grounded in Christ, and if he does not necessarily employ it in a bad sense, he at least restricts its use to the designation of a purely human affection"; this word is precisely *amicitia*. Against Fabre's thesis, however, it has been objected that despite the far greater frequency of *caritas* in connection with Christian friendships, Paulinus "does occasionally use *amicus* without implying that he is talking to a non-Christian," and that in his eleventh epistle he employs *amicitia* as well of his relationship with Sulpicius Severus, his revered soulmate:

Such instances show that Paulinus did not feel that the use of the word *amicitia* was anathema in Christian circles: while *caritas* is applied exclusively to the love in Christian relationships, *amicitia* can be used of either secular or Christian friendships. (White 1992: 158, 159)

---

[11] Brotherhood: cf. Hauck 1928: 220; Petré 1948: 17, 104–40; Vischer 1953: 174–6; Klauck 1991: 10–11; Sextus, Pythagorean sayings, Clitarchus: texts and commentary in Chadwick 1959.

[12] Paulinus' use of *caritas*: Fabre 1949: 142–8; cf. Petré 1948: 30–98;

In general, however, Paulinus does seem to draw some distinction between friendship and Christian affection.[13] For example, he exclaims to Severus (*Ep.* 11.3):

you, who have become my brother not only for succor in the present but also for eternal companionship [*consortium*], exceed in dearness my bodily relatives in the same degree as you are my brother by virtue of a greater parent than those who are united to me by mere flesh and blood. For where is that brotherhood in blood now? Where that former friendship [*amicitia*]? Where that previous comradeship [*contubernia*]? I have died to all of them.

Paulinus is here contrasting an old idea of friendship with the new relationship established in Christ.

In another letter, addressed to Pammachius (*Ep.* 13.2), Paulinus writes:

Therefore in the truth in which we stand in Christ, receive my spirit as it is expressed to you in this letter, and do not measure our friendship by time. For it is not as a secular friendship, which is often begotten more in hope than in faith, but rather that spiritual kind, which is produced by God as its source and is joined in a brotherhood of souls. Consequently, it does not develop toward love by daily familiarity nor does it depend on anticipation of proof but, as is worthy of a daughter of truth, it is born at once stable and great, because it arises out of fullness through Christ.

In this passage, Paulinus self-consciously contrasts his vision of Christian fellowship with the classical conception of friendship, which, unlike erotic love, was supposed to require time in which to mature and to demand proofs of loyalty.[14] Since Paulinus deliberately rejects or refashions this view, the phrase "our friendship" (*amicitia nostra*) seems to mean "our version of what is usually called friendship," i.e., a relationship in Christ, for which Paulinus immediately substitutes the term *amor* and, in the next sentence, *caritas*.

FRIENDSHIP AND VIRTUE

But even if Christian *caritas* is, in Paulinus' view, different from secular friendship as it was understood in the classical tradition, we may still inquire why he chooses to skirt the language of *amicitia* when he has no objection to adapting to the new vision of union in Christ classical terms like *amor*, *dilectio*, and *caritas* itself that were perfectly compatible with the relationship between *amici* (cf. Cicero, *Part. orat.* 88).

One motive seems to be that, for Paulinus, a profession of friend-

---

[13] Cf. White 1992: 250 n. 32; Fabre 1949: 149–52.
[14] Cf. Arist. *EN* 9.5; White 1992: 154–5.

ship represents a claim to qualities of goodness that runs contrary to the humble spirit of a man who, of all his contemporaries, seems to have taken Christian meekness most to heart. Thus, in a verse epistle addressed to Ausonius, his former teacher, that is designed to appease the older man for Paulinus' apparent withdrawal of his affections after his conversion, Paulinus assures Ausonius that Cicero and Virgil could hardly support their end of the yoke if they were teamed up with him, and then continues (*Poems* 11.39–43):

> If I am yoked by love,
> I'll dare to boast that I'm your yoke-mate only
> as small contends with great in common reins.
> My friendship in an eternal pact with you is sweet
> and fair by equal laws of always loving in return.

Although the expression is fairly contorted, White explains (1992: 150) that Paulinus "alludes to the importance of equality in friendship but denies that they are equals in merit, only in their love for each other." The posture of lowliness becomes even more intense when Paulinus writes to eminent Christians whom he deeply admires, often on short acquaintance or known only by their reputation and writings, such as Saint Augustine and Augustine's close friend Alypius. Take the greeting, for example, that introduces *Ep.* 3: "To his lord, deserving and honored and most blessed, father Alypius, from the sinners Paulinus and Therasia." Paulinus perceives himself and his wife to be at the farthest remove from the holiness of Alypius.[15]

Such protestations of unworthiness are incompatible with the classical notion of friendship, which at its best, on the traditional view, rested on an ideal of mutual regard for one another's character. It is respect for virtue that gives rise to amicable feelings, according to both Aristotle and Cicero, and this belief was commonplace outside the schools as well. Thus, Horace describes the type of the social climber who accosts one in the street as declaring (*Sat.* 2.5.32–3): "'Quintus,' it may be, or 'Publius' (their tender little ears delight in first names), 'your virtue has made me a friend of yours.'" Claiming to be a friend thus meant that one deserved to be so, and to Paulinus, imbued as he was with Christian modesty, such an avowal, above all with a person of Alypius' standing, would be a sign

---

[15] Contrast White 1992: 149, who sees in this humility a residue of the deference characteristic of Roman patronage.

of arrogance and presumption. In describing himself as a sinner, then, Paulinus has undercut the kind of friendship that classical writers ascribed to decent men. Since his humility prevents him from laying claim to moral excellence, Paulinus is, it appears, reluctant to pretend to friendship and prefers to invoke a conception of unprompted and uncompensated love, a charity that depends more on God's grace than on Paulinus' own merits. This, at least, is how Paulinus seems to interpret the love that those he holds dearest have for him.

In another letter (*Ep.* 11.12), Paulinus replies to Severus, who has made subtle excuses for not visiting him:

> If you believe that this virtue [*virtus*] has been bestowed on me, which you confess that you wish to but cannot achieve, namely that I am content with having food and clothing and think of nothing beyond today [cf. Matt. 6:25–34], why do you imagine that I must be overcome by the compulsion of my poverty so as to cease inviting you, whom I cannot help but miss, and why do you present yourself as so weak and lacking in confidence in Christ, that you fear to come to a friend [*amicus*] of the sort you proclaim me to be?

Severus had evidently linked his friendship with Paulinus to the latter's virtue, though this is not the classical sort but rather the Christian capacity to be content with little, and even this merit is said to have been granted, not earned. What is more, Severus seems to have affected so profound a humility as to hesitate to present himself before such a friend. It is in this context that Paulinus urges Severus to be mindful of his friend (*amicus*), and proceeds to compliment him at his own expense: "certainly you, as the more clever farmer, have the larger harvest"; "I, who am even weaker in intellect than in body, am far behind you," and so forth. In calling himself a friend, Paulinus is in fact deprecating the excessive veneration expressed or feigned by Severus, since he has equal grounds for admiring Severus in return.

In Paulinus, then, Christian humility seems to disrupt the classical conception of friendship based on a consciousness of virtue. For virtues, as Augustine says (*City of God* 19.25), are deceptive, and to imagine that one possesses them on one's own, rather than referring them to God, renders the virtues themselves haughty, and thereby converts them into vices (cf. the implicit contrast between civic virtue and Christian piety in Augustine, *Ep.* 86.1).

SOME CHRISTIAN VIEWS

It is not the case that all Christian writers in the fourth century consistently avoided language associated with friendship. Jerome and Augustine in Latin, for example, and Basil of Caesarea in Greek avail themselves of the classical terminology. Nevertheless, they too commonly resort to the metaphor of brotherhood and substitute *caritas* or *agapē* for *amicitia* or *philia*, preferring to represent themselves as brothers united in Christ by virtue of their faith rather than claim the name of friend on the basis of their own excellence.[16] Thus Basil writes to one Pergamius, to whom he evidently has owed a letter (*Ep.* 56; trans. Deferrari 1926: 353):

As for you, dear sir, cease in your brief expressions to bring serious charges, charges indeed that imply the utmost depravity. For "forgetfulness of friends [*philōn*]," and that "haughtiness which is engendered by power," embrace all the crimes there are. For if we fail to love [*agapan*] according to the commandment of the Lord, neither do we possess the character suitable to our position; and if we are filled with the conceit of empty pride and arrogance, then we are fallen into the sin of the devil from which there is no escape.

To the layman's accusation that he has neglected his *philoi*, Basil responds by appealing to the Christian duty of *agapē*. So too, Saint Augustine (*Ep.* 130.13, to Proba) stipulates that in his view, "friendship must not be confined in narrow boundaries: it embraces all to whom love and affection are due." To be sure, *amicitia* in Augustine sometimes "designates friendship in the strict sense, i.e., the bonds uniting two persons in mutual sympathy" (e.g. *Ep.* 84.1), but this usage seems most frequent in the *Confessions*, where Augustine is characterizing relationships formed prior to his conversion. In the *City of God* (19.8), Augustine expands on the vulnerability to grief that friendship entails, great enough at the death of friends but still worse should they lapse from faithfulness and rectitude. Given these dangers, one should congratulate friends of good character when they have died. Augustine indeed takes friendship here in its common acceptation; however, he is in this part of the treatise engaged in a critique of the values, including friendship, propounded

---

[16] Joly 1968 argues convincingly that the verb *agapan* began to replace *philein* in pagan literature well before the Christian era; this does not affect the fact, however, that certain Christian writers perceived a tension between the abstract nouns *agapē* and *philia* in ways foreign to pagan texts, and tended to avoid the term *philos* (or *amicus*) in contexts relating to Christian love.

by the classical philosophical sects. For good measure, Augustine adds that those sages, presumably Stoics, who have claimed that the gods are friends of theirs are deluded by demons, along with whom they will suffer eternal damnation (19.9).[17]

In his treatise *On the Priesthood* (1.1), John Chrysostom of Antioch (second half of the fourth century) remarks that, in his youth, he had "genuine and true friends [*philoi gnēsioi te kai alētheis*] who knew the laws of friendship [*tous tēs philias nomous*] and observed them carefully" (trans. Clark); the language suggests, as Elizabeth Clark notes, "that he had in mind the classical descriptions of friendship's requirements" (Clark 1979: 42).[18] Chrysostom particularly emphasizes the similarity between himself and his intimate friend Basil (not Basil the Great) in interests and background. Clark continues (42–3):

Basil made more progress toward asceticism than he did, John confesses, which jeopardized their "former equality" (*tēn isotēta ... tēn proteran*) until he advanced to the same self-discipline as his friend. In this brief description we can note all the classical assumptions regarding friendship's demand for equality of circumstances and similarity of interests.

But it is worth remarking that Chrysostom's account of friendship pertains precisely to the time before he assumed the priesthood. In his *Homily on Saint Paul's Epistle to the Colossians* (1, 325d-6e), Chrysostom describes human bonds generally as forms of *philia*, and further distinguishes between those attachments or *philiai* that arise during one's life (*biōtikai*) and those that are natural or by birth (*phusikai*), that is, family ties. He notes too that friends (*philoi*) are often more loyal than the closest kin. But the spiritual love (*pneumatikē agapē*) of God, he declares, is higher than all of these, and it alone is indissoluble. Nevertheless, Chrysostom's vocabulary is not rigid, and he concludes by recommending that we pursue those *philiai* that are of the spirit.[19]

---

[17] Broad sense of friendship in Augustine: cf. McNamara 1958: 194; McEvoy 1986: 80–91; friendship in the strict sense: McNamara 1958: 193 (cited in text); friendships prior to conversion: cf. Cassidy 1992: 134: "in comparison to *caritas* there are relatively few references to *amicitia* in the mature writings of Augustine."

[18] Cf. White 1992: 90; on Chrysostom's references to pagan sources, Coleman-Norton 1930: 305–17.

[19] Before assuming the priesthood: cf. Vischer 1953: 198–9; for Chrysostom's more traditional pronouncements on the value of friends, cf. *Homily on Saint Paul's Epistle to the Thessalonians 2* 2 = *PG* 62.474–5; the passage is excerpted by Maximus Confessor in his *Commonplaces* 6 (*PG* 91: 757); cf. also White 1992: 91.

GREGORY OF NAZIANZUS ON FRIENDSHIP

Gregory of Nazianzus, however, the intimate friend and lifelong colleague of Basil, although he does on occasion employ the term *agapē*, most often speaks of his relations to intimates in the vocabulary of *philia* and *philoi*. Thus, Kurt Treu observes:

Although Basil, under "friendship," clearly distinguishes between *philia* and *agapē*, and employs *philia* with various reservations but only *agapē* in an unequivocally positive way, Gregory of Nazianzus uses *philia* almost exclusively for the same semantic territory. It is not oversubtle to perceive in this an expression of a deeper difference between the two friends... Basil is more strongly tied to the ecclesiastical heritage, from which *agapē* derives, whereas Gregory remains more uninhibited in his debt to the ancient Greek tradition, in which *philia* is at home (Treu 1961: 427).[20]

When Gregory wants to specify Christian bonds, he may appeal to metaphors of kinship to reinforce the idea of friendship. Thus, in *Ep.* 11.2, he writes: "Since all are friends and relations of one another who live according to God and follow the same Gospel, why will you not hear from us in frankness [*parrhēsia*] what all men are muttering?" But Gregory has no hesitation in pronouncing himself conquered by friendship and friends (*hēttōn ... philias kai philōn, Ep.* 94.3; cf. 103), and he frankly declares (*Ep.* 39.1; cf. 39.4) that "by friends I mean those who are noble and good and bound to ourselves by virtue [*aretē*], since we too have some part in that."

In the funeral oration that he pronounced for Basil in the year 382, of which Raymond Van Dam remarks that "the narrative portions ... were as much about the nature of true friendship as about Basil" (1986: 72), Gregory recalls how Basil "used to correct many of the things I did both by the rule of *philia* and by a greater standard [*nomos*]– I am not ashamed to say it, because for everyone he was a standard of *aretē*" (*Or.* 43.2). Gregory had not been the first to eulogize Basil, who had died some three years earlier (there survives the speech delivered by Basil's brother, Gregory of Nyssa), and he goes on to explain that the delay was not a sign of his indifference to propriety: "I would never be so neglectful either of virtue or of the duty of friendship [*to philikon kathēkon*]." After praising Basil's family – he describes his father as "superior in *aretē* to all others, and prevented by his son alone from winning first prize" (43.10) – Gregory goes on to recount how he first became friends

---

[20] Cf. Ruether 1969: 127; Neuhausen 1975: 191, 212–15; Van Dam 1986: 70–2.

with Basil during their student days in Athens, when he took Basil's part against some disputatious Armenian scholars and together they routed the opposition with their syllogisms (43.17). Later, he and Basil were at the center of a phratry or club of Christians, distinguished for its nobility and learning, but the two friends in particular were a team (*xunōris*) so famous they surpassed all the Orestes and the Pylades in the eyes of the Athenians. Gregory catches himself up for slipping accidentally into self-praise, but adds that "it is no wonder if here too I have taken some advantage of that man's friendship in regard to my reputation now that he is dead, as I did in regard to my virtue when he was alive" (43.22).[21]

As a consequence of their training in Athens, Gregory and Basil were both steeped in pagan literature, and Gregory was not at all antagonistic to traditional learning. He roundly affirms (*Or.* 43.11): "I believe that all who have any sense are agreed that education [*paideusis*] is first among the goods we possess." Basil too admits that culture is necessary, and in his well-known epistle "To His Nephews on How They May Profit from Greek Literature," he goes so far as to acknowledge the value of classical *aretē*, such as that of Odysseus, as a model for young people entering upon their lives (ch. 5). Gregory of Nazianzus was, however, far more inclined to refer respectfully to classical philosophy than were his fellow Cappadocians, Basil and Gregory of Nyssa, and he eschewed their blanket denunciations of non-Christian learning. Indeed, he occasionally enjoys a little philosophizing for its own sake (e.g. *Ep.* 31.2). For example, he praises Aristotle's definition of happiness as the actualization of the soul in accord with virtue, though he rejects the further condition that happiness depends as well on external goods. Gregory endorses instead the Stoic conception of the complete independence of happiness in respect to extrinsic circumstances (*Ep.* 32.5–7). Nothing here suggests a perception of mankind as remote from virtue. Indeed, Gregory castigates Aristotle's position on external goods as "excessively humble" (*lian tapeinōs*, 32.6), as though to emphasize the confidence attaching to the Stoic and Christian views.[22]

---

[21] On the role of virtue, cf. Vischer 1953: 186–8, 191; also Gregory's use of the classical ideal of *kalokagathia* or "nobility," a reputation for which by itself, he says, wins a person friends (*Ep.* 71.1).

[22] Steeped in pagan literature: Pelikan 1993: 17; cf. Gregory, *Ep.* 5.1; Gregory's approval of education: cf. his remarks (*Or.* 43.23) on Basil's erudition; also *Ep.* 39.3 on the Christian ideal of *aretē* and *paideia*; on the Cappadocians' views of classical education, see Pelikan

But Gregory's use of the terms *philos* and *philia* is not just an expression of his indebtedness to pagan thought in general. Rather, he seems to draw specifically on the classical idea, derived principally from Aristotle, of achievable human virtue and mutual respect as the basis of friendship. It is of course true that, for Gregory, complete virtue entails commitment to the Christian faith, and that the Christian virtues do not altogether coincide with the classical conception. However, he does not hesitate to express himself in language that echoes the pagan tradition.

Basil of Caesarea and Gregory of Nazianzus are not likely to have differed over fundamental questions of faith. The choice between the vocabulary of friendship and that of brotherhood or *agapē* (*caritas*) among Christian writers was not so much a matter of doctrine as of sensibility. Undoubtedly, various factors conditioned their predilections, including a suspicion of particular friendships, as opposed to the universal love enjoined by Christian teachings, that was especially relevant, perhaps, to monastic life. Another element was the impulse to discriminate God's love from merely mortal attachments (cf. James, *Ep.* 4:4: "the friendship of this world is the enmity of God: therefore whoever wishes to be a friend of the world is rendered an enemy of God"). But those writers who most systematically avoided the terms *philos* and *amicus* were perhaps also moved by misgivings concerning the classical association between friendship and virtue, by which the claim to be a friend appeared to be not just a weaker avowal than Christian love, or a more partial one, but also carried with it an unwelcome hint of pride.[23]

JOHN CASSIAN AND MONASTIC FRIENDSHIP

The sixteenth *Conversation* by John Cassian (early fifth century), entitled *On Friendship*, is intended specifically for monastic communities (McGuire 1988: 79 remarks that the essay "would have been

---

1993: 176–7; "To His Nephews": see the edition by Wilson 1975; blanket denunciations: Pelikan 1993: 18–20.

[23] Questions of faith: cf. Pelikan 1993: 6: "Careful study ... has repeatedly confirmed the impression of 'a striking similarity among the Cappadocians' in thought and even in language" (quoting Norris, 1991: 185); matter of sensibility: cf. Van Dam 1986: 72–3; suspicion of particular friendship: cf. Basil's hostility to "partial affection and comradeship" (*merikē philia kai hetairia: Logos askētikos* = *PG* 31: 885; in general, see chs. 79–81); also *Ep.* 56, 204; Augustine, *Ep.* 258, cit. White 1992: 58; McGuire 1988: xxvi: "christian love is universal, not preferential"; Browning 1967: 205: "Particular friendship is ... an exclusive association and therefore detrimental to the universal charity due to all."

better entitled *De concordia in claustro* than *De amicitia*"). Cassian begins by defending the thesis, which he attributes to certain "elders" and "men of wisdom," that comradeship depends on the equality and perfection in virtue of both partners:

> Thus according to the stated opinion of elders, love [*caritas*] will not be able to remain stable and unbroken unless it is among men of like virtue and conduct. (16.24)

> Therefore the opinion of the wisest men is absolutely right, namely that true harmony and indivisible companionship [*societas*] cannot endure except among people with improved characters of like virtue and conduct. (16.28)

After a description of the several kinds of sentimental bonds or *amicitiae* – analogous to John Chrysostom's *philiai* (cf. Cicero *Part. Orat.* 88) – among both human beings and animals, including love for kin and for members of one's own species (16.2), Cassian proceeds to commend as indissoluble that solidarity which is based on a likeness of virtue (*similitudo uirtutum*, 16.3):

> This is true and unbroken affection [*dilectio*], which grows through the twin perfection and virtue of the friends [*amici*], and whose bond, once entered into, neither changeability in desires nor fractious conflict of wills will break.

This doctrine is surely indebted to the classical model of friendship. However, mentions of the word *amicitia* are few in Cassian's dialogue (nine in all), and are clustered in the beginning and end of the treatise (2–3, 5–6, and 28); so too for related terms such as *amicus*. In the body of the tractate, where advice is offered concerning relationships between ordinary people as opposed to those who are perfect in virtue, Cassian predominantly employs the language of brotherhood, *caritas*, and *affectio*. Cassian may have exploited the terminology relating to *amicitia* in the more theoretical frame of the colloquy in order to attach his treatment of friendship to the classical tradition, as well as to suggest an ideal toward which ascetics might strive (cf. 6: "the first basis of true friendship lies in the contempt for the physical world and disdain for all the goods we possess"); in the central part of the work, however, he reverted to language that was more at home in Christian discourse.[24]

24 Clustering of *amicus*-terms in Cassian's *Conference*: see Neuhausen 1975: 192–3; language of brotherhood: Neuhausen 1975: 225, 206–11; reversion to Christian discourse: cf. Fiske 1955: 168: "Cassian's identification of *amicitia* with *caritas* remains somewhat incomplete as a doctrine"; also Fiske 1970: ch. 3: 4; Markus 1990: 164.

FRIENDSHIP WITH GOD

Although many Christians, as opposed to Greeks and Romans in the classical period, were ambivalent about the classical vocabulary of friendship, Christians outdid the classical tradition in recognizing the possibility of friendship between mortals and God or angels. Thus McGuire (1988: 8) comments on Athanasius' *Life of Saint Antony*, written shortly after Antony's death in the year 356 at the age of 105:

The only friends mentioned in his *Life* are the angels with whom he spoke on his deathbed. They received and deserve the name *amici*, while his companions in the desert, who forced themselves on him, were *discipuli*, or, at best, *fratres*.

McGuire adds (9): "Even in his most human moments..., Antony never makes a friend on his own level."[25] Similarly, St. Hilary of Arles, in his "Sermon on the Life of St. Honoratus" pronounced for his kinsman and mentor (probably on the first anniversary of his death in January 429), mentions Honoratus' companions only in the context of the worldly associates whom the young Gaulish aristocrat seemed to be abandoning upon accepting his Christian calling (5): "his native district, his friends [*familiares*], his parents all felt that the shining jewel, as it were, and common glory of all was being snatched from them" (trans. Deferrari 1952: 365). Hilary concludes the sermon, however, by apostrophizing Honoratus (39): "Remember us, therefore, friend of God [*amice Dei*]" (*PL* 50.1252, 1272). Prudentius tends to describe martyrs as patrons (*patronus*) of their petitioners (the usage apparently originates with Ambrose), but the martyr's relation to Christ is described as *amicitia*.[26] Striking a more cautious note, Augustine feels the need to warn his readers that their angel friends might be demons in disguise (*City of God* 19.9).

The idea of friendship with God in Judaeo-Christian texts written in Greek and Latin has its roots in the Bible. The Greek translation (Septuagint) of the Old Testament identifies Moses as a "friend [*philos*] of God" (Exodus 33:11; cf. Genesis 18:17, Wisdom 7:27), and Abraham too came to be so regarded. From these passages, which influenced the Jewish writer Philo of Alexandria (early first century AD), as well as from Luke 12:4 and especially Jesus' words in John

---

[25] Antony: cf. the salutations to *Epp.* 4–5 (trans. Chitty 1975).
[26] See Roberts 1993: 21–5.

15:14 ("you are my *philoi* if you do whatever I command you"), the idea passed into Christian literature.[27]

Aristotle had categorically denied the possibility of friendship between a human being and a god because of the extreme degree of difference between the two (*EN* 8.7, 1158b33–6). In this, he was reflecting popular Greek attitudes. However, Erik Peterson, in a learned and still fundamental article on the topos published more than seventy years ago, argued that two distinct views circulated in classical antiquity, one of which admitted the possibility of such friendship while the other, represented by Aristotle, did not. He thus concluded that its presence in the works of Philo and the church fathers represented the confluence of two traditions.[28]

In fact, Peterson greatly overstated the case for friendship with gods in early classical sources. The Greeks happily spoke of a mortal being dear (*philos*) to the gods (the notion is captured in the compound *theophilēs*), and of course recognized that the gods were dear to human beings. These adjectival uses of the word *philos*, however, often in combination with a dative indicating the one to whom the other party is dear, must be distinguished more carefully than Peterson did from the nominal, which properly indicates friendship.

Consider, for example, the passage in Xenophon's *Symposium* (4.47–8) with which Peterson begins:

These gods, then, who are all-knowing and all-powerful, are so friendly [*philoi*] to me that on account of their care of me I never elude them, whether by night or day or wherever I may turn or whatever I am going to do.

The adverbial modifier "so" (*houtō*) makes it clear that *philoi* is an adjective rather than a substantive; the dative "to me" (*moi*), which alone would not be decisive, here clinches the case (in the next sentence Xenophon writes: "because you care for them you hold them so dear"). Xenophon says nothing about friendship with gods; he is speaking rather about being favored by the gods, a different notion that goes back to Homeric formulas such as *Dii philos*, "dear to Zeus."[29]

---

27 Abraham: see the Vulgate version of 2 Chronicles 22.7, whence apparently, in the New Testament, James 2:23; cf. Peterson 1923: 172–3, 177.
28 See Peterson 1923; for his influence, cf. Dedek 1967; Moltmann 1994.
29 For analysis of other cases adduced by Peterson, including Plato, *Tim.* 53d, *Rep.* 10.621c, Plotinus, *Enneads* 2.9.9, Maximus of Tyre, *Or.* 11.12, 14.6, Epictetus, *Disc.* 3.22.95, 3.24.60,

Peterson cites a clever bit of sophistry attributed to the Cynic Diogenes by Diogenes Laertius (6.72; cf. 6.37), which exploits the different senses of *philos* as "dear" and as "friend":

> He said that all things belong to wise men...: all things belong to the gods; the gods are dear [*philoi*] to wise men; the possessions of friends [*tōn philōn*] are in common; therefore, all things belong to wise men.

Peterson supposes (165) that the argument looks back to a Stoic formula according to which the wise man is a friend of the gods. This is to miss the joke. Diogenes has produced a parody of a formal syllogism, and the wit depends in part on the pun or slippage between adjectival *philos* ("dear to wise men") and the substantival use (marked here by the presence of the definite article) in the sense of "friend."

At some point, however, the Stoics did make the claim that the sage was a friend of the gods. Thus, the "Life of Homer" attributed to Plutarch (143) reports: "the Stoics, who declare that good men are friends of gods [genitive], took this too from Homer." Philodemus, writing in the first century BC, takes up the question of friendship between gods and mortals (*On the Gods*, col. 1.17–18), only to challenge the propriety of such expressions: "we do not seem to call such things friendship" (col. 1.19–20). Philodemus adds (col. 1.20–fr. 85.2) that it is preferable not to force the sense of words. Evidently, he is criticizing Stoic practice, which seemed to him a radical view and an abuse of ordinary language.[30]

In the lectures recorded by Arrian, the Stoic philosopher and former slave Epictetus (late first–early second century) declares his wish

> to lift up my neck toward trouble like a free man and look up at the sky like a friend of the god [*philos tou theou*], fearing nothing of the things that may befall. (*Disc.* 2.17.29)

Again (4.3.9), he asserts: "for I am free and a friend of the god." Both times, the formula is associated with being free (*eleutheros*); true freedom for Epictetus renders one equal to the Stoic divinity.

It is not clear that the Christian idea of friendship with God was in any way influenced by Stoic doctrine, as opposed to the biblical

---

and *Greek Anthology* 7.676, see Konstan 1996b: 91–7; on adjectival *philos*, see also above, p. 56.

[30] Life of Homer: cit. Peterson 1923: 161; Philodemus *On the Gods*: text in Diels 1916, cit. Peterson 166; criticizing Stoics: Diels 1916a: 7–8.

passages cited above. In Christianity, such a relationship implies nothing like equality.[31] Philo, in his *Life of Moses* (1.156), writes:

For if, according to the proverb, "possessions of friends are in common," and the prophet has been called a friend of god, then as a consequence he would have a share in his property too, according to need.

As Peterson notes (178), the argument recalls the syllogism attributed to Diogenes the Cynic. So too, Clement of Alexandria (*Protr.* 12.122.10):

If "the possessions of friends are in common," and a man is god-beloved [*theophilēs*] (for in fact he is dear [*philos*] to god, because reason mediates [between them]), then everything turns out to belong to man because everything does so to god and all things of both friends [*philoi*], god and man, are in common.

Clement uses the expression "friend of God" in numerous contexts, independently of any allusion to Diogenes' sophism.[32] The passage is of interest, however, as an indication of one way in which the classical and the Judaeo-Christian traditions concerning the friend of god intersected. Neither Philo nor Clement seems to have found inspiration for the idea of friendship with God in Platonism or in Stoicism; rather, they found in a curious play on words associated with the Cynics a point of contact with their own beliefs.

That Christians should have been too modest to claim friendship with fellow beings and yet acknowledge the possibility of being a friend of God is no doubt a sign of reverence for the sanctity of holy men. Ultimately, however, such righteousness itself was understood as a consequence, not a cause, of God's limitless love. Aristotle's reservations about friendship between men and gods are irrelevant in this context, because the basis of the relationship is wholly different.

FRIENDSHIP IN LATE ANTIQUITY

One must not overstate the divide that resulted from the spread of Christianity in the Roman Empire. Markus (1990: 12) affirms: "There just is not a different culture to distinguish Christians from their pagan peers, only their religion" – though that is a substantial enough divergence. Christians continued to meditate on the need that princes have for reliable friends, and with reason; as Alföldi

---

[31] For Saint Thomas' account of friendship with God in the context of Aristotle's stress on equality, see Bobik 1986: 7, 17–18; Bond 1941: 54.

[32] See Peterson 1923: 190–1; cf. Pizzolato 1993: 246–53.

(1952: 19) comments: "We can assert without fear of contradiction that whenever anyone in the fourth century secured an office, he at once brought in his dependants and friends with him" (cf. Eutropius, *Brev.* 10.7.2 on Constantine's generous treatment of friends, and 10.15 on Julian as *in amicos liberalis*). Thus, Synesius of Cyrene, comparing the poet Theotimus' role in the retinue of Anthemius (praetorian prefect in the east and the father-in-law of the historian Procopius) to that of Simonides at the court of Hiero, writes (*Ep.* 51, early fifth century): "to a man in power what possession is finer than a friend, if he has a non-mercantile character?" (cf. *Ep.* 63; *On Kingship* 10). Basil, in turn, (*Ep.* 20) differentiates between a friend and a flatterer in much the same spirit as do Plutarch, Maximus of Tyre, and Themistius (cf. *Ep.* 63).[33]

Again in a traditional vein, Basil writes to a Cappadocian aristocrat named Callisthenes (*Ep.* 73): "May you be most pleasing to your friends, most feared by your enemies, and respected by both." Synesius (*Ep.* 44 = 43 Garzya) insists that his code (*themis*) is to do everything in his power to do what is good for his friends (he then counsels his correspondent to turn himself in to the law, which he would not, he says, have urged upon his enemies). Maximus Confessor (seventh century), in his collection of *Commonplaces*, comfortably combines extracts on friendship from the Bible, the church fathers, and pagan sources (in that order) in his chapter on "Friends and Brotherly Love" (*PG* 91: 753–61; but contrast his four sets of "100 Chapters" on *agapē*, *PG* 90: 960–1073, which eschew the word *philia*).

Pagan thinkers, in turn, had expressed grave doubts about the trustworthiness of friends. Dio of Prusa (*Or.* 74.23, "On Faithlessness") cites the three or four famous friendships in mythology in order to demonstrate how rare such loyalty is. Maximus of Tyre, proclaiming that faithlessness (*apistia*) in friendship is the cause of all conflict, both at home and abroad, (*Or.* 35.8), insists that to produce a genuine peace one must first achieve *philia* within the soul:

I do not trust a festival until I see that the feasters are friends. This is the law and nature of a genuine respite, arranged under the god as legislator, which one cannot see without acquiring *philia*, no matter how often one has pledged a truce.

Fourth-century pagans took friendship seriously. Symmachus (*Ep.* 7.99) remarks, "I happily apply myself to the cultivation of friendship." Libanius of Antioch, who was tutor to the emperor Julian

---

[33] Simonidas: cr. Xen. *Hiero*; Basil: cf. White 1992: 74.

(whom he praised for his regard for friendship, *Or.* 14.1) and one of
John Chrysostom's teachers, devoted an oration (8) to the theme that
friends are riches. Libanius concludes on a personal note (8.14):

We may call millionaires poor in respect to what they have not acquired or
do not possess, and one may state that I too have grown poorer. In fact, one
who does not say it has not, I think, adequately noted my circumstances, or
how it would take a day to enumerate the friends of mine who have died.

Donatus, who taught Jerome, notes in his commentary on the plays
of Terence (ad *Eunuch* 148): "a lover is one thing, a friend another: a
lover is one who loves for the moment, a friend one who loves
forever."

John Chrysostom understood the value Libanius placed on friendship, as did Gregory of Nazianzus and Basil of Caesarea, who
corresponded with Libanius. Whether Christians or not, those at the
apex of Roman society constituted a small, interconnected world.
Granting all the resemblances in their habits of thought, however,
one must acknowledge that the Christians were in fact engaged in
profoundly reevaluating the kinds of solidarity that had characterized
the social life of classical antiquity. Bonds of love were held to obtain
among the faithful through God's dispensation rather than, in the
first instance, through personal attachment or affection: "He truly
loves a friend," Augustine preaches, "who loves God in his friend,
either because He is in him, or so that He be in him."[34]

The ideals of Christian love emerged in the context of millenarian
currents within Judaism and other religions in the Near East; while it
is true that the verb *agapan* had increasingly displaced *philein* as the
ordinary word for "love" in pagan texts well before the Christian
era, the noun *agapē* seems to have been a term of art in Christian
doctrine, and it, along with its cognates, were certainly charged with
new kinds of significance by Christian thinkers.[35] Over the first four
centuries AD, a history of intermittent persecution, often the result of
sectarian conflict within Christianity, generated a powerful awareness of the need for cohesion among the faithful; bonds between the
brethren acquired the emotional resonance of civic and ethnic
connections and even of family relationships, all of which were
relatively devalued as ties of the flesh rather than the spirit. One
must add that local churches were often instrumental in resisting the

[34] Augustine, *Sermons.* 361.1, cit. McNamara 1958: 206; cf. *On the Trinity* 9.7.13; *On Christian
Doctrine* 1.22.20.
[35] *Agapan* and *philein*: see Joly 1968.

invasions that unsettled life within the empire, and in maintaining self-respect among the populace both during and after periods of danger and exposure to atrocities. The church fathers almost all express at one time or another the sense of being acutely embattled. In these conditions, the dramatic development of monasticism provided a radical model of communal fellowship combined with a loathing for the body which exerted a powerful influence upon the church at large.

Christian brotherhood was a social force. It was proclaimed not only on state occasions or before a public schooled to admire the declamatory rhetoric of which Maximus of Tyre, John Chrysostom, Themistius, and Libanius were masters, but also in homilies addressed to congregations of simple worshipers who were, or could be roused to be, fierce in their devotion. The fourth century was, in many ways, an age of fanaticism. This too helps to explain why the classical ideal of friendship was displaced by other, more resonant forms of collective identification.

There is a curious aftermath to the Christian emphasis on brotherhood in the fourth century. Once the language of *caritas* had penetrated the sphere of relations previously denominated by *amicitia* and its cognates, the boundary between the semantic domains of love and friendship became more porous. In subsequent centuries, when a new interest in friendship emerged among Christian writers, poets like Venantius Fortunatus (sixth century) intermingled the vocabulary of *amor* with that of *amicitia* in ways that were foreign to classical practices (e.g. 11.17, 21).[36] There now begin to appear extravagant expressions of devotion between friends that resemble in tone the effusions inspired by Romanticism and other currents of the modern cult of friendship, as opposed to the altogether more restrained and chaste code that appears to prevail throughout classical antiquity. To trace the new turns in the idea of friendship into the middle ages and beyond, however, exceeds the scope of the present volume.

[36] Cf. Rogers 1970: 43; George 1992: 144, 173-4.

Bibliographical essay

Virtually everyone who writes on friendship, ancient or modern, is given to remarking that it has not, until recently, invited substantial attention from scholars. This situation has begun to change, but there are still few comprehensive studies of friendship in the classical world, and virtually nothing at all on the role of friendship in respect to many specific genres and periods (doctoral candidates, take note!).

The most up-to-date and readable survey of friendship in classical antiquity and the ancient Hebrew and Christian traditions is Pizzolato 1993. Dirlmeier 1931 is highly condensed and limited in scope, but contains a large quantity of evidence. Fraisse 1974 is confined to philosophy, and suffers from a disposition to trace a conceptual progress in ancient views that culminates in the modern ideal. Laín Entralgo 1985 is speculative and rather thin on antiquity, since it follows the subject down to modern times. The encyclopedia articles on *philos* by Stählin 1974 and Treu 1972 are compact and useful, but necessarily schematic. None of these works is in English.

Fitzgerald 1996a is a handy collection of studies, which examine the role of friendship in a miscellany of ancient authors; more of this kind of thing is needed. Gill, Postlethwaite, and Seaford (forthcoming) treats reciprocity in general, but there is some good material on friendship from this point of view.

When it comes to particular topics, philosophical treatments of friendship have received the fullest coverage, above all the work of Aristotle. Cooper 1977 remains a classic essay. Price 1989, covering both Plato and Aristotle, is dense but rich. Still on Aristotle, Stern-Gillet 1995 can be recommended as a recent, rather imaginative interpretation, with up-to-date bibliography. Pakaluk (forthcoming) will provide detailed commentary on the argument of *Nicomachean Ethics* 8–9. A great variety of specialized studies, indicated on pp. 67–78, may be consulted with profit.

Outside of philosophy, Homer has perhaps received most attention in relation to the topic of friendship. For a general survey of friendship terms in Homeric epic, one may consult H. Kakridis 1963. For the view that friendship is a purely objective relationship in archaic Greece, see Adkins 1963 (and cf. Donlan 1985). For Homeric friendship as a relationship based rather on affection, see especially Robinson 1990. Turning to the classical period, Blundell 1989 provides a thoughtful and wide-ranging study of friendship in Sophocles; the introductory chapters cover classical materials generally. Goldhill 1986 has a good chapter (with which I disagree) on *philia* in *Antigone*. Several dissertations have been written on friendship in Euripides; for bibliography, see Konstan 1985 on *Electra*. New Comedy is a rich field for friendship; unfortunately, Zucker 1950 is rather superficial.

On friendship in relation to history, Connor 1971 is a classic study of fifth-century BC Athens, with particular (perhaps even excessive) attention to the role of friendship in politics. Two chapters in Millett 1991 consider the place of *philia* in the Athenian economy. Herman 1980 is a fine introduction to kings and their retinues or "Friends" in Hellenistic courts. As for friendship in the Roman Republic, Brunt 1988 is indispensable: he scotches the old idea that *amicitia* represents little more than a political tie, and demonstrates the wide range of affective relations that it designates. Hutter 1978 offers a modern sociological analysis of Greek and Roman politics as grounded in friendship; the book is interesting but not always reliable. As for Christian friendship in the fourth century, C. White 1992 can be recommended as a broad and useful introduction.

On concepts that abut on friendship, Herman 1987 is an intriguing (though in my view flawed) interpretation of relations between foreigners or *xenoi* as an example of ritualized friendship. Joly 1968 is narrowly focussed but interesting on the relation between the verbs *philein* and *agapan*, the latter of which, he shows, is not specific to Christian writers. Halperin 1990 remains invaluable for an understanding of the contrast between *erōs* and *philia* in antiquity. Eernstman 1932 (in Dutch) examines the terms *hetairos*, *epitēdeios*, and *oikeios*, but there is room for much new work on these and other topics such as friends vs. neighbors or relations between age-mates vs. those between *philoi*.

The question of friends vs. flatterers, and along with this the idea of frank speech as the sign of the true friend, are treated in Fitzgerald 1996a (a collection of essays). On the role of the parasite in particular, one may consult Nesselrath 1985, and Damon 1996. On friendship and patronage in Rome, Saller 1982 and P. White 1993 are especially to be recommended.

There are several good treatments of modern friendship from a sociological point of view: I recommend Allan 1989, Reohr 1991, and Cucó Giner 1995 as clear, brief, and comprehensive. The fundamental study of the gift in pre-modern societies by Marcel Mauss (1967, orig. 1923–4) remains fascinating; I have some doubts, however, about the relevance of much anthropological literature to classical antiquity. Silver 1989 and 1990 are highly interesting on the emergence of the modern idea of sentimental friendship in the Scottish Enlightenment.

For modern philosophical interpretations of friendship, Pakaluk 1991 is a handy collection of the classical studies from Plato and Aristotle to Kant and beyond. A good set of recent philosophical papers is reprinted in

Badhwar 1993. Rouner 1994, a set of original essays, is not as consistently illuminating. Blum 1980 is thoughtful and readable. Among popular impressionistic accounts, Alberoni 1984 is fun.

The above works offer an introduction to various aspects of friendship and its role in the classical world. But it is worth repeating that there are many areas that still need to be investigated. I know of nothing that treats friendship in ancient comedy as a whole, and the same is true for friendship in Greek tragedy. A good study of *philoi* in Hellenistic poetry would be valuable; so too, a close examination of friendship in the ancient novels. Dionysius of Halicarnassus is discussed in one of the essays in Fitzgerald 1996a, but any number of historians writing in Greek (including Josephus) are still up for grabs. Despite his central importance for the topic, there is no comprehensive study of friendship in Plutarch.

On the Roman side, there is nothing that deals with *amicitia* in Roman elegy as a whole. Believe it or not, work remains to be done on friendship in Cicero's letters, especially with a view to discriminating his use of terms such as *amicus, familiaris, socius, necessarius,* and the like. Martial and Pliny remain vast unexplored territories. When it comes to late antiquity, the enormous correspondence of Symmachus, who has been undeservedly neglected in this book, would amply repay study from the point of view of friendship. The friends of Roman emperors, and the representation of friendship in panegyrics and discourses on kingship and the like, deserve closer attention. A great deal remains to be done as well on Christian friendship.

It would be easy to continue this list, but as a bibliography of works that do not exist, it is long enough. The field remains wide open.

Bibliography

ABELOVE, H., M. A. BARALE, and D. M. HALPERIN, eds. (1993) *The Lesbian and Gay Studies Reader*. New York

ACOSTA MÉNDEZ, E. (1983) "PHerc. 1089: Filodemo 'Sobre la adulación,'" *Cron. Erc.* 13: 121–38

ADKINS, A. W. H. (1963) "'Friendship' and 'self-sufficiency' in Homer and Aristotle," *CQ* 13: 30–45

    (1972) *Moral Values and Political Behaviour in Ancient Greece: From Homer to the End of the Fifth Century*. London

ALBERONI, F. (1984) *L'amicizia*. Milan

ALFÖLDI, A. (1952) *A Conflict of Ideas in the Late Roman Empire: The Clash Between the Senate and Valentinian I*. Trans. H. Mattingly. Oxford

ALLAN, G. (1989) *Friendship: Developing a Sociological Perspective*. Boulder, CO

ALLEN, R. E. (1991) *The Dialogues of Plato*. Vol. 2. *The Symposium*. New Haven, CT

ALMAGUER, T. (1993) "Chicano men: A cartography of homosexual identity and behavior," in Abelove, Barale, and Halperin 1993: 255–73

ALONSO, A. M. and M. T. KORECK. (1993) "Silences: 'Hispanics,' AIDS, and sexual practices," in Abelove, Barale, and Halperin 1993: 110–26

ALPERN, K. D. (1983) "Aristotle on the friendships of utility and pleasure," *Journal of the History of Philosophy* 21: 303–15

ANDERSON, M. (1971) *Family Structure in Nineteenth Century Lancashire*. Cambridge

ANDERSON, W. (1993) *Barbarian Play: Plautus' Roman Comedy*. Toronto

ANDREWES, A. (1978) "The opposition to Perikles," *JHS* 98: 1–8

ANHALT, E. K. (1993) *Solon the Singer: Politics and Poetics*. Lanham, MD

ANNAS, J. (1977) "Plato and Aristotle on friendship and altruism," *Mind* 86: 532–54

    (1988) "Self-love in Aristotle," *The Southern Journal of Philosophy* 27 (supplement): 1–18

ANNIS, D. B. (1987) "The meaning, value, and duties of friendship," *American Philosophical Quarterly* 24: 349–56

ANTONACCIO, C. M. (1995) *An Archaeology of Ancestors: Tomb Cult and Hero Cult in Early Greece*. Lanham, MD

ARCHIBALD, E. (1992) "Malory's ideal of fellowship," *Renaissance English Studies* n.s. 43 (no. 171): 311–28

ARIETI, J. A. (1985) "Achilles' guilt," *CJ* 80: 193–203

ARMSTRONG, D. (1994) "The addressees of the *Ars Poetica*: Herculaneum, the Pisones and Epicurean protreptic," in J. Strauss Clay, P. Mitsis and A. Schiesaro, eds., *Mega nepios: il ruolo del destinatario nell'epos didascalico = Materiali e Discussioni* 31: 185–230

ARMSTRONG, M. and W. M. CALDER III (1994) "The *damnatio* of Vergil in Theodor Mommsen, *Römische Kaisergeschichte*," *Vergilius* 40: 85–92

ARNAOUTOGLOU, I. (1994) "Associations and patronage in ancient Athens," *Ancient Society* 25: 5–17

ARNHEIM, M. T. W. (1977) *Aristocracy in Greek Society*. London

ARNOTT, W. G. (1970) *"Phormio parasitus*: a study in dramatic methods of characterization," *Greece & Rome* 17: 32–57

ATKINS, E. M. (1990) " 'Domina et regina virtutum': justice and societas in De officiis," *Phronesis* 35: 258–89

BADHWAR, N. K., ed. (1993) *Friendship: A Philosophical Reader*. Ithaca, NY

BAKER, R. J. (1988) "Maecenas and Horace Satires II.8," *CJ* 83: 212–32

BALCH, D. L. (1996) "Political friendship in the historian Dionysius of Halicarnassus, *Roman Antiquities*," in Fitzgerald 1996a: 124–45

BARKAS, J. L. (1985) *Friendship: A Selected, Annotated Bibliography*. New York

BARRETT, D. S. (1981) "The friendship of Achilles and Patroclus," *CB* 57: 87–93

BARTSCH, S. (1994) *Actors in the Audience: Theatricality and Doublespeak from Nero to Hadrian*. Cambridge, MA

BATSTONE, W. (1993) "Logic, rhetoric, and poiesis," *Helios* 20: 143–72

BAUSLAUGH, R. A. (1991) *The Concept of Neutrality in Classical Greece*. Berkeley, CA

BELL, R. R. (1981) *Worlds of Friendship*. Beverly Hills, CA

BELMONT, D. E. (1962) "Early Greek guest-friendship and its role in Homer's *Odyssey*." Princeton: Diss. Princeton University

BENVENISTE, E. (1973 [1969]) *Indo-European Language and Society*. Trans. E. Palmer. London

BLACK, J. D. (1980) *Friendship*. New York

BLUM, L. (1980) *Friendship, Altruism and Morality*. London

BLUNDELL, M. W. (1989) *Helping Friends and Harming Enemies. A Study in Sophocles and Greek Ethics*. Cambridge

BOBIK, J. (1986) "Aquinas on *communicatio*, the foundation of friendship and *caritas*," *Modern Schoolman* 64: 1–18

BODÉÜS, R. (1993) *The Political Dimensions of Aristotle's Ethics*. Trans. J. E. Garrett. Albany, NY

BOLLACK, J. (1975) *La pensée du plaisir*. Paris

BOND, L. M. (1941) "A comparison between human and divine friendship," *Thomist* 3: 54–94

BORZA, E. N. (1990) *In the Shadow of Olympus: The Emergence of Macedon*. Princeton, NJ

BOSWELL, J. (1994) *Same-Sex Unions in Premodern Europe*. New York

BOULARAND, E. (1972) "L'amitié d'après saint Ambroise dans le 'De officiis ministrorum,'" *Bulletin de Littérature Ecclésiastique* 73: 103–23

BOURDIEU, P. (1977 [1972]) *Outline of a Theory of Practice*. Trans. R. Nice. Cambridge

(1984 [1979]) *Distinction: A Social Critique of the Judgement of Taste*. Trans. R. Nice. Cambridge, MA

BOWDITCH, L. (1994) "Horace's poetics of political integrity: Epistle 1.18," *AJP* 115: 409–26

BOWIE, E. (1990) "Miles ludens," in Murray 1990: 221–9

BRAIN, R. (1976) *Friends and Lovers*. New York

BRAY, A. (1990) "Homosexuality and the signs of male friendship in Elizabethan England," *History Workshop Journal* 29: 1–19

BREMMER, J. N. (1980) "An enigmatic Indo-European rite: paederasty," *Arethusa* 13: 279–97

(1990) "Adolescents, *symposion*, and pederasty," in Murray 1990: 135–48

BRESCIA, C. (1955) "La φιλία in Epicuro," *Giornale Italiano di Filologia* 8: 314–32

BRENTON, M. (1974) *Friendship*. New York

BROKATE, C. (1913) "De aliquot Plutarchi libellis." Göttingen: Diss. University of Göttingen

BROWN, P. G. McC. (1992) "Menander, fragments 745 and 746 K-T, Menander's *Kolax*, and parasites and flatterers in Greek comedy," *ZPE* 92: 91–107

BROWNING, C. (1967) "Friendship, particular," in *The New Catholic Encyclopedia*. Vol. 6: 205–6. San Francisco

BRUNT, P. A. (1988) *The Fall of the Roman Republic and Related Essays*. Oxford

BUDÉ, G. DE, ed. (1919) *Dionis Chrysostomi Orationes*. Vol. 2. Leipzig

BUFFIÈRE, F. (1980) *Eros adolescent: la pédérastie dans la Grèce antique*. Paris

BURKERT, W. (1991) "Oriental symposia: contrasts and parallels," in Slater 1991: 7–24

BURTON, J. B. (1995) *Theocritus' Urban Mimes: Mobility, Gender, and Patronage*. Berkeley, CA

CAIAZZA, E., ed. (1993) *Plutarco: Precetti politici*. Naples

CALHOUN, D. H. (1989) "Friendship and self-love in Aristotle's ethics." Evanston: Diss. Northwestern University

CAMERON, A. (1981) "Asclepiades' girl friends," in H. P. Foley, ed., *Reflections of Women in Antiquity*, 275–302. New York.

CAMPBELL, D. A. (1982, 1988) *Greek Lyric*. Vols. 1 and 2. Cambridge, MA

CAPASSO, M., ed. (1988) *Carneisco: Il secondo libro del Filista (PHerc. 1027)*. Naples

CARNEY, E. (1995) "Women and *basileia*: legitimacy and female political action in Macedonia," *CJ* 90: 367–91

CARRIER, J. M. (1985) "Mexican male bisexuality," in F. Klein and T. J. Wolf, eds., *Bisexualities: Theory and Research*, 75–85. New York

CARRIÈRE, J.-C. (1984) *Plutarque: Oeuvres morales.* Vol. 11.2. Paris

CARTLEDGE, P. (1987) *Agesilaos and the Crisis of Sparta.* London and Baltimore, MD

(1993) *The Greeks: A Portrait of Self and Others.* Oxford

CARTLEDGE, P., P. MILLETT, and S. TODD, eds. (1990) *Nomos: Essays in Athenian Law, Politics and Society.* Cambridge

CARTLEDGE, P., P. MILLETT, and S. VON REDEN, eds. (forthcoming) *Kosmos: Order, Conflict and Community in Classical Athens.* Cambridge

CARY, E., trans. (1939, 1945) *The Roman Antiquities of Dionysius of Halicarnassus.* Vols. 2 and 5. Cambridge, MA

CASSIDY, E. (1992) "The recovery of the classical ideal of friendship in Augustine's portrayal of *caritas,*" in T. Finan, ed., *The Relationship between Neoplatonism and Christianity,* 127–40. Dublin

CASSIRER, E. (1953) *The Philosophy of Symbolic Forms.* Trans. R. Mannheim. Vol. 1: *Language.* New Haven, CT

CERRI, G. (1968) "La terminologia sociopolitica di Teognide: I. l'opposizione semantica tra ἀγαθός-ἐσθλός e κακός-δειλός," *QUCC* 6: 7–32

CHADWICK, H. (1959) *The Sentences of Sextus: A Contribution to the History of Early Christian Ethics.* Cambridge

CHAPLAIS, P. (1994) *Piers Gaveston: Edward II's Adoptive Brother.* Oxford

CHELUNE, G. J. and associates. (1979) *Self-Disclosure: Origins, Patterns, and Implications of Openness in Interpersonal Relationships.* San Francisco

CHITTY, D. J., trans. (1975) *The Letters of St. Antony the Great.* Fairacres, Oxford

CHONG, K.-C. (1984) "Egoism, desires, and friendship," *American Philosophical Quarterly* 21: 349–57

CLARK, E. (1979) *Jerome, Chrysostom, and Friends.* New York and Toronto

CLARK, M. E. and J. S. REUBEL. (1985) "Philosophy and rhetoric in Cicero's *Pro Milone,*" *Rheinisches Museum* 128: 57–72

CLARKE, W. M. (1978) "Achilles and Patroclus in love," *Hermes* 106: 381–96

CLAY, J. STRAUSS. (1983) *The Wrath of Athena: Gods and Men in the Odyssey.* Princeton, NJ

CLOUD, D. (1989) "The client-patron relationship: Emblem and reality in Juvenal's first book," in Wallace-Hadrill 1989: 205–18

COHEN, D. (1991) *Law, Sexuality, and Society: The Enforcement of Morals in Classical Athens.* Cambridge

COHEN, E. E. (1992) *Athenian Economy and Society: A Banking Perspective.* Princeton, NJ

COHEN, Y. A. (1961) "Patterns of friendship," in Y. A. Cohen, ed., *Social Structure and Personality: A Casebook,* 351–86. New York

COLDSTREAM, J. N. (1984) *The Formation of the Greek Polis: Aristotle and Archaeology.* Düsseldorf-Rheinisch-Westfälische Akademie der Wissenschaften Vorträge G 272

COLEMAN, K. M. (1988) *Statius Silvae IV.* Oxford

COLEMAN-NORTON, P. R. (1930) "St. Chrysostom and the Greek philosophers," *CP* 25: 305–17

CONNOR, W. R. (1971) *The New Politicians of Fifth-Century Athens.* Princeton, NJ [repr. with new intro. 1992]

COOPER, F. and S. MORRIS. (1990) "Dining in round buildings," in Murray 1990: 66–85

COOPER, J. M. (1977) "Aristotle on the forms of friendship," *Review of Metaphysics* 30: 619–48

(1990) "Political animals and civic friendship," in Patzig 1990: 220–41

COTTON, H. (1984) "The concept of *indulgentia* under Trajan," *Chiron* 14: 245–66

COYLE, A. F. (1955) "Cicero's De officiis and De officiis ministrorum of St. Ambrose," *Franciscan Studies* 15: 224–56

CROOK, J. (1955) *Consilium Principis: Imperial Councils and Counsellors from Augustus to Diocletian.* Cambridge

CUCÓ GINER, J. (1995) *La amistad: Perspectiva antropológica.* Barcelona

CUMMINS, W. J. (1981) "*Eros, epithumia,* and *philia* in Plato," *Apeiron* 15: 10–18

DAMON, C. (1996) *The Mask of the Parasite: A Pathology of Roman Patronage.* Ann Arbor, MI

D'ARMS, J. (1990) "The Roman *convivium* and equality," in Murray 1990: 308–20

DEDEK, J. F. (1967) "Friendship with God," in *The New Catholic Encyclopedia.* Vol. 6: 207–8. San Francisco

DEFERRARI, R. J., ed. and trans. (1926, 1928) *Saint Basil: The Letters.* 2 vols. Cambridge, MA

DEFERRARI, R. J., trans. (1952) "A sermon on the Life of St. Honoratus," in R. J. Deferrari, ed. *Early Christian Biographies,* 361–94. Washington, DC

DEMAND, N. (1994) *Birth, Death, and Motherhood in Classical Greece.* Baltimore, MD and London

DENTZER, J.-M. (1982) *Le motif du banquet couché dans le proche-orient et le monde grec du VIIe au IVe siècle avant J.-C.* Rome

DERRIDA, J. (1982 [1972]) *Margins of Philosophy.* Trans. A. Bass. Chicago

(1993) "Politics of friendship," *American Imago* 50: 353–91

DE WITT, N. W. (1935) "Parresiastic poems of Horace," *CP* 30: 312–19

DIELS, H. (1916) *Philodemus Über die Götter: Drittes Buch, I. Griechischer Text,* in *Abhandlungen der königlich preussischen Akademie der Wissenschaften.* Berlin (1917)

(1916a) *Philodemus Über die Götter: Drittes Buch, II. Erläuterung des Textes,* in *Abhandlungen der königlich preussischen Akademie der Wissenschaften.* Berlin (1917)

DILLON, J. and J. HERSHBELL, ed. and trans. (1991) *Iamblichus: On the Pythagorean Way of Life.* Atlanta, GA

DIRLMEIER, F. (1931) *ΦΙΛΟΣ und ΦΙΛΙΑ im vorhellenistischen Griechentum.* Munich: Inaugural-Dissertation, Ludwig-Maximilians-Universität

DIXON, S. (1993) "The meaning of gift and debt in the Roman elite," *Echos du Monde Classique/Classical Views* 37: 451–64

DONLAN, W. J. (1980) *The Aristocratic Ideal in Ancient Greece: Attitudes of Superiority from Homer to the End of the Fifth Century B.C.* Lawrence, KA

(1985) "*Pistos philos hetairos,*" in Figueira and Nagy 1985: 223–44

(1985a) "The social groups of dark age Greece," *CP* 80: 293–308

(1989) "The pre-state community in Greece," *SO* 64: 5–29

DOVER, K. J. (1964) "The poetry of Archilochus," in *Entretiens Hardt* 10: 181–212. Geneva

(1971) *Theocritus: Select Poems.* London

DREWS, R. (1983) *Basileus: The Evidence for Kingship in Geometric Greece.* New Haven

DUBOIS, P. (1995) *Sappho is Burning.* Chicago

DUCK, S. (1983) *Friends, for Life: The Psychology of Close Relationships.* New York

DUNBABIN, K. M. D. (1991) "Triclinium and stibadium," in Slater 1991: 121–48

DYCK, A. R. (1983) *Epimerismi homerici.* Berlin

DZIAZKO, K. (1898) *P. Terentius Afer: Phormio.* 3rd ed. Rev. E. Hauler. Leipzig

EBELING, H. (1963 [orig. 1880–5]) *Lexicum homericum.* 2 vols. Hildesheim

ECO, U. (1976) *A Theory of Semiotics.* Bloomington, IL

EERNSTMAN, J. P. A. (1932) "Οἰκεῖος, Ἑταῖρος, Ἐπιτηδεῖος, Φίλος: Bijdrage de kennis van de terminologie der vriendschap bij de Grieken." Gröningen: Diss. University of Utrecht

EICHENBAUM, L. and S. ORBACH. (1988) *Between Women: Love, Envy, and Competition in Women's Friendships.* New York

EISENSTADT, S. N. and L. RONIGER. (1984) *Patrons, Clients and Friends: Interpersonal Relations and the Structure of Trust in Society.* Cambridge

ELSE, G. F. (1963) *Aristotle's Poetics: The Argument.* Cambridge, MA

ENGLAND, E. B., ed. (1921) *The Laws of Plato.* 2 vols. Manchester

ENRIGHT, D. J. and D. RAWLINSON, eds. (1991) *The Oxford Book of Friendship.* Oxford

ERBSE, H., ed. (1969–88) *Scholia graeca in Homeri Iliadem.* Berlin

EVANS, K. G. (1996) "Friendship in Greek documentary papyri and inscriptions: a survey," in Fitzgerald 1996a: 185–207

EVANS-PRITCHARD, E. E. (1940) *The Nuer.* Oxford

FABRE, P. (1949) *Saint Paulin de Nole et l'amitié chrétienne.* Paris

FARAONE, C. A. (1994) "Deianira's mistake and the demise of Heracles: erotic magic in Sophocles' *Trachiniae,*" *Helios* 21: 115–35

FIGUEIRA, T. J. and G. NAGY, eds. (1985) *Theognis of Megara: Poetry and the Polis.* Baltimore, MD

FINLEY, M. I. (1977 [1954]) *The World of Odysseus.* 2nd edn. London

(1985) *The Ancient Economy.* 2nd edn. London

(1986) *The Use and Abuse of History.* Rev. edn. New York

FISCHER, C. S. (1982) *To Dwell Among Friends: Personal Networks in Town and City.* Chicago

FISHER, N. R. E., ed. (1976) *Social Values in Classical Athens.* Toronto and London

FISKE, A. M. (1955) "The survival and development of the ancient concept of friendship in the Early Middle Ages." New York: Diss. Fordham University

(1970) *Friends and Friendship in the Monastic Tradition.* Cuernavaca, Mexico (Cuaderno 51)

FITZGERALD, J. T., ed. (1996) *Friendship, Flattery, and Frankness of Speech: Studies in Friendship in the New Testament World.* Leiden

(1996a) *Greco-Roman Perspectives on Friendship.* Atlanta, GA

FORNARA, C. W. and L. J. SAMONS II (1991) *Athens from Cleisthenes to Pericles.* Berkeley, CA

FORTENBAUGH, W. W. (1984) *Quellen zur Ethik Theophrasts.* Amsterdam

FORTENBAUGH, W. W., P. M. HUBY, R. W. SHARPLES, and D. GUTAS, eds. (1992) *Theophrastus of Eresus: Sources for his Life, Writings, Thought and Influence.* Vol. 2. Leiden

FOUCAULT, M. (1984) *Histoire de la sexualité,* vol. 2: *L'usage des plaisirs.* Paris. English trans. by R. Hurley: *The History of Sexuality,* vol. 2: *The Use of Pleasure.* 1985. New York

(1984a) *Histoire de la sexualité,* vol. 3: *Le souci de soi.* Paris. English trans. by R. Hurley: *The History of Sexuality,* vol. 3: *The Care of the Self.* 1986. New York

FOWLER, H. N., trans. (1927) *Plutarch's Moralia.* Vol. 10. Cambridge, MA

FRAISSE, J. C. (1974) *Philia: La notion d'amitié dans la philosophie antique.* Paris

FRIEDMAN, M. (1993) *What Are Friends For? Feminist Perspectives on Personal Relationships and Moral Theory.* Ithaca, NY

FROST, F. J. (1976) "Tribal politics and the civic state," *AJAH* 1: 66–75

FURBANK, P. N. (1995) "Yours intimately" (review of Kermode and Kermode 1995) *TLS* 4814 (7 July): 36

GALLANT, T. W. (1991) *Risk and Survival in Ancient Greece: Reconstructing the Rural Domestic Economy.* Cambridge

GALLO, I. and E. PETTINE, eds. (1988) *Plutarco: Como distinguere l'adulatore dall' amico.* Naples

GANTAR, K. (1976) "La préhistoire d' *amicus sibi* chez Horace," *Les Études Classiques* 44: 209–21

GARGIULO, T. (1981) "PHerc. 222: Filodemo sull' adulazione," *Cron. Erc.* 11: 103–27

GARNSEY, P. (1988) *Famine and Food Supply in the Graeco-Roman World: Responses to Risk and Crisis.* Cambridge

GEDDES, A. G. (1984) "Who's who in Homeric society," *CQ* 34: 17–36

GEHRKE, H.-J. (1984) "Zwischen Freundschaft und Programm: politische Parteiung im Athen des 5. Jahrhunderts v. Chr," *Historische Zeitschrift* 239: 529–64

GELZER, M. (1969 [1912]) *The Roman Nobility.* Trans. Robin Seager. New York

GEMELLI, B. (1978) "L'amicizia in Epicuro," *Sandalion* 1: 59–72

GEORGE, J. W. (1992) *Venantius Fortunatus: A Latin Poet in Merovingian Gaul.* Oxford

GERNET, L. (1981 [1968]). *The Anthropology of Ancient Greece*. Trans. J. Hamilton and B. Nagy. Baltimore, MD

GHINATTI, F. (1970) *I gruppi politici ateniesi fino alle guerre persiane*. Rome

GIANNANTONI, G., ed. (1983–5) *Socraticorum Reliquiae*. 4 vols. Naples

GIBBS, J. L., Jr. (1962) "Compensatory blood-brotherhood: a comparative analysis of institutionalized friendship in two African societies," *Proceedings of the Minnesota Academy of Science* 30: 67–74

GIL, L. (1981–3) "El 'alazón' y sus variantes," *Estudios Clásicos* 86: 39–57

GILL, C. (1994) "Peace of mind and being yourself: Panaetius to Plutarch," *ANRW* II.36.7: 4599–4640

(forthcoming) "Altruism or reciprocity in Greek ethical philosophy?," in Gill *et al.*

GILL, C., N. POSTLETHWAITE and R. SEAFORD, eds. (forthcoming) *Reciprocity in Ancient Greece*. Oxford

GLAD, C. E. (1992) "Early Christian and Epicurean psychagogy. Paul and Philodemus." Providence: Diss. Brown University

(1995) *Paul and Philodemus: Adaptability in Epicurean and Early Christian Psychagogy*. Leiden

GLIDDEN, D. K. (1981) "The *Lysis* on loving one's own" *CQ* 31: 39–59

GOITEIN, S. D. (1971) "Formal friendship in the medieval Near East," *Proceedings of the American Philosophical Society* 115: 484–9

GOLD, B. K. (1987) *Literary Patronage in Greece and Rome*. Chapel Hill, NC

GOLDEN, M. and P. TOOHEY, eds. (1996) *Inventing Ancient Culture? Historicism, Periodization and the "New Classics."* London

GOLDHILL, S. D. (1986, [corr. repr. 1988]) *Reading Greek Tragedy*. Cambridge

GÓMEZ MUNTÁN, J. L. (1966) "La concepción platonica del amor según el Lysis," *Pensamiento* 22: 23–53

GOULD, G. (1993) *The Desert Fathers on Monastic Community*. Oxford

GRAHAM, A. J. (1995) "The *Odyssey*, history, and women," in B. Cohen, ed. *The Distaff Side: Representing the Female in Homer's Odyssey*, 3–16. New York

GRAINGER, J. D. (1990) *The Cities of Seleucid Syria*. Oxford

GRAVER, M. (1995) "Therapeutic Reading and Seneca's Moral Epistles." Providence: Diss. Brown University

GRAY, V. (1989) *The Character of Xenophon's Hellenica*. London and Baltimore, MD

GREENE, E. (1994) "Apostrophe and women's erotics in the poetry of Sappho," *TAPA* 124: 41–56

GRUEN, E. S. (1984) *The Hellenistic World and the Coming of Rome*. Vol. 1. Berkeley, CA

HADEN, J. (1983) "Friendship in Plato's *Lysis*," *Review of Metaphysics* 37: 327–56

HÄGG, R., ed. (1983) *The Greek Renaissance of the Eighth Century* BC: *Tradition and Innovation*. Stockholm

HÄGG, T. (forthcoming) "A professor and his slave: conventions and values in the *Life of Aesop*," in P. Bilde, T. Engberg-Pedersen, L. Hannestad, and J. Zahle, eds., *Conventional Values of the Hellenistic World*. Aarhus

HALL, E. (1993) "Political and cosmic turbulence in Euripides' *Orestes*," in A. H. Sommerstein, S. Halliwell, J. Henderson, and B. Zimmermann, eds., *Tragedy, Comedy and the Polis*, 263–85. Bari

HALPERIN, D. M. (1985) "Platonic *erōs* and what men call love," *AP* 5: 161–204

(1990) *One Hundred Years of Homosexuality and Other Essays on Greek Love*. New York

HAMILTON, J. R. (1969) *Plutarch Alexander: A Commentary*. Oxford

HANDS, A. R. (1968) *Charities and Social Aid in Greece and Rome*. London

HANSEN, M. H. (1991) *The Athenian Democracy in the Age of Demosthenes: Structure, Principles and Ideology*. Trans. J. A. Crook. Oxford

HANSEN, M. H., ed. (1993) *The Ancient Greek City-State*. Copenhagen

HANSEN, P. A., ed. (1983) *Carmina epigraphica graeca saeculorum VIII–V a. Chr. n.* Berlin

HARDIE, W. F. R. (1980) *Aristotle's Ethical Theory*. 2nd edn. Oxford

HARKINS, P. W., trans. (1963) *Galen on the Passions and Errors of the Soul*. Columbus, OH

HARMON, A. M., ed. and trans. (1936) *Lucian*. Vol. 5. Cambridge, MA

HARNACK, A. (1905) *The Mission and Expansion of Christianity in the First Three Centuries*. Trans. J. Moffatt. Vol. 2. London

HARTOG, F. (1988 [1980; rev. ed. 1992]) *The Mirror of Herodotus: The Representation of the Other in the Writing of History*. Trans. J. Lloyd. Berkeley, CA

HAUCK, F. (1928) "Die Freundschaft bei den Griechen und im Neuen Testament," *Festgabe Th. Zahn*, 211–28. Leipzig

HEATH, M. (1987) *The Poetics of Greek Tragedy*. Stanford, CA

HECKEL, W. (1992) *The Marshals of Alexander's Empire*. London

HENSE, O., ed. (1909) *Teletis reliquiae*. 2nd edn. Tübingen

HERMAN, G. (1980–81) "The 'friends' of the early Hellenistic rulers: servants or officials?," *Talanta* 12/13: 103–49

(1987) *Ritualised Friendship and the Greek City*. Cambridge

HEUBECK, A., S. WEST, and J. B. HAINSWORTH, eds. (1988) *A Commentary on Homer's Odyssey*. Vol. 1. Oxford

HEUBECK, A. and A. HOEKSTRA, eds. (1989) *A Commentary on Homer's Odyssey*. Vol. 2. Oxford

HEUSS, A. (1956) "Cicero und Matius," *Historia* 5: 53–73

HEYLBUT, G. (1889). *Aspasii in Ethica nicomachea quae supersunt commentaria*. Berlin (*CAG* 19)

HIRSCH, S. W. (1985) *The Friendship of the Barbarians: Xenophon and the Persian Empire*. Hanover, NH

HOLDER, A., ed. (1967 [orig. 1894]) *Pomponi Porfyrionis commentum in Horatium Flaccum*. Hildesheim

HOLZBERG, N. (1994) "Der griechische Briefroman. Versuch einer Gattungstypologie," in N. Holzberg, ed., *Der griechische Briefroman: Gattungstypologie und Textanalyse*, 1–52. Tübingen

HOOKER, J. "Homeric φίλος," *Glotta* 65: 44–65

(1989) "Homer, Patroclus, Achilles," *SO* 64: 30–5

HORSFALL, N. (1981) *Poets and Patron: Maecenas, Horace and the Georgics, Once More*. North Ryde

HUMMEL, P. (1988) "*Philos/pistos*: étude d'un cas de complémentarité métrique," *Informations Grammaticales* 36: 17–9

HUMPHREYS, S. C. (1978) *Anthropology and the Greeks*. London

(1986) "Kinship patterns in the Athenian courts," *GRBS* 27: 57–91

HUNTER, R. L. (1985) "Horace on friendship and free speech (*Epistles* 1.18 and *Satires* 1.4)," *Hermes* 113: 480–90

HUTSON, L. (1994) *The Usurer's Daughter: Male Friendship and Fictions of Women in Sixteenth-Century England*. London

HUTTER, H. (1978) *Politics as Friendship: The Origins of Classical Notions of Politics in the Theory and Practice of Friendship*. Waterloo, Ont.

IRWIN, T., trans. (1985) *Nicomachean Ethics*. Indianapolis, IN

(1990) "The good of political activity," in Patzig 1990: 73–98

JAEGER, C. S. (1991) "L'Amour des rois: structure sociale d'une forme de sensibilité aristocratique," *Annales ESC* 46 no. 3: 547–71

JAEKEL, S., ed. (1964) *Menandri sententiae; Comparatio Menandri et Philistionis*. Leipzig

JAMESON, M. (1990) "Private space and the Greek city," in Murray and Price 1990: 171–95

JOCELYN, H. D., ed. (1969) *The Tragedies of Ennius*. Cambridge

JOHNSON, T. S. (1994) "Horace, *C.* IV.12, Vergilius at the symposion," *Vergilius* 40: 49–66

JOLY, R. (1968) *Le vocabulaire chrétien de l'amour est-il original? Φιλεῖν et ἀγαπᾶν dans le grec antique*. Brussels

JOURARD, S. M. (1971) *Self Disclosure*. New York

KAHN, C. H. (1981) "Aristotle and altruism," *Mind* 90: 20–40

KAKRIDIS, H. J. (1963) *La notion de l'amitié et de l'hospitalité chez Homère*. Thessaloniki

KAKRIDIS, J. T. (1949) *Homeric Researches*. Lund

KENNEDY, R. (1986) "Women's friendships on Crete: a psychological perspective," in J. Dubisch, ed. *Gender and Power in Rural Greece*, 121–38. Princeton, NJ

KENNY, M. (1962) *A Spanish Tapestry: Town and Country in Castile*. Bloomington, IN

KERMODE, F. and A. KERMODE, eds. (1995) *The Oxford Book of Letters*. Oxford

KILPATRICK, R. S. (1986) *The Poetry of Friendship: Horace, Epistles I*. Edmonton, Alta

KLAUCK, H.-J. (1991) "Kirche als Freundesgemeinschaft? Auf Spurensuche in Neuen Testament," *Münchener Theologische Zeitschrift* 42: 1–14

KLEIN, E. (1957) "Studien zum Problem der 'römischen' und 'griechischen' Freundschaft." Freiburg: Diss. Albert-Ludwigs-Universität

KONSTAN, D. (1985) *"Philia* in Euripides' *Electra,"* *Philologus* 129: 176–85

(1993) "Friends and lovers in ancient Greece," *Syllecta Classica* 4: 1–12

(1994) *Sexual Symmetry: Love in The Ancient Novel and Related Genres.* Princeton, NJ

(1994/5) "Friendship and the state: the context of Cicero's *De amicitia,"* *Hyperboreus* 2: 1–16

(1995) "Patrons and friends," *CP* 90: 328–42

(1995a) *Greek Comedy and Ideology.* New York

(1996) "Greek friendship," *AJP* 117: 71–94

(1996a) "Friendship, frankness and flattery," in Fitzgerald 1996: 7–19

(1996b) "Problems in the history of Christian friendship," *Journal of Early Christian Studies* 4: 87–113

(forthcoming) "Reciprocity and friendship," in Gill *et al.* forthcoming

KRAUT, R. (1989) *Aristotle on the Human Good.* Princeton, NJ

KRISTEVA, J. (1994) "Entrevista," *Babelia (Revista de cultura de El País)* 148 (20 August): 2–3

KROLL, W. (1933) *Kultur der ciceronischen Zeit.* Vol. 1. Leipzig

KURKE, L. (1991) *The Traffic in Praise: Pindar and the Poetics of Social Economy.* Ithaca, NY

KYTZLER, B. (1960) "Matius und Cicero," *Historia* 9: 96–121

LAFLEUR, R. A. (1979) *"Amicitia* and the unity of Juvenal's first book," *ICS* 4: 158–77

LAÍN ENTRALGO, P. (1985) *Sobre la amistad.* Madrid

LANCASTER, R. N. (1988) "Subject honor and object shame: the construction of male homosexuality and stigma in Nicaragua," *Ethnology* 28.2: 111–26.

LANDFESTER, M. (1966) *Das griechische Nomen "Philos."* Hildesheim = Spudasmata 11

LA PENNA, A. (1983) "Lettura del nono libro dell'Eneide," in M. Gigante, ed. *Lecturae vergilianae.* Vol. 3: 301–40. Naples

LARDINOIS, A. (1994) "Subject and circumstance in Sappho's poetry," *TAPA* 124: 57–84

LA ROCHEFOUCAULD, F., duc de (1964) *Oeuvres complètes.* Ed. L. Martin-Chauffier. Paris

LATTIMORE, R., trans. (1951) *Homer: The Iliad.* Chicago

LEACH, E. R. (1968) *A Runaway World?* London

LEGON, R. P. (1981) *Megara: The Political History of a Greek City-State to 336 B.C.* Ithaca, NY

LEISEGANG, I. (1926–30) *Philonis Alexandrini opera quae supersunt.* Vol. 7: Indices. Berlin

LESKY, A. (1976 [1963]) *Historia de la literatura griega.* Trans. J. M. Díaz Regañón and B. Romero. Madrid

LESSES, G. (1986) "Plato's *Lysis* and Irwin's Socrates," *International Studies in Philosophy* 18: 33–43

(1993) "Austere friends: the Stoics and friendship," *Apeiron* 26: 57–75

LEVI, A. (1950) "La teoria della φιλία nel *Liside*," *Giornale di Metafisica* 5: 285–96

LEWIS, J. M. (1985) "Eros and the *polis* in Theognis book II," in Figueira and Nagy 1985: 197–222

LEWIS, N. (1986) *Greeks in Ptolemaic Egypt: Case Studies in the Social History of the Hellenistic World.* Oxford

LISSARRAGUE, F. (1990 [1986]) *The Aesthetics of the Greek Banquet: Images of Wine and Ritual.* Trans. A. Szegedy-Maszak. Princeton

LITTLE, G. (1993) *Friendship: Being Ourselves with Others.* Melbourne

LLOYD, G. E. R. (1966) *Polarity and Analogy: Two Types of Argumentation in Early Greek Thought.* Cambridge [repr. Bristol 1987]

LONG, A. A. and D. N. SEDLEY, eds. (1987) *The Hellenistic Philosophers.* Vol. 1. Cambridge

LONGO AURICCHIO, F. (1986) "Sulla concezione filodemea dell' adulazione," *Cron. Erc.* 16: 79–91

LORD, A. B. (1960) *The Singer of Tales.* Cambridge, MA

LUALDI, M. (1974) *Il problema della philia e il Liside platonico.* Milan

LUFTIG, V. (1993) *Seeing Together: Friendship between the Sexes in English Writing, from Mill to Woolf.* Stanford, CA

LYNCH, J. J. (1977) *The Broken Heart: The Medical Consequences of Loneliness.* New York

MACDOWELL, D. M., ed. (1990) *Demosthenes: Against Meidias (Oration 21).* Oxford

MACINTYRE, A. (1984) *After Virtue: A Study in Moral Theory.* 2nd edn. Notre Dame, IN

MADIGAN, A. (1985) "*EN* IX 8: beyond egoism and altruism," *The Modern Schoolman* 62: 1–20

MAGAGNA, V. (1991) *Communities of Grain.* Ithaca, NY

MALINOWSKI, B. (1922) *Argonauts of the Western Pacific.* London

MANVILLE, P. B. (1990) *The Origins of Citizenship in Ancient Athens.* Princeton, NJ

MARKUS, R. A. (1990) *The End of Ancient Christianity.* Cambridge

MARQUARDT, I., ed. (1884) *Claudii Galeni Pergameni scripta minora.* Vol. 1. Leipzig

MAUSS, M. (1967 [1923/24]) *The Gift: Form and Functions of Exchange in Archaic Society.* Trans. I. Cunnison. New York

MCEVOY, J. (1986) "*Anima una et cor unum*: friendship and spiritual unity in Augustine," *Recherches de Théologie Ancienne et Médiévale* 53: 40–92

MCGUIRE, B. P. (1988) *Friendship & Community: The Monastic Experience.* Kalamazoo = Cistercian Studies 95

MCKECHNIE, P. (1989) *Outsiders in the Greek Cities in the Fourth Century B.C.* London and New York

MCKERLIE, D. (1991) "Friendship, self-love, and concern for others in Aristotle's Ethics," *AP* 11: 85–101

MCNAMARA, M. A. (1958) *Friendship in Saint Augustine*. Fribourg

MEILAENDER, G. (1994) "When Harry and Sally read the *Nicomachean Ethics*: friendship between men and women," in Rouner 1994: 183–96

MICHELS, A. K. (1944) "Παρρησία and the satire of Horace," *CP* 39: 173–7

MILLAR, F. (1984) "The political character of the classical Roman republic, 200–151 BC," *JRS* 74: 1–19

(1986) "Politics, persuasion and the people before the Social War, 150–90 BC," *JRS* 76: 1–11

(1989) "Political power in mid-republican Rome: *curia* or *comitium*?" Rev. of K. A. Raaflaub, ed., *Social Struggles in Archaic Rome* (Los Angeles 1986) and K.-J. Hölkeskamp, *Die Entstehung der Nobilität* (Stuttgart 1987). *JRS* 79: 138–50

(1993) "The Greek city in the Roman period," in Hansen 1993: 232–60

(1995) "The Roman *libertus* and civic freedom," *Arethusa* 28: 99–105

MILLER, S. (1983) *Men and Friendship*. Boston

MILLER, W., trans. (1914) *Xenophon: Cyropaedia*. 2 vols. Cambridge, MA

MILLETT, P. (1984) "Hesiod and his world," *Proceedings of the Cambridge Philological Society* n.s. 30: 84–116

(1989) "Patronage and its avoidance in classical Athens," in Wallace-Hadrill 1989: 15–47

(1990) "Sale, credit and exchange in Athenian law and society," in Cartledge, Millett, and Todd 1990: 167–94

(1991) *Lending and Borrowing in Ancient Athens*. Cambridge

MILLGRAM, E. (1987) "Aristotle on making other selves," *Canadian Journal of Philosophy* 17: 361–76

MITCHELL, A. C. (1992) "The social function of friendship in Acts 2:44–47 and 4:32–37," *Journal of Biblical Literature* 111: 255–72

MITSIS, P. (1987) "Epicurus on friendship and altruism," *Oxford Studies in Ancient Philosophy* 5: 127–53

(1988) *Epicurus' Ethical Theory. The Pleasures of Invulnerability*. Ithaca, NY

MOLTMANN, J. (1994) "Open friendship: Aristotelian and Christian concepts of friendship," in Rouner 1994: 29–42

MOMIGLIANO, A. (1973) "Freedom of speech in antiquity," in P. P. Wiener, ed., *Dictionary of the History of Ideas: Studies of Selected Pivotal Ideas*. Vol. 2: 252–63. New York

MOMMSEN, T. (1992) *Römische Kaisergeschichte nach den Vorlesungs-Mitschriften von Sebastian und Paul Hensel 1882/86*. Ed. B. and A. Demandt. Munich

MOORE, M. B. (1987) "The Amasis Painter and Exekias: approaches to Narrative," in *Papers on the Amasis Painter and His World: Colloquium J. Paul Getty Museum*, 153–67. Malibu, CA

MORAVCSIK, J. (1988) "The perils of friendship and conceptions of the self," in J. Dancy, J. M. E. Moravcsik, and C. C. W. Taylor, eds., *Human Agency: Language, Duty, and Value*, 132–51. Stanford, CA

MORISSON, J. V. (1994) "A key topos in Thucydides: the comparison of cities and individuals," *AJP* 115: 525–41

MORRIS, I. (1992) *Death-Ritual and Social Structure in Classical Antiquity.* Cambridge

MUÑOZ MOLINA, A. (1987) *El invierno en Lisboa.* Barcelona

MURRAY, O. (1983) "The Greek symposion in history," in E. Gabba, ed. *Tria corda: Scritti in onore di Arnaldo Momigliano,* 257–72. Como

   (1983a) "The symposion as social organisation," in Hägg 1983: 195–9

   (1991) "War and the symposium," in Slater 1991: 83–103

MURRAY, O., ed. (1990) *Sympotica: A Symposium on the Symposion.* Oxford [repr. with add. 1994]

MURRAY, O. and S. PRICE, eds. (1990) *The Greek City from Homer to Alexander.* Oxford

MUSTI, D. (1984) "Syria and the East," in Walbank *et al.* 1984: 175–220

NAGEL, T. (1970) *The Possibility of Altruism.* Oxford

NAGY, G. (1979) *The Best of the Achaeans: Concepts of the Hero in Archaic Greek Poetry.* Baltimore, MD

   (1985) "Theognis and Megara: a poet's vision of his city," in Figueira and Nagy 1985: 22–81

   (1990) *Pindar's Homer: The Lyric Possession of an Epic Past.* Baltimore, MD

NESSELRATH, H.-G. (1985) *Lukians Parasitendialog: Untersuchungen und Kommentar.* Berlin

   (1990) *Die attische mittlere Komödie.* Berlin

NEUHAUSEN, K. A. (1975) "Zu Cassians Traktat De amicitia (Coll. 16)," in C. Gnilka and W. Schetter, eds., *Studien zur Literatur der Spätantike,* 181–218. Bonn

NIMIS, S. A. (1986) "The language of Achilles: Construction vs. representation," *Classical World* 79: 217–25

   (1987) *Narrative Semiotics in the Epic Tradition: The Simile.* Bloomington, IL

NORRIS, F. W., ed. (1991) *Faith Gives Fullness to Reasoning: The Five Theological Orations of Gregory Nazianzen.* Trans. L. Wickham and F. Williams. Leiden

NUSSBAUM, M. C. (1986) *The Fragility of Goodness.* Cambridge

   (1994a) "Poetic justice: a reply to Nancy Sherman," *Internationale Zeitschrift für Philosophie* 2: 220–38

   (1994b) *The Therapy of Desire: Theory and Practice in Hellenistic Ethics.* Princeton, NJ

OBER, J. (1989) *Mass and Elite in Democratic Athens: Rhetoric, Ideology, and the Power of the People.* Princeton, NJ

O'CONNOR, D. K. (1989) "The invulnerable pleasures of Epicurean friendship," *GRBS* 30: 165–86

OLIENSIS, E. (1995) "Life after publication: Horace *Epistles* 1.20," *Arethusa* 28: 209–24

OLIVIERI, A., ed. (1914) *Philodemi Περὶ παρρησίας.* Leipzig

ONIANS, R. B. (1954) *The Origins of European Thought about the Body, the Mind, the Soul, the World, Time, and Fate.* 2nd edn. Cambridge

OSBORNE, R. (1985) *Demos: The Discovery of Classical Attika.* Cambridge

(1990) "The *demos* and its divisions in classical Athens," in Murray and Price 1990: 265–93

OXLEY, H. G. (1978) *Mateship in Local Organization: A Study of Egalitarianism, Stratification, Leadership, and Amenities Projects in a Semi-Industrial Community of Inland New South Wales*. 2nd. edn. Brisbane

PAGE, D. L. (1962) *Poetae Melici Graeci*. Oxford

PAINE, R. (1969) "Anthropological approaches to friendship," *Humanities* 6: 139–59

(1969a) "In search of friendship: an exploratory analysis in 'middle-class' culture," *Man* 4: 505–24

PAKALUK, M., ed. (1991) *Other Selves: Philosophers on Friendship*. Indianapolis, IN

PAKALUK, M. (1994) "Political friendship," in Rouner 1994: 197–213

(forthcoming) *Aristotle Nicomachean Ethics VIII–IX*. Oxford

PANOFSKY, E. (1961) *Gothic Architecture and Scholasticism*. New York

PAREKH, B. (1994) "An Indian view of friendship," in Rouner 1994: 95–113

PARKER, H. N. (1993) "Sappho schoolmistress," *TAPA* 123: 309–51

PARRY, M. (1971) *The Making of Homeric Verse: The Collected Papers of Milman Parry*. Ed. Adam Parry. Oxford

PATZIG, G., ed. (1990) *Aristoteles' "Politik."* Göttingen

PELIKAN, J. (1993) *Christianity and Classical Culture: The Metamorphosis of Natural Theology in the Christian Encounter with Hellenism*. New Haven, CT

PELLIZER, E. (1990) "Outlines of a morphology of sympotic entertainment," in Murray 1990: 177–84

PETERSON, E. (1923) "Der Gottesfreund: Beiträge zur Geschichte eines religiösen Terminus," *Zeitschrift für Kirchengeschichte* 42: 161–202

(1929) "Zur Bedeutungsgeschichte von παρρησία," in Wilhelm Koepp, ed., *Reinhold-Seeberg Festschrift von Wilhelm Koerr*. Vol. 1: 283–97. Leipzig

PETRÉ, H. (1948) *Caritas: Étude sur le vocabulaire latin de la charité chrétienne*. Louvain

PITT-RIVERS, J. A. (1954) *The People of the Sierra*. New York (2nd edn. 1971. Chicago)

(1973) "The kith and the kin," in J. Goody, ed. *The Character of Kinship*, 89–105. Cambridge

PIZZOLATO, L. F. (1974) "L'amicizia nel *De officiis* di Sant'Ambrogio e il *Laelius* di Cicerone," *Archivio Ambrosiano* 27: 53–67

(1993) *L'idea di amicizia nel mondo antico classico e cristiano*. Turin

POLANYI, K. (1944) *The Great Transformation*. New York

(1968) *Primitive, Archaic, and Modern Economies: Essays of Karl Polanyi*. Ed. G. Dalton. Boston

PORTER, J. R. (1994) *Studies in Euripides' Orestes*. Leiden

PÖSCHL, V. (1940) *Grundwerte römischen Staatsgesinnung in den Geschichtswerken des Sallust*. Berlin

POWELL, J. G. F. (1995) "Friendship and its problems in Greek and Roman thought," in D. Innes, H. Hine, and C. Pelling, eds., *Ethics and Rhetoric: Classical Essays for Donald Russell on his Seventy-Fifth Birthday*, 31–45. Oxford

POWELL, J. G. F., ed. (1990) *Cicero: Laelius, On Friendship and the Dream of Scipio.* Warminster

POWELL, J. U., ed. (1925) *Collectanea alexandrina.* Oxford

PREISIGKE, F. (1925–71) *Wörterbuch de griechische Papyrusurkunden.* Berlin

PRICE, A. W. (1989) *Love and Friendship in Plato and Aristotle.* Oxford

PRICE, S. R. F. (1984) *Rituals and Power: The Roman Imperial Cult in Asia Minor.* Cambridge

PROCOPÉ, J. (1991) "Höflichkeit," in *RAC* 15: 930–86

PUGLIA, E., ed. (1988) *Demetrio Lacone: Aporie testuali ed esegetiche in Epicuro.* Naples

PUTNAM, M. C. J. (1986) *Artifices of Eternity: Horace's Fourth Book of Odes.* Ithaca, NY

QUILLER, B. (1981) "The dynamics of the Homeric society," *SO* 56: 109–55

RAAFLAUB, K. A. (1991) "Homer und die Geschichte des 8. Jh.s v. Chr.," in J. Latacz, ed., *Zweihundert Jahre Homer-Forschung: Rückblick und Ausblick*, 205–56. Stuttgart and Leipzig

(1993) "Homer to Solon: the rise of the polis. The written sources," in Hansen 1993: 41–106

RAMSØY, O. (1968) "Friendship," in D. L. Sills, ed., *International Encyclopedia of the Social Sciences.* Vol. 6: 12–17. New York

RAPHAEL, F. (1993) "Frederic Raphael on friendship," *The Independent Magazine* 24 April 1993: 16–17

RAYMOND, J. G. (1986) *A Passion for Friends: Toward a Philosophy of Female Affection.* Boston

REDFIELD, R. (1956) *Peasant Society and Culture.* Chicago

REECE, S. (1993) *The Stranger's Welcome: Oral Theory and the Aesthetics of the Homeric Hospitality Scene.* Ann Arbor, MI

REINER, P. (1991) "Aristotle on personality and some implications for friendship," *AP* 11: 67–84

RENGSTORF, K. H., ed. (1983) *A Complete Concordance to Flavius Josephus.* Vol. 4. Leiden

REOHR, J. R. (1991) *Friendship: An Exploration of Structure and Process.* New York

RHODES, P. J. (1986) "Political activity in classical Athens," *JHS* 106: 132–44

RIBBECK, O. 1883. *Kolax: Eine ethologische Studie.* Leipzig

RICHLIN, A. (1983) *The Garden of Priapus: Sexuality and Aggression in Roman Humor.* New Haven (2nd edn. 1992. New York)

(1991) "Zeus and Metis: Foucault, feminism, classics," *Helios* 18: 160–80

RIHLL, T. (1986) "'Kings' and 'commoners' in Homeric society," *LCM* 11: 86–91

RITTER, R. (1963) "Die aristotelische Freundschaftsphilosophie nach der Nikomachischen Ethik." Munich: Diss. Ludwig-Maximilians-Universität

ROBERTS, M. (1993) *Poetry and the Cult of the Martyrs: The Liber Peristephanon of Prudentius.* Ann Arbor, MI

ROBINSON, D. (1986) "Plato's *Lysis*: the structural problem," *ICS* 11: 63–83
(1990) "Homeric φίλος: love of life and limbs, and friendship with one's θυμός," in E. M. Craik, ed., *"Owls to Athens": Essays on Classical Subjects Presented to Sir Kenneth Dover,* 97–108. Oxford

ROGERS, B. J. (1970) "The Poems of Venantius Fortunatus: A Translation and Commentary." New Brunswick, NJ: Diss. Rutgers University

ROLLER, M. B. (1994) "Early Imperial Literature and the Crisis of Aristocratic Authority." Berkeley: Diss. University of California

ROSÉN, H. B. (1959) "Die Ausdrucksform für 'veräusserlichen' und 'unveräusserlichen' Besitz im Frühgriechischen. Das Funktionsfeld von hom. φίλος," *Lingua* 8: 264–93

ROSIVACH, V. J. (1988) "The tyrant in Athenian democracy," *QUCC* 59:43–57

RÖSLER, W. (1980) *Dichter und Gruppe: Eine Untersuchung zu den Bedingungen und zur historischen Funktion früher griechischer Lyrik am Beispiel Alkaios.* Munich
(1990) *"Mnemosyne* in the *symposion,"* in Murray 1990: 230–7

ROSSI, L. E. (1983) "Il simposio arcaico e classico come spectacolo a se stesso," in *Spectacoli conviviali dall'antichità classica alle corti italiane dell'400,* 41–50. Viterbo

ROULAND, N. (1979) *Pouvoir politique et dépendance personnelle dans l'antiquité romaine: Genèse et rôle des rapports de clientèle.* Brussels: Collection Latomus no. 166

ROUNER, L. S., ed. (1994) *The Changing Face of Friendship.* Notre Dame, IN

ROUSSEAU, P. (1985) *Pachomius: The Making of a Community in Fourth-Century Egypt.* Berkeley, CA

ROUSSEL, D. (1976) *Tribu et cité.* Paris: Les Belles Lettres = Annales Littéraires de l'Université de Besançon 193

RUBIN, L. B. (1959) *Just Friends: The Role of Friendship in our Lives.* New York

RUBINSTEIN, L. (forthcoming) "The *idiotes* of Athens or what's in a name?" in Cartledge, Millett and von Reden (forthcoming)

RUDICH, V. (1993) *Political Dissidence under Nero: The Price of Dissimulation.* London

RUETHER, R. R. (1969) *Gregory of Nazianzus: Rhetor and Philosopher.* Oxford

RUNCIMAN, W. G. (1982) "Origins of states: the case of archaic Greece," *Comparative Studies in Society and History* 24: 351–77

RUSSELL, D., trans. (1993) *Plutarch: Selected Essays and Dialogues.* Oxford

SADLER, W. A., Jr. (1970) "The experience of friendship," *Humanities* 6: 177–209

SAINT-EVREMOND, C. (1966) "Sur l'amitié," in *Oeuvres en Prose,* vol. 7, ed. René Ternois. Paris

SAKELLARIOU, M. B. (1989) *The Polis-State: Definition and Origin.* Athens

SALLER, R. P. (1982) *Personal Patronage Under the Early Empire.* Cambridge
(1989) "Patronage and friendship in early imperial Rome: drawing the distinction," in Wallace-Hadrill 1989: 49–62

SARTON, M. (1977) *The House by the Sea: A Journal.* New York

SARTORI, F. (1967) *Le eterie nella vita politica ateniese del VI e V secolo a.C.* Rome

SCAFURO, A. (forthcoming) *The Forensic Stage: Settling Disputes in Graeco-Roman New Comedy.* Cambridge

SCARPAT, G. (1964) *Parrhesia: Storia del termine e delle sue traduzioni in latino.* Brescia

SCHEID-TISSINIER, E. (1990) "Remarques sur la représentation de l'étranger dans le monde homérique," *Civiltà Classica e Cristiana* 11: 7–31

SCHEIN, S. L. (1984) *The Mortal Hero: An Introduction to Homer's Iliad.* Berkeley, CA

SCHENKL, H., G. DOWNEY, and A. F. NORMAN, eds. (1971) *Themistii orationes quae supersunt.* Vol. 2. Leipzig

SCHMITT-PANTEL, P. (1990) "Sacrificial meal and *symposion*: two models of civic institutions in the archaic city?," in Murray 1990: 14–33

(1990a) "Collective activities and the political in the Greek city," in Murray and Price 1990: 199–213

(1992) *La cité au banquet: Histoire des repas publics dans les cités grecques.* Rome

SCHOFIELD, M. (1991) *The Stoic Idea of the City.* Cambridge

SCHOLLMEIER, P. (1994) *Other Selves: Aristotle on Personal and Political Friendship.* Albany, NY

SCOTT, M. (1982) "*Philos, philotēs* and *xenia*," *Acta Classica* 25: 1–19

SCULLY, S. (1990) *Homer and the Sacred City.* Ithaca, NY

SEAFORD, R. (1989) "The attribution of Aeschylus, *Choephoroi*, 691–9," *CQ* 39: 302–6

(1994) *Reciprocity and Ritual: Homer and Tragedy in the Developing City-State.* Oxford

SEAGER, R. (1977) "Amicitia in Tacitus and Juvenal," *AJAH* 2: 40–50

SEDLEY, D. (1989) "Is the Lysis a dialogue of definition?" *Phronesis* 34: 107–8

SERGENT, B. (1986 [1984]) *Homosexuality in Greek Myth.* Trans. Arthur Goldhammer. Boston

SHACKLETON BAILEY, D., ed. (1977) *Cicero: Epistulae ad Familiares.* 2 vols. Cambridge

(1982) *Anthologia Latina.* Vol. 1, fasc. 1. Stuttgart

SHACKLETON BAILEY, D., ed. and trans. (1965–8) *Cicero's Letters to Atticus.* 6 vols. Cambridge

SHARABANY, R. (1994) "Continuities in the development of intimate friendships: object relations, interpersonal, and attachment perspectives," in R. Erber and R. Gilmour, eds., *Theoretical Frameworks for Personal Relationships,* 157–78. Hilldale, NJ

SHARP, R. A. (1986) *Friendship and Literature: Spirit and Form.* Durham, NC

SHAY, J. (1994) *Achilles in Vietnam: Combat Trauma and the Undoing of Character.* New York

SHOEMAN, F. (1985) "Aristotle on the good of friendship," *Australasian Journal of Philosophy* 63: 269–82

SIDER, D., ed. (1997) *The Epigrams of Philodemus*. New York

SILVER, A. (1989) "Friendship and trust as moral ideals: an historical approach," *European Journal of Sociology* 30: 274–97

(1990) "Friendship in commercial society: eighteenth-century social theory and modern sociology," *American Journal of Sociology* 95: 1474–504

(1996) " 'Two different sorts of commerce,' or, friendship and stranger-ship in civil society," in J. Weintraub and K. Kumar, eds., *Public and Private in Thought and Practice*, Chicago

SIMMEL, G. (1950) *The Sociology of Georg Simmel*. Trans. and ed. K. H. Wolff. Glencoe, IL

SINCLAIR, R. K. (1988) *Democracy and Participation in Athens*. Cambridge

SINFIELD, A. (1994) *Cultural Politics – Queer Reading*. Philadelphia

SINOS, D. S. (1980) *Achilles, Patroklos and the Meaning of Philos*. Innsbruck = Innsbrucker Beiträge zur Sprachwissenschaft 29

SISSA, G. (1988 [1986]) "La familia en la ciudad griega (siglos V-IV a.C.)," in A. Burguière, C. Klapische-Zuber, M. Segalen, and F. Zonabend, eds., *Historia de la familia*. Vol. 1: 169–201. Madrid = *A History of the Family*. Vol. 1:194–227. Cambridge

SKINNER, M. B. (1979) "Parasites and strange bedfellows: a study in Catullus' political imagery," *Ramus* 8: 137–52

(1993) "Woman and language in archaic Greece, or why is Sappho a woman?," in N. S. Rabinowitz and A. Richlin, eds., *Feminist Theory and the Classics*, 125–44. Ithaca, NY

SLATER, W. J., ed. (1986) *Aristophanis Byzantii fragmenta*. Berlin

(1991) *Dining in a Classical Context*. Ann Arbor, MI

SLATKIN, L. (1988) "Les amis mortels: à propos des insultes dans les combats de *L'Iliade*," *L'Ecrit du Temps* 19: 119–32

SMITH, M. F., ed. (1993) *Diogenes of Oenoanda: The Epicurean Inscription*. Naples

SNELL, B. (1953) *The Discovery of the Mind*. Trans. T. G. Rosenmeyer. Oxford

SNODGRASS, A. M. (1983) "Two demographic notes," in Hägg 1983: 167–71

(1990) "Survey archaeology and the rural landscape of the Greek city," in Murray and Price 1990: 113–36

SPINA, L. (1986) *Il cittadino alla tribuna: Diritto e libertà di parola nell' Atene democratica*. Naples

SPINELLI, E. (1983–4) "Le massime di Democrito sull'amicizia," *Annali dell'Istituto Italiano per gli Studi Storici* 8: 47–74

SPRINGBORG, P. (1986) "Politics, primordialism, and orientalism: Marx, Aristotle, and the myth of Gemeinschaft," *American Political Science Review* 80: 185–211

STÄDELE, A. (1980) *Die Briefe des Pythagoras und der Pythagoreer*. Meisenheim am Glan

STAGAKIS, G. (1975) *Studies in the Homeric Society*. Wiesbaden: Franz Steiner = *Historia* Einzelschriften 26

STÄHLIN, G. (1974) "Philos, philē, philia," in G. Friedrich, ed., *Theological*

Dictionary of the New Testament. Trans. G. W. Bromiley. Vol. 9. Grand Rapids, MI

STANTON, G. R. (1990) "Φιλία and ξενία in Euripides' 'Alkestis,'" *Hermes* 118: 42–54

STEHLE, E. M. (1994) "Cold meats: Timokreon on Themistokles," *AJP* 115: 507–24

STEIN-HÖLKESKAMP, E. (1989) *Adelskultur und Polisgesellschaft: Studien zum grieschischen Adel in Archaischer und klassischer Zeit*. Stuttgart

STEINMETZ, F.-A. (1967) *Die Freundschaftslehre des Panaitios nach einer Analyse von Ciceros "Laelius de amicitia"*. Wiesbaden

STERN-GILLET, S. (1995) *Aristotle's Philosophy of Friendship*. Albany, NY

STOCK, ST. G. (1913) "Friendship (Greek and Roman)," in J. Hastings, ed., *Encyclopedia of Religion and Ethics*. Vol. 6: 134–8. Edinburgh

STRAUSS, B. S. (1986) *Athens After the Peloponnesian War: Class, Faction and Policy 403–386 BC*. London and Ithaca, NY

STRAWSON, G. (1991) "On friendly terms," Review of Enright and Rawlinson 1991. *TLS* 3 May: 5–6

SUTTLES, G. D. (1970) "Friendship as a social institution," in G. J. McCall, M. M. McCall, N. K. Denzin, G. D. Suttles, and S. B. Kurth, eds., *Social Relationships*, 95–135. Chicago

SYME, R. (1939) *The Roman Revolution*. Oxford

TAKABATAKE, S. (1988) "The idea of ξένος in classical Athens: its structure and peculiarities," in T. Yuge and M. Doi, eds., *Forms of Control and Subordination in Antiquity*, 449–55. Leiden

TAYLOR, C. (1989) *Sources of the Self: The Making of the Modern Identity*. Cambridge, MA

TAYLOR, L. R. (1949) *Party Politics in the Age of Caesar*. Berkeley, CA

THESLEFF, H. (1961) *An Introduction to the Pythagorean Writings of the Hellenistic Period*. Åbo = Acta Academiae Aboensis, Humaniora 24.3

THESLEFF, H., ed. (1965) *The Pythagorean Texts of the Hellenistic Period*. Åbo = Acta Academiae Aboensis, Ser. A, Humaniora 30.1

THOMAS, L. (1987) "Friendship," *Synthese* 72: 217–36

(1993) "Friendship and other loves," in Badhwar 1993: 48–72

TREGGIARI, S. (1991) *Roman Marriage: Iusti Coniuges from the Time of Cicero to the Time of Ulpian*. Oxford

TREU, K. (1961) "Φιλία und ἀγάπη: zur Terminologie der Freundschaft bei Basilius und Gregor von Nazianz," *Studii Classice* 3: 421–7

(1972) "Freundschaft," in *RAC* 8: 418–34

TRILLING, L. (1972) *Sincerity and Authenticity*. Cambridge, MA

ULF, C. (1990) *Die homerische Gesellschaft: Materialen zur analytischen Beschreibung und historischen Lokalisierung*. Munich

USSHER, R. G., ed. (1993) *The Characters of Theophrastus*. 2nd edn. London

VAN BROCK, N. (1959) "Substitution rituelle," *Revue Hittite et Asianique* 65: 117–46

VAN DAM, H.-J. (1984) *P. Papinius Statius Silvae Book II: A Commentary*. Leiden

VAN DAM, R. (1986) "Emperor, bishops, and friends in late antique Cappadocia," *Journal of Theological Studies* n.s. 37: 53–76

VAN WEES, H. (1992) *Status Warriors: War, Violence and Society in Homer and History.* Amsterdam

VICKERS, M. (1990) "Attic symposia after the Persian Wars," in Murray 1990: 105–21

VINAVER, E. ed. (1990) *The Works of Sir Thomas Malory.* 3rd. edn., rev. P. J. C. Field. Oxford

VISCHER, L. (1953) "Das Problem der Freundschaft bei den Kirchenvätern: Basilius der Grosse, Gregor von Nazianz und Chrysostomus," *Theologische Zeitschrift* 9: 173–200

VLASTOS, G. (1973) "The individual as an object of love in Plato," in G. Vlastos, *Platonic Studies,* 3–42. Princeton, NJ

VOGEL, C. J. DE. (1966) *Pythagoras and Early Pythagoreanism: An Interpretation of Neglected Evidence on the Philosopher Pythagoras.* Assen

WADELL, P. J. (1989) *Friendship and the Moral Life.* Notre Dame, IN

WALBANK, F. W. (1984) "Monarchies and monarchic ideas," in Walbank *et al.* 1984: 62–100

WALBANK, F. W., A. E. ASTIN, M. W. FREDERIKSEN, and R. M. OGILVIE, eds. (1984) *The Cambridge Ancient History.* 2nd edn. Vol. vii.1. Cambridge

WALKER, A. D. M. (1979) "Aristotle's account of friendship in the Nicomachean Ethics," *Phronesis* 24: 180–96

WALLACE-HADRILL, A. (1982) "Civilis princeps: Between citizen and king," *JRS* 72: 32–48

WALLACE-HADRILL, A., ed. (1989) *Patronage in Ancient Society.* London

WARD, J. K. (1995) "Focal reference in Aristotle's account of φιλία: Eudemian Ethics VII.2," *Apeiron* 28: 183–205

WELLES, C. B. (1934) *Royal Correspondence in the Hellenistic Period.* New Haven, CT

WEST, M. L., ed. (1989, 1992) *Iambi et Elegi Graeci.* Vols. 1 and 2 (second edn.) Oxford

(1980) *Delectus ex iambis et elegiis graecis.* Oxford

WEST, M. L., ed. and trans. (1987) *Euripides Orestes.* Warminster

WHITE, C. (1992) *Christian Friendship in the Fourth Century.* Cambridge

WHITE, P. (1978) "*Amicitia* and the profession of poetry in early imperial Rome," *JRS* 68: 74–92

(1993) *Promised Verse: Poets in the Society of Augustan Rome.* Cambridge, MA

WILLIAMS, R. (1977) *Marxism and Literature.* Oxford

WILSON, N. G., ed. (1975) *Saint Basil on the Value of Greek Literature.* London

WISEMAN, J. P. (1986) "Friendship: bonds and binds in a voluntary relationship," *Journal of Social and Personal Relationships* 3: 191–211

WITTGENSTEIN, L. (1958) *The Blue and Brown Books.* Oxford

WOLF, E. R. (1966) "Kinship, friendship, and patron-client relations in complex societies," in M. Banton, ed., *The Social Anthropology of Complex Societies,* 1–22. New York

WOYTEK, E., ed. (1982) *T. Maccius Plautus, Persa: Einleitung, Text und Kommentar.* Vienna

WRIGHT, G. H. VON., ed. and trans. (1974) *Ludwig Wittgenstein: Letters to Russell, Keynes and Moore.* Ithaca, NY

WRIGHT, P. H. (1982) "Men's friendships, women's friendships and the alleged inferiority of the latter," *Sex Roles* 8: 1–20

YAKOBSON, A. (1992) "*Petitio et largitio*: popular participation in the centuriate assembly of the late Republic," *JRS* 82: 32–52

ZANKER, G. (1994) *The Heart of Achilles: Characterization and Personal Ethics in the* Iliad. Ann Arbor

ZHMUD, L. (1996) *Wissenschaft, Philosophie und Religion im frühen Pythagoreismus.* Berlin

ZUCKER, F. (1950) *Freundschaftsbewährung in der neuen attischen Komödie: Ein Kapitel hellenistischer Ethik und Humanität.* Berlin

Index

Printed in the United Kingdom
by Lightning Source UK Ltd.
107431UKS00002B/289-291